The Civil War and Pop Culture

Favorite Stories and Fresh Perspectives
from the Historians at Emerging Civil War

Edited by
Chris Mackowski & Jonathan Tracey

Also from the
Emerging Civil War 10th Anniversary Series

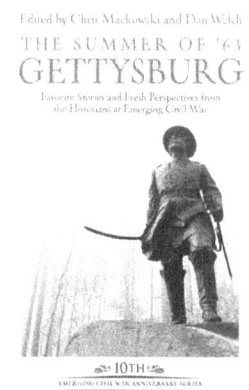
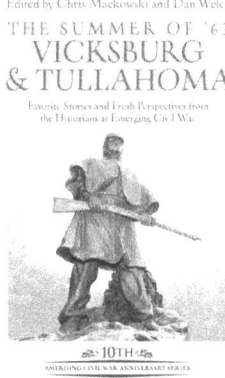

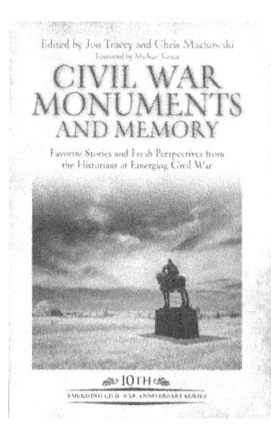
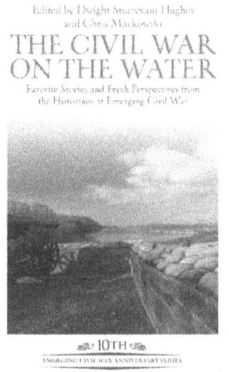

For a complete list of titles,
visit www.emergingcivilwar.com.

The Civil War and Pop Culture

Favorite Stories and Fresh Perspectives
from the Historians at Emerging Civil War

Edited by
Chris Mackowski & Jonathan Tracey

SB
Savas Beatie
California

© 2023 Emerging Civil War

All rights reserved. No part of this publication may be reproduced, stored in a retrieval system, or transmitted, in any form or by any means, electronic, mechanical, photocopying, recording, or otherwise, without the prior written permission of the publisher.

First edition, first printing

ISBN-13 (hardcover): 978-1-61121-635-6
ISBN-13 (ebook): 978-1-61121-636-3

Library of Congress Cataloging-in-Publication Data

Names: Tracey, Jon, editor. | Mackowski, Chris, editor.
Title: The Civil War and pop culture : favorite stories and fresh perspectives from the historians at emerging Civil War / edited by Jon Tracey and Chris Mackowski.
Description: California : Savas Beatie, [2023] | Series: Emerging Civil War Anniversary Series | Includes bibliographical references and index. | Summary: "This collection of essays explores some of the ways people have imagined and re-imaged the war, at the tension between history and art, and how those visions have left lasting marks on American culture"-- Provided by publisher.
Identifiers: LCCN 2023006363 | ISBN 9781611216356 (hardcover) | ISBN 9781611216363 (ebook)
Subjects: LCSH: United States--History--Civil War, 1861-1865--Influence. | United States--History--Civil War, 1861-1865--Historiography | United States--History--Civil War, 1861-1865--Literature and the war. | United States--History--Civil War, 1861-1865--Motion pictures and the war. | United States--In popular culture.
Classification: LCC E468.9 .C4743 2023 | DDC 973.7--dc23/eng/20230329
LC record available at https://lccn.loc.gov/2023006363

Savas Beatie
989 Governor Drive, Suite 102
El Dorado Hills, CA 95762
916-941-6896 / sales@savasbeatie.com / www.savasbeatie.com

All of our titles are available at special discount rates for bulk purchases in the United States. Contact us for information.

Proudly published, printed, and warehoused in the United States of America.

CHRIS:
To my friends Brad Buck, Ric Tyler,
and the great and glorious Bubba Cheese,
as well as to the lovely Elizabeth

JON:
To past and present members
of Emerging Civil War's Editorial Board,
who tirelessly review guest post submissions
and help guide the writing of "emerging" voices.

Chris and Jon jointly
dedicate this book to Dan Welch,
ECW's "Music Man"
and a good friend to us both.

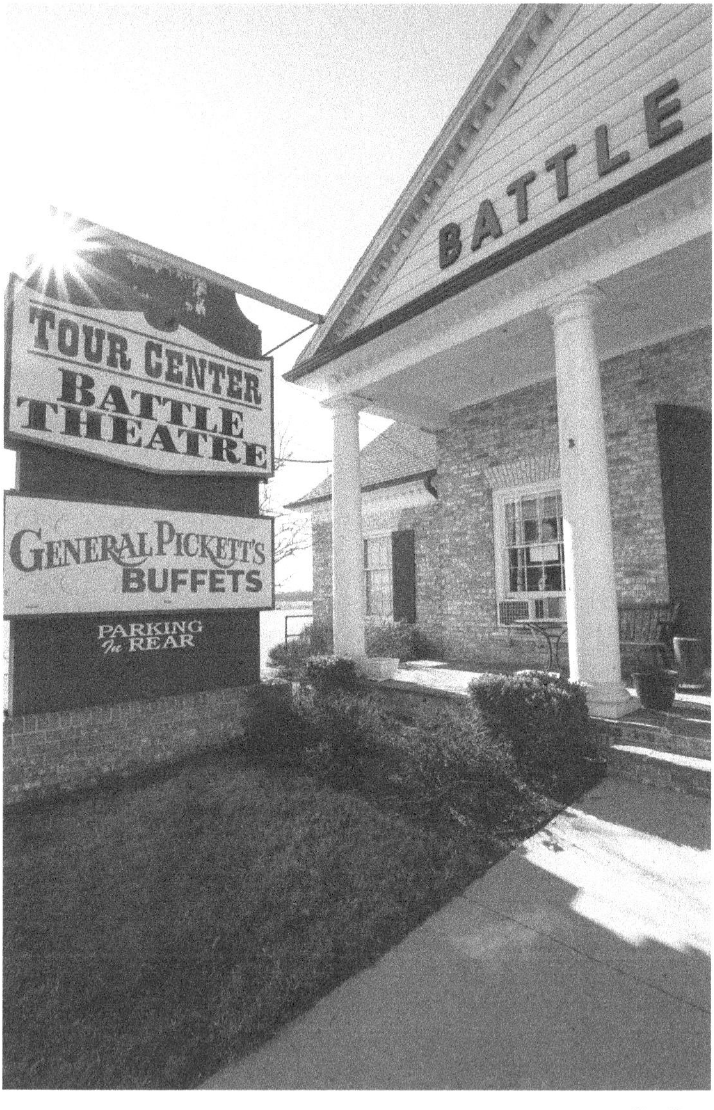

Chris Heisey

www.emergingcivilwar.com

Table of Contents

Editors' Note
xii

Acknowledgments
xiv

Foreword
Brian Matthew Jordan
xvi

Photographing Pop Culture
Chris Heisey
xxxii

Nineteenth-Century Social Media:
Civil War Photography Was 150 Years Ahead of the Game
Garry Adelman
1

The Confederate Flag in Popular Culture
John M. Coski
14

The Gray Ghost on TV Made Me a Civil Warrior
Stephen Davis
34

Telling History vs. Making Art
Chris Mackowski
59

Birth of a (Lost Cause) Nation
Sheritta Bitikofer
85

A Fun Civil War Movie: *The General*
Dwight S. Hughes
94

Gone with the Wind: Some Thoughts
Sarah Kay Bierle
97

Charlton Heston's Civil War
Brian Steel Wills
108

Violence and Forgetting in the Crater
Kevin M. Levin
114

Glory: Rediscovering the USCT in Popular Culture
Steward Henderson
121

Reconsidering *Gettysburg*
Tom McMillan
130

A Conversation with *Gettysburg* Actor
Patrick Gorman (Maj. Gen. John Bell Hood)
Frank Jastrzembski
136

The *Gettysburg* Soundtrack
Dan Welch
142

The 2nd South Carolina String Band
and the Pop Music of the Civil War
Chris Mackowski
147

Driving Dixie Down
Patrick Vecchio
155

Steve Earle's "Ben McCulloch"
Jon-Erik Gilot
160

Steve Earle, "Dixieland,"
and the Irresistible Charm of Buster Kilrain
Chris Mackowski
163

Dwight Yoakam Sings "Dixie"
Chris Mackowski
166

Hurrah for Homespun!
Sherrita Bitikofer
169

"I Heard the Bells on Christmas Day . . ."
Meg Groeling
177

The Civil War in Surprising Places:
The Pop Culture Delights of Emily Dickinson's Poetry
Cecily Nelson Zander
181

Uncle Remus, Brer Rabbit,
and Their Continued Influence
Ashley Webb
185

The Book I Threw
(and Then Picked Up Again)
Sarah Kay Bierle
193

Andersonville Offers Wonderful Writing
Amidst Horrific Suffering
Chris Mackowski
198

Thoughts on *Madame Castel's Lodger*
Sean Michael Chick
202

Richard Adams, Author of *Traveller*, Dies at 96
Chris Mackowski
206

A Beautiful, Despairing Journey
with a Coal-Black Horse
Chris Mackowski
209

The Delicious "If": MacKinlay Kantor's
If the South Had Won the Civil War and Alternative History
Stephen Davis
211

Holiday Village Reenactments and Reflections
Neil P. Chatelain
217

Civil War Wargaming
Scott L. Mingus Sr.
221

Gaming the Civil War
Sean Michael Chick
231

Ready, Aim, Click!:
A Look at the Civil War Through Video Games
Tyler McGraw
241

Battlefield to Football Field:
Civil War Ties to College Football
Christopher L. Kolakowski
246

Re-Creating War in Peaceful Fields:
Catharsis Through Reenacting
Derek D. Maxfield
253

The Civil War Art Boom (and Bust)
Richard Heisler
271

The Stream of American History
Chris Mackowski
275

What If There Were No Civil War Epics?
Sarah Kay Bierle
280

Contributors' Notes
283

Postscript
289

Index
290

Editors' Note

Emerging Civil War serves as a public history-oriented platform for sharing original scholarship related to the American Civil War. The scholarship we present reflects the eclectic background, expertise, interests, and writing styles of our cadre of historians. We've shared that scholarship not only on the Emerging Civil War blog, but also in the pages of the Emerging Civil War Series published by Savas Beatie, in other general-audience and academic publications, at our annual Emerging Civil War Symposium at Stevenson Ridge, on our monthly podcasts, and even through social media.

Our Emerging Civil War 10th Anniversary Series captures and commemorates some of the highlights from our first ten years.

This compendium includes pieces originally published on our blog; podcast transcripts; and transcripts of talks given at the ECW Symposium. It also includes an assortment of original material. Previously published pieces have been updated and, in most cases, expanded and footnoted. Our attempt is to offer value-added rather than just reprint material available for free elsewhere.

Between the covers of this series, readers will find military, social, political, and economic history; memory studies; travelogues; personal narratives; essays; and photography. This broad range of scholarship and creative work is meant to provide readers with a diversity of perspectives. The combined collection of material is *not* intended to serve as a complete narrative of events or comprehensive overview. Rather, these are the stories and events our historians happened to be interested in writing about at any given time. In that way, the collection represents the sort of eclectic ongoing conversation you'll find on our blog.

As a collective, the individuals who comprise ECW are encouraged to share their own unique interests and approaches. The resulting work—and the respectful discussions that surround it—forward ECW's overall effort to promote a general awareness of the Civil War as America's defining event.

Another of ECW's organizational priorities is our ongoing work to identify and spotlight the next generation of "emerging" Civil War historians and the fresh ideas they bring to the historical conversation. (Some of us were "emerging" when ECW started up ten years ago and have perhaps since "emerged," but the quest to spotlight new voices continues!)

Most importantly, it is the common thread of public history and the ideals of interpretation that so strongly tie our seemingly disparate bodies of work together. America's defining event should not be consigned to forgotten footnotes and dusty shelves. As public historians, we understand the resonance and importance history's lessons can have in our modern world and in our daily lives, so we always seek to connect people with those great stories and invaluable lessons. Emerging Civil War remains committed to making our history something available for all of us—writers, readers, historians, hobbyists, men, women, young, old, and people of all races and ethnicities—and by doing so, making it something we can engage, question, challenge, and enjoy.

Please join us online at www.emergingcivilwar.com.

A Note About This Volume:

In 2020, as part of ECW's "Engaging the Civil War" Series with Southern Illinois University Press, ECW produced a book titled *Entertaining History: The Civil War in Literature, Film, and Song*. The book focused on texts—books, movies, TV shows, songs—with a planned second book to look at other cultural connections. Alas, Illinois's legendary state budget woes forced us to part ways with SIUP (amicably!) before we could do that companion volume.

The book you hold in your hand collects some of the original pieces for that second volume, coupled with a bunch of our "greatest hits" from the blog during our first ten years. We also have a few original pieces. The Civil War in pop culture is an area of particular interest to Chris, so he's written a lot about it over the years (which is why there's so much "Chris Mackowski" in this collection and for which he asks your indulgence).

There is, we hope, a lot of fun stuff in this volume that conjures good memories for you about your favorite books, movies, and art, as well as other ways you have experienced the war. But we also hope there's a lot of material here for you to think about, too. Many of us became hooked on the Civil War because of pop culture; for others, though, pop culture may be the only way they ever interact with Civil War history. For those reasons, the influence the Civil War has had—and continues to have—through pop culture should be of keen interest to us all.

Acknowledgments

First and foremost, as editors, we'd like to thank our colleagues at Emerging Civil War, past and present. ECW has always been and remains a team effort. We've worked with some wonderful historians, writers, and "emerging voices" over the past decade, and we're proud to show off some of that work here.

Thanks, too, to Theodore Savas and his entire team at Savas Beatie, with a special thanks to our editorial liaison, Sarah Keeney, and production manager, Veronica Kane. Ted took a chance on ECW when we were still a young blog, accepting Kris White's pitch for the Emerging Civil War Series. That proved to be a game-changer for us. Together, ECW and Savas Beatie have produced some great work, and we're thankful to Ted for agreeing to help us celebrate ECW's tenth anniversary by allowing us to produce more great work. We thank everyone at Savas Beatie for all they do to support the work of Emerging Civil War.

Sarah Kay Bierle, as ECW's managing editor, manages the content on the blog on a daily basis. Her work made it a lot easier for us to collect the material we've assembled in this volume. Our official un-official archivist, Jon-Erik Gilot, has helped us make it easier to access our past work.

Cecily Nelson Zander, as our chief historian, provides overall quality control for our work. She joins a list of distinguished historians—Kristopher D. White, Christopher Kolakowski, and Dan Davis—who have served in that role. Our thanks to all of them over the years for ensuring a high bar for our writers in service to our readers.

Thanks to Patrick McCormick, who reviewed the text and made valuable suggestions and observations. And a big thank-you to Chris Heisey for always being willing to contribute *one more* photograph as the design of this book continued to evolve.

Finally, a special thanks to co-founders Chris Mackowski, Jake Struhelka, and Kristopher D. White, whose brainstorming over beers, cigars, and history led to ECW's creation. To quote Kris's wife, "Not too bad for three idiots sitting on a porch."

* * *

Jon:

Naturally I have to acknowledge my parents for being the first to introduce me to these forms of pop culture when I was young, through fiction books and the film *Gettysburg*. The natural second half of that is additional thanks to my parents for supporting my appetite for those things, and thanks to my teachers who helped complicate the narratives imparted by the art.

I'd also like to acknowledge those who create art about the Civil War era, whether they're fiction writers, filmmakers, artists, musicians, video game developers, or work in other mediums. While popular culture adaptations may not always get the complicated history perfectly right, which can certainly be an issue sometimes, they often have great value in connecting us to the past.

Chris:

Foremost, I offer my thanks to Jon Tracey, who kindly indulged me with this volume. We're both memory guys, although we come at it from different directions, so as we compiled material for *Civil War Monuments and Memory*, we realized we had enough material for two books. He let me run with this one, and it was a lot of fun. So, my thanks to him for that latitude and support.

This was a wonderful line-up of authors to work with, so I offer them my gratitude. I offer my particular thanks to Garry Adelman, John Coski, Steve Davis, Steward Henderson, Derek Maxfield, Scott Mingus, and Pat Vecchio. They had written pieces for a book that ended up not getting made, and they've waited patiently as I've sat on their excellent essays, waiting for a chance to get them into print. I am grateful for their patience because their material is excellent.

My thanks to my dean, Aaron Chimbel, for the support he constantly offers. I also thank the Jandoli School of Communication at St. Bonaventure University as well as my colleagues in the university's Office of Marketing and Communications.

Finally, my thanks to my wife, Jenny Ann, and my children, Steph and her husband, Thomas (and my granddaughter, Sophie—the Pip!); Jackson; and Maxwell James. Family is everything.

1. Foreword

by Brian Matthew Jordan

"Almost nothing renders us human," historian David Blight contends, "as much as our unique capacity for memory." No other species "can use memory to create, to record experience, to forge self-conscious associations, to form and practice language, to know, collect, narrate and write their pasts."[1] For better or for worse, memory is the medium through which most Americans engage with the past. As many theorists have pointed out, historical memories are shaped by anxieties in the present, rather than the realities of the past. Encumbered by few of the concerns that animate academic historians—under no obligation to render the past accurately or objectively, and shorn of the responsibility to evaluate nettlesome or uncomfortable evidence—popular audiences frequently approach the past as a wellspring of solace; they rummage history for affirmation or to escape contemporary life, contented in their evaluation of the past as a "simpler" or "nobler" time.[2]

Throughout much of the last century, the Civil War loomed as an ironic touchstone for white Americans. Even as the decades demonstrated the utter prescience of W. E. B. DuBois's turn-of-the-century contention that

---

[1] David W. Blight, "The Memory Boom: Why and Why Now?" in Pascal Boyer and James V. Wertsch, *Memory in Mind and Culture* (Cambridge: Cambridge University Press, 2009), 238.

[2] The literature on the social constructedness of memory is vast, but a foundational text is Maurice Halbwachs, *The Collective Memory*, trans. Francis J. Ditter, Jr., and Vida Yazdi Ditter (New York: Harper & Row, 1980). For an early definition of "memory studies" in American historical scholarship, see David Thelen, "Memory and American History," *Journal of American History* 75, no. 4 (March 1989): 1117–29.

"the problem of the Twentieth Century is the problem of the color-line," most Americans preferred to see the war as an inspired test of the nation's mettle rather than an unheeded mandate for racial equality. Despite their chronological convergence, the modern Black freedom struggle and the Civil War Centennial were, as Blight has written, "like planets in separate orbits around different suns." By staging battle reenactments, hawking gimmicky souvenirs, and waving rebel flags, the nation celebrated the triumph of sectional reconciliation—even as a high school in Little Rock, a Baptist church in Birmingham, and a steel bridge in Selma became new battlefields in the nation's long struggle for equal rights.[3]

The Civil War even served as something of an unlikely antidote during America's long and painful "reckoning" with Vietnam. Even amid the "living room war," the "romance" of 1861–65 was remarkably irresistible. Civil War titles sold surprisingly well during the Vietnam years. In 1972, for instance, E. B. Long reported to fellow Civil War scholar Bell I. Wiley that his encyclopedic tome, *The Civil War Day by Day*, had "done better than we (or Doubleday) expected. We will even make a few dollars for once." Wiley had penned a foreword for Long's exhaustive almanac. "Over 6,000 trade sales by April 30," Long crowed, "and in addition the History Book Club and four other book clubs distributed it in one form or another." The final volume of novelist Shelby Foote's Civil War trilogy, tracking the war from the banks of the Red River to Appomattox, appeared in 1974.[4]

Only days after the image of a helicopter evacuating Saigon dominated Americans' television screens, Columbia University bestowed the 1975 Pulitzer Prize for Fiction on author Michael Shaara's novel of the battle of Gettysburg, *The Killer Angels*. Two years later, Gerald Ford honored fellow Michigander Bruce Catton, the "preeminent historian" who "made us hear the sounds of battle," with the Presidential Medal of Freedom. All the same, historian William C. Davis, the editor of *Civil War Times Illustrated*, marveled that his magazine's readership grew significantly during "a decade

---

3 W. E. B. DuBois, *The Souls of Black Folk*, ed. Jonathan Scott Holloway (New Haven, CT: Yale University Press, 2015), 1; David W. Blight, *American Oracle: The Civil War in the Civil Rights Era* (Cambridge, MA: Harvard University Press, 2011), 2; Robert J. Cook, *Troubled Commemoration: The American Civil War Centennial, 1961–1965* (Baton Rouge: Louisiana State University Press, 2008).

4 E. B. Long to Bell Irvin Wiley, letter, August 23, 1972, E. B. Long Collection, Box 3, Folder 85, Texas A&M University, College Station, Texas.

filled with the most penetrating soul searching about war and violence." "We like to think that there is meaning to this—that despite the turmoil of our years and the seeming rejection by many of our traditions, still at heart there is a basic, almost instinctive, bond between Americans and their past." "The Civil War is going to be with us for a long time to come," Long predicted on the 111th anniversary of Lee's surrender at Appomattox, unable to conceal his misty-eyed reverence for the spirit of Johnny Reb and Billy Yank. "No, the Civil War is far from exhausted, though it may be exhausting."[5]

True to form, the Civil War was invoked as a national search for healing begun in the confounding wake of Vietnam and Watergate. In 1975, framed by the stately columns of Arlington House, President Gerald R. Ford signed a congressional resolution restoring citizenship to Robert E. Lee—a pardon decidedly more popular than the one he issued for his predecessor, Richard M. Nixon. The president understood and used the politics of Civil War memory. Just three years later, Ford's successor, Jimmy Carter—only the second southerner to serve as president since Appomattox—signed into law S.J. Res. 16, fully restoring citizenship rights to Confederate President Jefferson Davis. "Our Nation needs to clear away the guilts and enmities and recriminations of the past," Carter asserted, "to finally set at rest the divisions that threatened to destroy our Nation and to discredit the principles on which it was founded."[6]

---

5 William C. Davis, "Behind the Lines," *Civil War Times Illustrated* (December 1974): 2. The magazine boasted more than 100,000 subscribers in January 1975. E. B. Long, comment on Civil War Historiography Panel, Chicago, Illinois, April 9, 1976, E. B. Long Collection, Box 4, Folder 20, Texas A&M University, College Station, Texas. "Civil warriors, students, scholars, nuts, or whatever, are indomitable," Long continued, "and they will not rest nor are they resting on their very considerable laurels, nor should they. The historiography of the Civil War era is a proud one, perhaps the brightest of any period in American historiography. No other period can boast the galaxy of serious scholars, great writers, and seminal books." Contrary to the arguments presented here, Gary W. Gallagher, *Causes Won, Lost, and Forgotten: How Hollywood and Popular Art Shape What We Know about the Civil War* (Chapel Hill: University of North Carolina Press, 2008), posits that interest in the war waned during Vietnam, only to be revived by James McPherson and Ken Burns.

6 Christian G. Appy, *American Reckoning: The Vietnam War and Our National Identity* (New York: Viking, 2015); Michael Shaara, *The Killer Angels* (New York: David McCay, 1974); Gerald R. Ford, "Remarks upon Presenting the Presidential Medal of Freedom," January 10, 1977, http://www.presidency.ucsb.edu/ws/index.php?pid=5550; Andrew Glass, "House Restores Citizenship to Robert E. Lee, July 22, 1975," *Politico*, July 22, 2010; William A. Blair, *With Malice toward Some: Treason and Loyalty in the Civil War Era* (Chapel Hill: University of North Carolina Press, 2013), 240; Jimmy Carter, "Restoration of Citizenship Rights to Jefferson F. Davis, Statement on Signing S.J. Res 16 into Law, October 17, 1978, https://www.presidency.ucsb.edu/documents/restoration-citizenship-rights-jefferson-f-davis-statement-signing-s-j-res-16-into-law.

* * *

While the restoration of Davis's citizenship demonstrated the enduring, mainstream appeal of the Lost Cause in the last quarter of the twentieth century, President Carter's discussion of "enmities" and "recriminations" also evoked the fiercely contested nature of Civil War memory. Although the Southern narrative of the war achieved supremacy by the war's jubilee anniversary, many Northerners—especially wizened veterans—preserved potent counter-memories. Indeed, the triumph of the Lost Cause in popular culture only steeled the tenacity and resolve of those who remembered the Civil War as a treasonous rebellion waged on behalf of slavery. In the margins, these men and women ensured that if beleaguered, emancipationist memories would not perish.[7]

By the mid-1930s, the war that the soldiers fought bore almost no resemblance to the war that was dramatized on stage and in celluloid. The war peddled in school textbooks and depicted on postage stamps minimized the horrors of slavery, effaced the crime of treason, and denied the sobering history of Reconstruction. Brimming with offense, altogether unwilling to submit to the "systematic misrepresentation of everything connected with the Civil War," the daughters of a Union veteran took matters into their own hands. Determined to dam an unremitting flood of "Confederate propaganda," Lucy Stewart and her Tallahassee-based sister, Helen Stewart Claassen, became instrumental in a national organization known as the "Society for Correct Civil War Information." Helen acted as the society's president, while Lucy functioned as its secretary, devotedly typing the group's monthly newsletter from her home on tree-lined Orrington Avenue

---

[7] David W. Blight, *Race and Reunion: The Civil War in American Memory* (Cambridge, MA: Harvard University Press, 2001). A growing body of scholarship has challenged Blight's thesis by focusing on the endurance of emancipationist memory well into the twentieth century. See, for example, Barbara A. Gannon, *The Won Cause: White and Black Comradeship in the Grand Army of the Republic* (Chapel Hill: University of North Carolina Press, 2011); Caroline E. Janney, *Remembering the Civil War: Reunion and the Limits of Reconciliation* (Chapel Hill: University of North Carolina Press, 2013); John Neff, *Honoring the Civil War Dead: Commemoration and the Problem of Reconciliation* (Lawrence: University Press of Kansas, 2005); M. Keith Harris, *Across the Bloody Chasm: The Culture of Commemoration among Civil War Veterans* (Baton Rouge: Louisiana State University Press, 2014); and Brian Matthew Jordan, *Marching Home: Union Veterans and Their Unending Civil War* (New York: Liveright, 2015). For a probing survey of this literature, see Nina Silber, "Reunion and Reconciliation, Reviewed and Reconsidered," *Journal of American History* 103, no. 1 (June 2016): 59–83.

in Evanston—a suburban community perched on Lake Michigan, about a dozen miles north of Chicago. "Today it is virtually impossible to glean Civil War facts from present century writings, either in school or other histories, biographies, novels, or magazine articles," Lucy lamented in the society's first newsletter, mailed in October 1935. "In later issues," she explained, establishing the bulletin's raison d'être, "other questions will be asked and answered, all in the interest of stimulating a desire to search the records to the end that the truth may be known." The sisters paid out of pocket to print the free newsletter, issuing it "in honor of the Union soldiers of the Civil War" and "in memory" of their father, who "fought with Thomas at Chickamauga and marched with Sherman from the mountains to the sea." In fact, more than once, the sisters politely declined offers of financial aid from grateful readers; so it was that the newsletter served both memorial and didactic purposes.[8]

Despite the sisters' remarkable industry—in six years, for subscribers scattered across the country, the society produced nearly seventy bulletins—their organization is not well known. While their contemporary influence was perhaps negligible, the Stewarts' energies nonetheless supplied an important venue for men and women—including some prominent Northern public intellectuals—to maintain a coherent memory of the Union Cause. "There seems to be no publication that sets forth systematically data concerning this Confederate propaganda," Lucy explained. "The many letters and messages of approval we have received since issuing the first two bulletins," she reported in December 1935, "have been most gratifying and encouraging." "Some patriotic groups use the bulletins as part of their programs, editors use the data in editorials, and others . . . use the data in open letters and otherwise to refute published misrepresentations," the sisters optimistically reported the following year. Today, the Stewarts' efforts challenge those historians who have implied that white Northerners—and in particular white Northern women—ceded authority over the war's history to white Southerners or reconciliationists. Demonstrating that the Lost Cause

---

8 *Bulletin of the Society for Correct Civil War Information*, no. 1 (October 19, 1935): 1–4; "Announcements," *Bulletin of the Society for Correct Civil War Information*, no. 49 (January 1940): 1; *Bulletin of the Society for Correct Civil War Information*, no. 12 (September 1936): 1; see also *Bulletin of the Society for Correct Civil War Information*, no. 37 (January 1939): 1, and *Bulletin of the Society for Correct Civil War Information*, no. 61 (January 1941): 1. Samuel Franklin Stewart fought in the 31st Ohio Volunteer Infantry.

myth did not go unopposed even at the apex of its influence, the bulletins of the Society for Correct Civil War Information afford modern scholars a remarkable index of how the Civil War was remembered in the early to mid-twentieth century.[9]

* * *

"More than seventy years have passed since the Civil War ended in victory for the defenders of the Union," Lucy Stewart wrote in November 1935. "But now a paradoxical situation has arisen, steadfastly developed, through which the vanquished slaveholders are held up as deserving of the highest honors for their attempt to disrupt this Nation in order that they might perpetuate and extend their 'peculiar institution' of slavery." Over the next six years, with the help of her readers, Stewart cataloged nearly every official statement, public monument, or cultural production that honored Confederate leaders, disparaged the Union Cause, or otherwise effaced the cause, course, and consequences of the Civil War. Seemingly nothing escaped scrutiny—from a Jefferson Davis biopic bankrolled by the WPA's Federal Theatre Project to wall calendars ("a petty form of forcing recognition of Confederates upon our people"). Lucy filled many pages of the *Bulletin* with her meticulous review of legislation pending in Congress, rallying opposition to any offending bills and their sponsors. Often, prominent members of the society, including noted Boston attorney Norman F. Hesseltine and the Pulitzer Prize–winning biographer Charles Edward Russell of New York, contributed essays and book reviews. Hesseltine, for instance, repudiated the "many false" and "malicious" claims advanced

---

9 *Bulletin of the Society for Correct Civil War Information*, no. 1 (October 19, 1935): 2; *Bulletin of the Society for Correct Civil War Information*, no. 3 (December 19, 1935): 1; "Statement," *Bulletin of the Society for Correct Civil War Information*, no. 12 (September 1936): 1. Almost nothing has been written about the Stewarts or the Society for Correct Civil War Information, save a two-and-a-half page, Centennial-era retrospective. See Robert Dykstra, "The Continuing War," *Civil War History* 9, no. 4 (December 1963): 430–33. The society's membership roster included Albert Bushnell Hart, a professor emeritus of history at Harvard University, and Philemon Tecumseh Sherman, the son of U.S. General William Tecumseh Sherman. The African-American civil rights activist Mary McLeod Bethune may have been a subscriber; a finding aid for the microfilm edition of her personal papers notes 20 frames related to the "Society for Correct Civil War Information." See Randolph H. Boehm, comp., "A Guide to the Microfilm Edition of Black Studies Research Sources: Microfilms from Major Archival and Manuscript Collections, Mary McLeod Bethune Papers: The Bethune-Cookman College Collection, 1922–1955," 14.

81

BULLETIN

Society for Correct Civil War Information

Number 23   August,

To members of the Society and other friends of the Union:

THE U.D.C. AND THE BATTLE HYMN OF THE REPUBLIC
The Atlanta Journal of August 1,1937, publishes an article from Anniston,Alabama,entitled "Alabama U.D.C.Declares War On 'Battle Hymn'", which we quote in full as follows:

"A campaign to expunge the song,'Battle Hymn of the Republic,'from songbooks used in churches and schools in the south, was started Saturday by Mrs.C.W.Daugette,president of the Alabama division of the United Daughters of the Confederacy.

"'The song slanders the south and as a war song it certainly is out of place in official church hymnals and books used in the schools,' Mrs. Daugette said in letters mailed to various state leaders. 'This poem hypocritically presents the soldiers of the south as heathens and barbarians and the northern invaders as ministers of God on their holy way to smite the southern hosts.It is not a hymn to be sung in our schools and churches by southern-born boys and girls.It is entirely sectional and the whole tenor of the hymn is untrue to the south.It is the product of the inflamed mind and hardened heart of a northern woman,a strong Abolitionist and bitter enemy of the south, Julia Ward Howe.'

"Mrs.Daugette is the wife of the president of the State Teachers College at Jacksonville, Ala."

There is nothing new in this attitude of the United Daughters of the Confederacy:in the issue of December 4,1919,the National Tribune has an article by Isabell Worrell Ball,discussing the action of the Georgia U.D.C. in placing the Battle Hymn of the Republic under the ban in a resolution adopted at Valdosta,Georgia, in which they "refuse to sing or teach songs that celebrate the victory of former foes," for "such action would,in view of southern loyalty, 'profane the temple of patriotism.'"

Mrs. Ball compares the Hymn with Dixie,and as many of our readers may not have made this interesting comparison, we here invite attention to the words and sentiment of the two songs:

Battle Hymn of the Republic
Mine eyes have seen the glory of the coming of the Lord,
He is trampling out the vintage where the grapes of wrath are stored;
He hath loosed the fateful lightning of his terrible swift sword,
His truth is marching on.
I have seen Him in the watch-fires of a hundred circling camps;
They have builded Him an altar in the evening dews and damps;
I can read his righteous sentence by the dim and flaring lamps,
His day is marching on.
I have read a fiery gospel, writ in burnished rows of steel;
"As ye deal with my contemners,so with you my grace shall deal;
Let the Hero,born of woman,crush the serpent with His heel,
Since God is marching on."
He has sounded forth the trumpet that shall never call retreat;
He is sifting out the hearts of men before His judgment seat;
Oh, be swift,my soul, to answer Him! be jubilant my feet,
Our God is marching on.

The August 1937 issue of the *Bulletin of the Society for Correct Civil War Information* shows the type-written sensibility driving the newsletter. *Author's Collection*

about "the birth and parentage of Abraham Lincoln," while Russell offered a tart assessment of the revisionist historian Avery Odelle Craven's synthesis, *The Repressible Conflict.*[10]

Perhaps no source was more valuable to the society than the *Official Records of the War of the Rebellion*. Compiled by the U.S. War Department between 1881 and 1901, the 128 volumes of the *Official Records* presented the after-action reports and correspondence of both Union and Confederate regimental, brigade, division, corps, and army commanders. "All the volumes contain a vast store of information on both sides," Lucy Stewart explained, "but the last volumes contain revelations concerning the inside workings of the confederacy that are priceless to a real historian and damning to present day claims of the beauty and unanimity of the Confederate cause 'that rose so white and fell so pure of stain.'" The Stewarts urged their subscribers to mine the *Official Records*, assuring that the "clear and indisputable" record of "the Union soldiers" set forth therein would prompt any loyal heart to throb with pride. "Searching them," Lucy wrote on another occasion, "one learns how honorable was the Union cause . . . and how far from unified, and how far from stainless was the Confederate cause."[11]

A fidelity to wartime evidence and a near obsession with statistics ran through every issue of the *Bulletin*. By presenting cold hard "facts," the sisters did their best to rebut the most fanciful claims of Southern propagandists. When the *Woman's Home Companion* not only alleged that "the Army of

---

10 *Bulletin of the Society for Correct Civil War Information*, no. 2 (November 19, 1935): 1; *Bulletin of the Society for Correct Civil War Information*, no. 5 (February 19, 1936): 1; *Bulletin of the Society for Correct Civil War Information*, no. 26 (November 1937): 14; *Bulletin of the Society for Correct Civil War Information*, no. 15 (December 1936): 24; Norman F. Hesseltine, "Lincoln's Parentage," *Bulletin of the Society for Correct Civil War Information*, no. 32 (May 1933): 58–59; Charles Edward Russell, "The Glories of Good Old Slavery," *Bulletin of the Society for Correct Civil War Information*, no. 47 (November 1939): 73–76; Avery Odelle Craven, *The Repressible Conflict, 1830–1861* (Baton Rouge: Louisiana State University Press, 1939).

11 *Bulletin of the Society for Correct Civil War Information*, no. 1 (October 19, 1935): 2; *Bulletin of the Society for Correct Civil War Information*, no. 3 (December 19, 1935): 1; "Statement," *Bulletin of the Society for Correct Civil War Information*, no. 52 (April 1940): 25; see also *Bulletin of the Society for Correct Civil War Information*, no. 37 (January 1939): 1. Historian Yael A. Sternhell has recently argued that the *Official Records* was a tool of reconciliation, but Lucy Stewart—together with the Union veterans who maintained complete sets of the *OR* in their GAR halls—suggests that the tellingly titled records of the "rebellion" more often served as a potent weapon against Lost Cause propaganda. See Yael A. Sternhell, "The Afterlives of a Confederate Archive: Civil War Documents and the Making of Sectional Reconciliation," *Journal of American History* 102, no. 4 (March 2016): 1025–50.

the Union could only be kept at full strength by means of conscription," but simultaneously ignored the rather farreaching effects of Confederate conscription, Lucy responded in kind. Pointing out that "the total number of Union volunteers was 1,933,779," and that the draft yielded only "119,954" men, "of which 46,347 served," she gleefully contrasted the manpower situation in the loyal states with conditions in the South. The Confederacy, after all, turned to conscription nearly a year before the draft began in the North. Especially damning was an August 1862 letter, reproduced in the *Official Records* and brandished by Stewart, in which the Confederate Secretary of War conceded to Jefferson Davis that "voluntary enlistment" had "failed." By wielding statistics, the society also attempted to set the record straight on the treatment of prisoners of war, a subject that had produced decades of notorious invective above and below the Mason-Dixon Line. Citing numbers from official Confederate reports of Andersonville, the infamous rebel prison, Lucy pointedly asked, "What can we think of Southern chivalry if they find honor in this record which the Confederates themselves characterized as a reproach to them as a nation, a disgrace to civilization?"[12]

By the 1930s, nobody personified the spirit of Southern chivalry more than Robert E. Lee. As historian Gary Gallagher has persuasively argued, "for many white southerners Robert E. Lee and the Army of Northern Virginia came to embody Confederate national identity after the second year of the war." Thus it should come as little surprise that, as Robert Dykstra has noted, the *Bulletin* trained significant attention on the general. "Our readers cannot fail to note how insistently Robert E. Lee is dangled before the public eye," Lucy bemoaned. "We are now told that the valor and courage of Lee belongs to all Americans," but "why should the valor and courage of treason be considered a thing of value?" In January 1937, radios crackled with a Sunday afternoon broadcast revering Lee as a "Great American." General Motors sponsored the offending segment. "It takes a good deal of effrontery," Lucy snarled, "for General Motors to present Lee as an upholder of our traditions when he could not even wait to be out of the Union Army before accepting a command elsewhere." Elsewhere, the *Bulletin* not only

---

12 *Bulletin of the Society for Correct Civil War Information*, no. 1 (October 19, 1935): 3; *Bulletin of the Society for Correct Civil War Information*, no. 47 (November 1939): 79. See also Benjamin G. Cloyd, *Haunted by Atrocity: Civil War Prisons in American Memory* (Baton Rouge: Louisiana State University Press, 2010).

called into question Lee's reputation as a talented military strategist ("his Maryland Campaign was a ghastly failure," Lucy wrote, highlighting the "brilliant success for Union arms at South Mountain, a battle usually ignored by writers"), but also challenged popular notions that the rebel commander, "duty-bound" to follow the Old Dominion out of the Union, was indifferent on questions of slavery and race. Especially bold was an editorial titled "Lee and the Klan," which built connections between the beloved rebel general and white supremacist terrorism. "Lee was the first choice of the old Klan for commander; he is recognized and honored in the new Klan, although a traitor. . . . Is it a far cry to guess that the Klan or Klan influence is abetting the United Daughters of the Confederacy in putting Lee forward as the great exemplar of all the virtues of humanity, especially 'white supremacy?'"[13]

With this brand of unflinching candor, the *Bulletin* sought to remind its readers of just how much was at stake between 1861 and 1865—something that decades of radio broadcasts and postage stamps, commemorative coins and congressional resolutions had altogether effaced. Perhaps nothing better demonstrates the extent to which the war had been divested of all meaning and ideology than the way ordinary Americans referred to it. As historian William Pencak has observed, in the years immediately after Appomattox, the conflict was rarely pronounced a "civil war"; the struggle was often styled the "War of the Rebellion" or the "War for the Union," two names that kept the crime of treason in full view. Yet in the late nineteenth century, as Americans "clasped hands across the bloody chasm," they yearned for new ways to refer to the war. "The period from 1873 to 1889 was marked by terminological diversity," Pencak noted. By the early twentieth century, the term "War between the States," which "can imply either that the individual states were sovereign and had a right to secede, or that the two combatants

---

13 Gary Gallagher, *The Confederate War: How Popular Will, Nationalism, and Military Strategy Could Not Stave Off Defeat* (Cambridge, MA: Harvard University Press, 1997), 72; "The Lee Cult," *Bulletin of the Society for Correct Civil War Information*, no. 59 (November 1940): 79–80; *Bulletin of the Society for Correct Civil War Information*, no. 18 (March 1937): 44; "The Antietam Memorial Coin," *Bulletin of the Society for Correct Civil War Information*, no. 23 (August 1937): 86; "Lee and the Klan," *Bulletin of the Society for Correct Civil War Information*, no. 25 (October 1937): 4–5; see also "Facts about Robert E. Lee," *Bulletin of the Society for Correct Civil War Information*, no. 6 (March 19, 1936): 1–3, and "Lee and the Ku Klux Klan," *Bulletin of the Society for Correct Civil War Information*, no. 9 (June 19, 1936): 2–3. Robert Dykstra accurately reported that "the *Bulletin* expended much of itself defending 'Uncle Billy' and sparring with 'Ol Marse Robert.'" See Dykstra, "The Continuing War," 431.

were equally independent 'states' or nations," had become common. Predictably, railing against that label became "a second favorite campaign" of the *Bulletin*. "Did you ever notice that the phrase 'War between the States,' which the slavery sympathizers are trying so hard to substitute for Civil War, is ungrammatical as well as historically absurd?" queried Charles Edward Russell in December 1936. He ridiculed the notion that the Confederates were merely "defending themselves against an invader when they fired upon Sumter." This was nothing more than a "grim joke," Russell affirmed, but "not quite so monstrous as the notion that there can be anything nobly heroic about a war carried on to establish a slave empire."[14]

The *Bulletin* made no mistake of why the Confederates went to war. "The flag of the so-called Confederate States of America," one issue declared, "is the emblem of national destruction and human slavery."[15] But the Stewarts also sought to correct the historical record with respect to the conduct and character of Union soldiers and abolitionists. "To conceal the odium of their cause," Lucy wrote, "the Confederate sympathizers have steadily presented propaganda misrepresenting the Union Cause and defenders, as if to blacken the Union cause would whiten their own dark cause.[16] "While Union leaders and soldiers are discredited," she wrote, "and abolitionists are pictured as ruthless fanatics, the Confederates are presented as upholding a 'stainless cause.'"[17] Lucy cataloged the many affronts: "General Butler," who afforded sanctuary to freedom-seeking slaves at Fortress Monroe before demanding unconditional loyalty in New Orleans, was "usually referred to as 'Beast

---

14 William Pencak, "The American Civil War Did Not Take Place: With Apologies to Baudrillard," *Rethinking History* 6, no. 2 (2002): 217-221; Charles Edward Russell, "The Term 'War Between the States' Discussed," *Bulletin of the Society for Correct Civil War Information*, no. 15 (December 1936): 22; "Use of 'War Between the States,'" *Bulletin of the Society for Correct Civil War Information*, no. 38 (February 1939): 9-10; Dykstra, "The Continuing War," 431.

15 "Confederate Flag Flies Again," *Bulletin of the Society for Correct Civil War Information*, no. 30 (March 1938): 41.

16 "The Andersonville Scheme," *Bulletin of the Society for Correct Civil War Information*, nos. 44–45 (August–September 1939): 54; "Reconstruction," *Bulletin of the Society for Correct Civil War Information*, no. 41 (May 1939): 33–34.

17 *Bulletin of the Society for Correct Civil War Information*, no. 7 (April 14, 1936): 1.

Butler,'" while "Generals Hunter and Sheridan," she added, "come in for their share of defamation."[18]

Vindicating the conduct of Union soldiers became especially time consuming after the release of producer David O. Selznick's *Gone with the Wind* (1939), which indicted the Union army for pillage, plunder, and wholesale destruction. The blockbuster film earned a predictable ire in the pages of the *Bulletin*. "The frenzy with which Scarlett and her cause are permeating our country has the symptoms of a dangerous fever inoculating the body politic with a virus that destroys pride in our Nation and its defenders," Lucy wrote just two months after the film's theatrical debut.[19] One of the most remarkable contributions to the *Bulletin* came from the pen of J. C. Arbuckle, an Iowa infantryman who fought with Uncle Billy and lived long enough to read Margaret Mitchell's novel. "The author is simply a plain Rebel," the veteran snarled. "She cannot say anything too bad in regard to Sherman's army, the Yankees."[20]

Rescuing the reputation of carpetbaggers and Radical Republicans—and, in truth, the historical narrative of Reconstruction itself—was a concurrent project. "Perhaps next to Lincoln and Sherman no one is more vilified than Thaddeus Stevens, the Great Equalitarian," Lucy wagered. "In our reading we find him referred to, almost universally, with slurs and innuendoes reflecting on him, yet he was one of our great men."[21] If the facts of treason and the cause of slavery had been purposefully forgotten, then the means and ends of Reconstruction had been badly remembered. In Lucy's estimation, popular and scholarly descriptions of Reconstruction as

---

18 *Bulletin of the Society for Correct Civil War Information*, nos. 65–66 (May–June 1941): 36.

19 Dykstra, "The Continuing War," 431; "The Great March," *Bulletin of the Society for Correct Civil War Information*, no. 14 (November 1936): 9–10; "The 'Scarlett' Fever Epidemic," *Bulletin of the Society for Correct Civil War Information*, no. 50 (February 1940): 11.

20 Revisionist historians believed that the war was "needless" and "avoidable," the result of "blundering" politicians who perfected the art of "self righteousness" in the years leading to Fort Sumter. This interpretation, perfectly congruent with a contemporaneous scholarship that sentimentalized slavery as the "schoolhouse of civilization," held sway for several decades. See J. G. Randall, "The Blundering Generation," *Mississippi Valley Historical Review* 27, no. 1 (June 1940): 3–28. *Bulletin of the Society for Correct Civil War Information*, no. 22 (July 1937): 76–77.

21 *Bulletin of the Society for Correct Civil War Information*, nos. 65–66 (May–June 1941): 36.

the corrupt reign of vindictive, bayonet-wielding carpetbaggers made "a bid for sympathy for those who tried to bring about our Nation's destruction."[22]

* * *

In November 1941, Lucy Stewart informed her loyal readers that "the publication of future numbers depends on the war situation; we do not expect to publish any *Bulletins* if we are plunged into active warfare against the will of the great majority of American citizens." The nation entered the war the following month, after the Japanese attack on Pearl Harbor prompted most Americans to forsake reservations about U.S. intervention.[23] As promised, the *Bulletin* ceased—and never resumed—publication. Ironically, despite her initial opposition to American intervention, the enormous demands of the Second World War on the country as a whole served only to underscore Lucy's arguments about the importance of loyalty, the perils of sectionalism, and the liabilities of "the insidious propaganda that the Negro would be better off as a slave than free." "As we sow, we shall reap," Lucy had once admonished. "If treason is made to appear more noble than loyalty, sooner or later we shall reap treason."[24] "Those who extol the Confederate cause," she wrote on another occasion, "extol the principle of national destruction and endorse the establishment of another government within the territory of the United States of America."[25]

* * *

---

22 *Bulletin of the Society for Correct Civil War Information*, nos. 65–66 (May–June 1941): 38; see also "Reconstruction," *Bulletin of the Society for Correct Civil War Information*, no. 41 (May 1939): 33. See also Bruce E. Baker, *What Reconstruction Meant: Historical Memory in the American South* (Charlottesville: University of Virginia Press, 2007), and Carole Emberton and Bruce E. Baker, eds., *Remembering Reconstruction: Struggles over the Meaning of America's Most Turbulent Era* (Baton Rouge: Louisiana State University Press, 2017).

23 Lucy Stewart, "Notice," *Bulletin of the Society for Correct Civil War Information*, nos. 71–72 (November–December 1941): 61.

24 *Bulletin of the Society for Correct Civil War Information*, no. 23 (August 1937): 88; *Bulletin of the Society for Correct Civil War Information*, no. 4 (January 19, 1935): 1.

25 *Bulletin of the Society for Correct Civil War Information*, no. 64 (April 1941): 25.

Its prescience notwithstanding, the memory work of the Society for Correct Civil War Information was quickly forgotten; the homespun newsletter could hardly compete with the extravagance of the cultural productions it so pungently critiqued. But that was fine with Lucy Stewart, who believed that the Civil War had been commemorated to excess. Anniversaries, she wrote, offered only "another opportunity to distinguish treason."[26] "It is not clear why the 75th anniversary of the Battle of Gettysburg was celebrated," she protested after the final meeting of the Blue and Gray on that Pennsylvania battlefield. "As an indication of unity reestablished it was not necessary. The valor of the Union soldiers preserved that unity, and as victors they have forgiven, but have not condoned, the effort to destroy our Government."[27]

The erasure of the Union Cause over the course of the twentieth century entailed the erasure of its most ardent defenders. So it was that at the height of the Centennial, Robert Dykstra's "discovery" of the society's efforts "came as a shock." In a brief note that he published in the new academic journal *Civil War History*, the leading historian regarded the *Bulletin of the Society for Correct Civil War Information* as "a curious little publication" that "maintain[ed] a constant invective—which varied from venomous to merely waspish." Dykstra concluded his piece with the observation that the nation's entry into "a new war" brought an end to the Stewarts' "old campaign."[28]

But the campaign that Lucy Stewart, Helen Claassen, and their faithful readers and contributors waged—the one that they inherited from legions of Lincoln's battle-scarred veterans, former slaves, and free Blacks—had persisted. What is more, that campaign would persist well beyond the 1960s. Indeed, the gap between nuanced academic history and romanticized popular memory has so narrowed in recent years that were it around today, the society might claim a tentative victory. Unlike previous anniversaries, the Civil War Sesquicentennial was noted for stellar National Park Service programs that tracked the war in real time, from the perspective of ordinary soldiers, civilians, and the enslaved; pioneering digital projects and museum

---

26 *Bulletin of the Society for Correct Civil War Information*, no. 23 (August 1937): 88.

27 *Bulletin of the Society for Correct Civil War Information*, no. 35 (August 1938): 86.

28 Dykstra, "The Continuing War," 430–32.

exhibits that deepened our knowledge of the conflict and its long-term consequences; and public symposia that reached beyond the battlefield and into the contraband camp, the hospital, and the horrors of Reconstruction. More dramatically, as the Sesquicentennial years came to a close, a national debate about the appropriateness of Confederate iconography on town squares—a debate that would have been unimaginable at any point in the twentieth century—resulted in the removal of venerable monuments to Robert E. Lee, "Stonewall" Jackson, and common Confederate soldiers. Even Hollywood, once an unofficial province of the Lost Cause, has embraced a less romanticized Civil War. Director Gary Ross's film *Free State of Jones* (2016), for example, celebrated the Mississippi anti-Confederate Newton Knight, while director Nate Parker appropriated the title of D. W. Griffith's racist epic *The Birth of a Nation* (1915) for his 2016 drama about the life of the Southside Virginia slave rebel Nat Turner.

Why this dramatic shift in Civil War memory? For one, 9/11 did much to shatter enduring illusions of "American exceptionalism," obviating the need for consensus, flag-waving narratives of the nation's past. The global war on terrorism, now the longest war in U.S. history and, as of this writing, a conflict spanning four presidencies, not only renewed suspicions about the wisdom of military conflict but also supplied sobering reminders of the many human costs of war. Finally, white supremacist terrorism of the sort put on display in Charleston, South Carolina, in 2015 and Charlottesville, Virginia, in 2017 urged many to come to terms with the nation's racist past—and made abundantly clear that celebrations of the United States as "post-racial" in the first years of the twenty-first century were nothing if not premature.[29]

While not everyone has embraced a "new" Civil War history, it seems that now, more than ever, the public is mindful that memories of the past need not restrain us; as the Stewart sisters trusted so many decades ago,

---

29 The Sesquicentennial commemoration has not yet produced a voluminous literature, but the postmodern thread running through Thomas J. Brown, ed., *Remixing the Civil War: Meditations on the Sesquicentennial* (Baltimore: Johns Hopkins University Press, 2011), is suggestive of the larger takeaway here—that a consensus Civil War memory, or one that celebrates and uplifts—has collapsed. Informing my argument here is Yael A. Sternhell's important essay, "Revisionism Reinvented? The Antiwar Turn in Civil War Scholarship," *Journal of the Civil War Era* 3, no. 2 (June 2013): 239–56, which considers the effects of 9/11, the modern political climate, and the ongoing war on terror on Civil War historiography.

they can also set us free.[30] Understanding how and why we engage with the past—appreciating how popular culture has informed our ideas about history—is the necessary first step in that process of liberation. On this score, the book that you hold in your hands—surveying popular imaginings of the Civil War from Stephen Crane to Shelby Foote, from *Gone with the Wind* to *Roots*—is essential reading.

---

30 Neo-Confederatism is alive, though the urgency with which its exponents level their claims suggests its increasingly marginal position in culture and society. Much more troubling is the trend that Sternhell identifies—a "neo-revisionism" that regards the Civil War as both "avoidable" and "unnecessary."

xxxii *The Civil War and Pop Culture*

Photographing Pop Culture xxxiii

1. Photographing Pop Culture

by Chris Heisey

For many Civil War enthusiasts, books, especially so in our youth, turned us on to studying this nation's defining event. Perhaps it was the enduring prose of Bruce Catton and his many works chronicling the Union's eastern theater travails. Perhaps it was Douglas Southall Freeman capturing Robert E. Lee and the exploits of his Confederate armies in Virginia.

For me, the book was *In the pursuit of the General: A History of the Civil War Railroad Raid* by William Pittenger, which I read in seventh grade. It's one of the few books in my life that I can honestly say was worth the "I could not put it down" moniker. The 1965 reprint with its flashy red dust jacket and pencil sketch illustrations were a feast for a young artist about to bloom. Civilian James Andrews and his band of 21st and 33rd Ohioians and their daring theft of a Confederate locomotive on April 12, 1862—right from under the eyes of Atlanta residents deep in the city's heart—is the stuff that makes 13-year-olds into daredevil wannabes.

Little did I care that Pittenger was self-serving while mostly embellishing his eyewitness accounts. That he was he was locked in one of the attached boxcars for most of the 100-mile jaunt into north Georgia hardly made him witness to much of the chase, but he was privy to enough of the story to spin a fascinating yarn. The General locomotive ran out of fuel as the Texas locomotive closed in on a part of track just north of Ringgold, Georgia.

When I saw Walt Disney's 1956 movie about the chase soon after reading that book, I was even more hooked. The swashbuckling tale starring

Fess Parker (who went on the star in the TV series *Daniel Boone* in the 1960s) included embellishments and fact-void drama, yet the essence of the daring several-hour chase on my black-and-white TV at home was worth the popcorn and soda I downed while being mesmerized.

Some 40 years later, my still-thriving captivation with the tale led me to finally trace the steps of the legendary chase along the Western and Atlantic Railroad line right up to the point where the General conked out near Tunnel Hill. There, a small, humble marker denotes the climatic scramble that ended the chase with the thieves' capture. Many fields of battle stir my soul, but—with no embellishment on my part—I can say I have never been more moved to put my feet in the footsteps of history than I had been when I stood where my childhood heroes did something so daring.

Just a couple of years ago, I traveled to Chattanooga and there, on a rainy December day, I found the memorial marker to the Andrews Raiders and the gravestone of James Andrews, who was hung on June 7, 1862, as a guilty spy by Confederates whose embarrassment demanded lethal restitution.

Never do I underestimate the power pop culture can have in igniting a lifelong interest in a young person. It's priceless.

* * *

The rows and rows of graves at Andersonville speak to the immense horror the notorious prison inflicted upon Union prisoners of war in the conflict's waning days. Some 50 miles off the nearest main highway, it's a journey to reach the hallowed place—only a hillside, really—where thousands died in southern Georgia, a place where the sun bakes you with no mercy. Every time I have made the sojourn, I am the only person walking among the graves, the names on them long forgotten, it seems. The harrowing first-hand accounts of prison survivors stir me more than any of the places of hell men experienced in the war. It's a quiet, solemn, lonely, moving, gut-wrenching place worthy of mass visits by this nation's populace. A visit may just instill a sense of awe and reverence that seems so gone these days in our culture. It's one of my favorite places to photograph as light, form, and mood combine for dramatic images.

Back in 2014, on Christmas Eve, I was gifted with a rare opportunity to see the 75th anniversary, 70mm restored film release of *Gone with the Wind* on

vi: General Pickett's Buffet and the Battle Theater were Gettysburg icons dating back to the days when the Lincoln Highway brought carloads of families to the battlefield for family-fun vacations. *Chris Heisey*

xxxii-xxxiii: Father Corby's statue at Gettysburg—and a twin on the Notre Dame campus—are better known to football fans as "Fair Catch" Corby. *Chris Heisey*

xxxvi: The sun beats down on Morris Island. *Chris Heisey*

xxxviii-xxxix: Andersonville *Chris Heisey*

xl-xli: The monument to Andrews Raiders in Chattanooga National Cemetery features a sculpture of the General. *Chris Heisey*

xlii: Abraham Lincoln appears in more statues—nearly 200—than any other American. *Chris Heisey*

a huge movie screen in a small Pennsylvania college town's vintage theater. I'd never seen the movie. Given that it's a 3.5-hour sit, I nonetheless took the gift offered. I must confess, I rarely have time for anything that glorifies or romanticizes the manners of the peculiar culture from the Ninteenth-Century South, yet seeing this movie was a visual treat and an experience I will never forget. Nor will I ever underestimate its power to tell a story.

There are cringe-worthy moments that any sensible Twenty-First Century historian would have issues with. But, the Hollywood adaptation of

Ms. Mitchell's 1,000-plus-page novel is nothing short of miraculous since the movie was shot in the late 1930s—truly in Hollywood's infancy. As a visual artist, I was just mesmerized by the light, set, and shot angles. For a movie so old, it dazzled. I walked out of the theater realizing that preconceived opinions or prejudices never make good learning companions and, that Christmas, I made up my mind that I will never bad-mouth any artist's attempt at sharing this war.

* * *

Far from the glitz of Hollywood sits Morris Island, a barrier island that protects Charleston, South Carolina, from the pounding surf of the Atlantic Ocean. There on July 18, 1863, while the public was still digesting the news of Vicksburg and Gettysburg, the 54th Massachusetts stormed Battery Wagner in one of the war's most desperate charges. The movie *Glory* (1989), which depicts this action, remains my favorite Civil War movie by far. Beautifully acted by Oscar-winning actors, the movie depicts the hardships the African-American regiment endured to earn the right to die in glory among the dunes in the humid summer twilight.

Spending an entire torrid July day on the island with my young adult son a few years ago remains my favorite Civil War day of my life. He was old enough to fight and die like those brave men did 160 years ago. And he knew it. I could see it in his eyes.

It is well war is so terrible, the famous R.E. Lee quote goes. Those who are fond of violence and war never realize the justice and immense peace our Civil War can still bring to our aching culture.

xxxviii The Civil War and Pop Culture

Photographing Pop Culture xxxix

Photographing Pop Culture xli

1. Nineteenth-Century Social Media: Civil War Photography Was 150 Years Ahead of the Game

by Garry Adelman

A young man learns that a train has derailed near his office. He thinks he can be first on the scene with a camera to document the fresh destruction. With a friend in tow, he arrives at the site and shoots some photos. He selects his favorite image—one in which he appears, standing stoically. He perfects the view, provides a snappy caption, and shares it. Before long, thousands of people have seen the image.

Perhaps you picture a shaggy-haired hipster toting his smartphone to see a CSX freight disaster, but the above fictitious scenario depicts the Civil War era. Although taking a photograph was considerably more laborious, the steps toward 1860s photo virality were very much the same as today's—create, manipulate, caption, share. With easy access to digital scans of thousands of rights-free photos and the technology to cast them about with ease, it's no surprise that Civil War photography has gone viral again . . . this time in the forms of memes, videos, closely cropped photos and "then and now" pairs, comparing the site over time.

The original glass plate negatives (top) on which most Civil War documentary photos were taken could be printed and mounted (bottom left) with descriptive captions on the back, designed to sell the photo (bottom right). *Library of Congress*

Images of the past represent an opportune confluence of history, place, and people who, upon inspection, act very much like people of today. Grabbing attention in modern mainstream culture is difficult, but historic photos have an especially simple on-ramp—Civil War photos are as easily grasped, at least on the surface, as Instagram images. When viewers dig a bit deeper, they find that the people of the past were not only like us but managed to be ahead of us in several ways. Even as the broader Civil War subject is as controversial as it has been in decades, enthusiasm surrounding one of its most fundamental primary sources—the photographs—resurges.

A New App

Photographs have been viral ever since photography was successfully demonstrated in 1839. Inventor Louis Daguerre's daguerreotypes were positive photographs on copper plates. But daguerreotypes, as electrifying as they were to mankind, were one of a kind, like a Polaroid photograph,

Photographers who left their studios often slept in, or next to, mobile darkrooms complete with bulky cameras, glass plates, chemicals, and many other supplies from their studios. The scene at left showing camera and subject was recorded south of Knoxville, Tennessee, and the mobile rig at right was captured on glass at Cold Harbor, Virginia. Note the sitting photographer is holding a 4" x 10" glass plate for stereoscopic negatives. *Library of Congress*

which almost eliminated any level of distribution. To produce a duplicate photograph, a photographer had to take a photo of the original. Tintypes—positives on a thin piece of iron—were the same, except far more affordable. Your friends needed to be with you to see your photos because you almost certainly retained the only version of it—the original plate.

The 1850s' proliferation of the "wet plate" process, however, changed the game. Now, a fixed image on plate of glass coated with a light-sensitive, sticky chemical created a dual-purpose image. If the glass plate was put against a black background, the image appeared as a positive, which was known as an ambrotype. Without the black background, however, the glass plate was a negative, which could be used to expose a print on lightsensitive paper. This could be done again and again, limitless times. Copy negatives could be made to make even more prints, faster. At length, thousands of prints of a person, place, or thing could be made and sold.

This technology was profitable for the thousands of mid-nineteenth-century photographers spread across the United States, almost all of whom made their money inside their studios by taking portraits of individuals and groups and selling plates and prints thereof. Although technology did not allow the conversion of photos into photomechanical "half-tone" reproductions that could be printed in newspapers and magazines until 1880, Civil War–era photos could be converted into engravings or "woodcuts" for

Photographs could not be mass-printed in Civil War newspapers and periodicals. If a publisher wanted to issue real photos, they had to be printed and issued individually. Publishers could and did, however, convert photos into woodcut engravings, allowing for mass reproduction of a facsimile, such as the photo and engraving shown here of the U.S. Army officers who later surrendered at Fort Sumter. *Library of Congress*

printing in mass media, which allowed hundreds of thousands of people to see artistic renditions of photographs.

Just as today's mainstream media and social media lock onto the biggest and most interesting stories, nineteenth-century illustrated magazines and newspapers such as *Frank Leslie's* and *Harper's Weekly* did so, too. Back then, as today, the goal was to secure more subscribers.

The Civil War reached every community, and portrait photographers were already working in most of these communities. For the most part, these photographers stayed put. The cost and rigor of toting glass or tin plates to a war zone, stockpiling and staging photo chemicals, outfitting a mobile darkroom wagon or box, making needed connections with political and military stakeholders and photograph distributors, and embarking on an ultimately speculative and dangerous venture in the name of documenting history for mass sales was beyond the means, inclination, and skills of all but a few dozen photographers. Some removed much of the risk by working in the field as camp photographers taking soldier portraits, sanctioned by army commands that also used them to make photographic maps. A few Northern firms, however, took the expensive and speculative route and began following the armies and taking shots of battlefields, camps, hospitals, and more. Who would pay for such an endeavor? Was the photographer a historian or businessman? A documentarian or photojournalist? It's no surprise that millions of portraits were made during the Civil War compared to an estimated 10,000 outdoor, documentary photos.[1]

The coverage of documentary photographs is uneven. Most were taken by Northern photographers, and they skew heavily toward photos in the east at accessible sites—the places the Union army won or controlled. So, the most-photographed places are the respective capital cites of Washington and Richmond, followed by places where Union forces stayed for a while: Petersburg, Brandy Station, Charleston, Port Hudson, and Chattanooga, to name a few. Despite the gaps in coverage, the thousands of photographs that do exist allow today's historians not only to locate the places where these images were taken but also to provide an extra dimension. At some places, visitors can tour the battlefield by hopping from the site of one wartime photo to the next, a form of virtual reality that can intimately connect people with the past.

Clickbait

Photo historian William A. Frassanito calls war itself "the most disgusting of obscenities," and Civil War photographers came to realize that the public would respond to images of the terrible, dramatic, or intriguing aspects of warfare.[2] Before the emergence of photojournalism, war was usually portrayed as glorious, with brave soldiers wearing determined faces, fighting and dying "good deaths" atop enemy parapets. In 1862, however, photos of fresh graves, dead horses, and ultimately American battlefield carnage brought this glorified portrayal into conflict with reality. Now, a horrified but fascinated public could see that battlefield deaths were not necessarily so "good." Bloated, decomposing, and unidentified corpses of soldiers far from home with faces pressed to the earth was about as far as one could get from a good death.

---

1 The 10,000 estimate is based on the number of documentary photos in the contemporary catalogs of the most prolific photographers and on the photo holdings of the major Civil War photo repositories: The Library of Congress, National Archives, Smithsonian Institution, and the Army Heritage Education Center.

2 William A. Frassanito, *Gettysburg: A Journey in Time* (New York: Charles Scribner's Sons, 1975), 216.

Pets, mascots, and other animals appeared in Civil War photos, just like they do on social media today. The detail at top with soldiers in a Washington fort shows, upon closer examination, a dog perched atop an artillery limber chest. At bottom left is the most photographed canine of the Civil War: Union army quartermaster Rufus Ingalls's coach dog. Appearing in no fewer than six photos, the dog was more photographed than most Civil War generals . . . and you can even go and pose where it posed on the steps of Appomattox Manor at City Point, as the author did in 2008. *Library of Congress; Justin A. Shaw*

The 97 known documentary photos showing dead soldiers—some Union and some Confederate—sold well during and after the Civil War.[3] They still do. Any look at sales on eBay reveals that these images win higher bids. Likewise, my social media posts of photographs that include dead soldiers generally receive substantially more reactions and comments than other Civil War photos. Interestingly, the rules that govern the proliferation of such photos are still unwritten. When Civil War photographers took photos of battlefield dead, it was new—the public had never seen images of dead soldiers on battlefields before. What was appropriate? Would it shock the public into an antiwar stance or propel them to support this war so that the "dead shall not have died in vain"?[4] Today's Facebook posts that include

---

3 The 97 number is based on the author's long study of documentary photography, including the work of William A. Frassanito, which addresses 92 of the 97 photos in his works. The 97 images were photographed on eight occasions: 20 photos at Antietam; 3 at Corinth, 1 at Fredericksburg (1863), 37 at Gettysburg, 8 at Fredericksburg (1864), 6 at Spotsylvania, and 22 at Petersburg.

4 Abraham Lincoln, Draft of the Gettysburg Address: Nicolay Copy, November 1863; Series 3, General Correspondence, 1837–1897; The Abraham Lincoln Papers at the Library of Congress, Manuscript Division (Washington, DC: American Memory Project, [2000–02]).

dead soldiers are increasingly likely to be "covered" by Facebook, warding off the possibility of users seeing potentially offensive content unless they choose to.

Nineteenth-century "clickbait" also went beyond dead soldiers. Photos of famous people, pretty women, technological marvels, or piles of horse dung might draw customers into a photographer's gallery. Americans proudly displayed their photo collections in albums, not unlike shareable digital albums of today. Digital albums tend to be deeply personal to each creator, just as physical albums were in the past, and often included not only family photos, but images of celebrities or other notable people.

Way Ahead of You

In the most literal sense, and in most other ways that count, Civil War photographers beat you to the punch. Their cameras had better resolution than yours do. They used large screens to project images. They made panoramas, colored their photos as they pleased, and licensed their photos for wider distribution. They created forms of virtual reality and not only took most of their documentary photos in 3D but created 4D opportunities—the ability to stand at the very spot a Civil War stereo photo was taken and immerse yourself in the historic scene, thereby adding time to the traditional three dimensions.

Most Civil War documentary photographs were shot as stereographs with twin-lens cameras holding 4″ x 10″ glass plates. The two lenses were spaced an eye-width apart, mimicking how our eyes see and thus creating the potential to duplicate the 3D capability of our eyesight. The invention of the 3D photograph came almost simultaneously with the invention of photography. But the advent of the glass plate negative as well as a simple, handheld viewer paved the way for the mass production and marketing of 3D photos just before the war began. During the war, 3D photos were sold on cards called "stereo views" or "stereographs." When placed in a viewer, the images became more than a regular photograph. They were a photographic viewing experience. Stereo viewers and a stack of stereo view cards became commonplace in living rooms across the country beginning in the late 1850s and allowed people to visually travel the world, seeing the

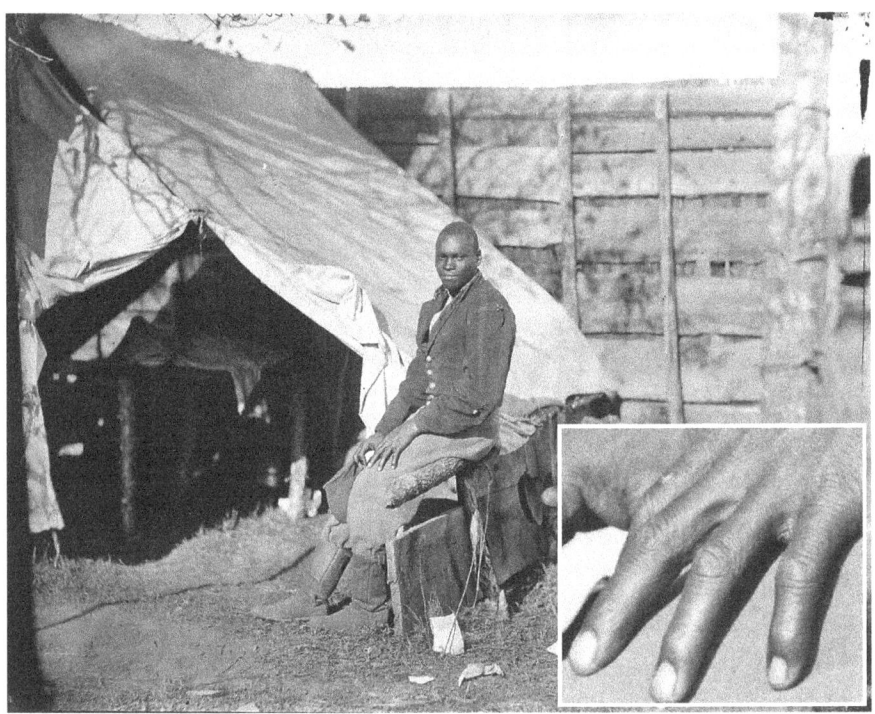

It is doubtful that Civil War photographers expected that unborn generations would zoom in on their photos the way we can today. And given our general propensity to pinch, pan, and zoom around imagery, we are fortunate that Civil War technology was so far ahead of us in terms of resolution. This photo was taken in the winter of 1863–64 at Brandy Station, Virginia, from approximately 15 feet away from the subject. Zooming in on the high-resolution TIFF scan of the original negative at the Library of Congress, we can see the small cracks in his hands. If his palms were up, we could see his fingerprints. Today's best digital cameras are just beginning to approach the resolution of nineteenth-century glass plate negatives. *Library of Congress*

Egyptian Pyramids in one moment and inaccessible Civil War battlefields in the next. The stereo viewer was the streaming service or internet of its day.

Documentary photographers also recorded images with single-lens cameras, and these negatives were often even larger, 7″ x 9″ for instance. The resultant 63-square-inch negative features a high level of resolution that 1.5 square inch, 35mm modern negatives do not approach and are comparable only to today's best, large-format digital cameras. It's not just the size of the negatives but the way Civil War negatives were created. Film negatives have grain. Digital images have pixels. But wet plate images are created on a chemical surface with no grain or pixels. The result is a historic document rich in detail and visual information and eminently zoomable.

In rare instances, Civil War cameramen recorded then-and-now photo pairs showing the same place over time, such as Fort Moultrie, South Carolina, in 1860 and 1861, and more modern times. Not only can one compare the prewar fort in 1860 at top left to the wartime fort of 1861 at top right, but one can also visit the site today and take a photo from a similar position, bottom left. Moreover, one can bring the historic photo with them and hold it up to the modern scene as at bottom right, which in this author's opinion creates a 4D experience. *Library of Congress; Garry Adelman*

Just download some of the thousands of scans at 100+ megabytes of Civil War glass plates at www.loc.gov to see the inadequacy of your camera's resolution! Under perfect conditions, can you photograph a person from 15 feet away and zoom in to see every crease in their fingers? I thought not.

In addition to creating and employing the art of photojournalism, Civil War photographers secured distant photos of actual fighting at Charleston Harbor and Fredericksburg, established full-scale map-copying operations, sometimes used "shutters" that allowed exposures of less than 1/10th of a second for stop-action photos (called "Instantaneous Views"), and took photos at the same place at different times over the years to show changes, adding time to the three dimensions inherent in 3D photos, creating a 4D experience long before that was even a thing. I would suggest that when time intersects with place and photography, the frequent expressions of those who experience it ("wow!" or "cool!") are simply struggling to describe the addition of a new dimension.

The idea that Civil War people did not smile for the camera (or did not smile at all) is easily dismissed by simply zooming in on some Civil War photos. There are hundreds of "smilers" in the depths of the images, including, clockwise from top left: a soldier on a bridge over the North Anna River; Kate Chase, a Washington belle and daughter of Salmon P. Chase; a soldier watching a cockfight at Petersburg; a soldier standing atop Petersburg fortifications at war's end; and, oddly, a girl at the Miller farm at Antietam—one of the battle's bloodiest places—soon after America's bloodiest day. *Library of Congress*

Just Like Us

The enduring fascination of Civil War photographs has less to do with the preservation of the plates and prints that "hold" the images and more to do with the subject matter, which continues to be relatable to succeeding generations. The more you see and the closer you zoom in to the people and places portrayed in these old images, the more familiar they all seem. Despite persistent beliefs that people didn't smile for nineteenth-century photos, hundreds of Civil War characters smirk, smile, beam uncomfortably, and even tilt their heads much like today's subjects. Civil War people had bad hair days and grew bad beards that they likely may have come to regret. Subjects fidgeted during photo exposures, and photographers even took selfies of a sort, regularly placing themselves or their photo assistants into their scenes, "tagging" the images as theirs.

The photo at top right has long been portrayed as United States Colored Troops in action near Dutch Gap, Virginia, but National Park Service historian Mike Gorman compared it with the image at left, which clearly demonstrates that the scene is posed. The photographer, T. C. Roche, who recorded several images at this dilapidated structure and whose darkroom and camera are visible at left, likely directed the moving of the barrel, the position of the men, and more. We should respect but be skeptical of what we see. Are we supposed to believe that the photographer parked his darkroom between the hostile battle lines and likely risked his life to secure this photo? *Library of Congress*

Our news feeds of today are filled with manipulated scenes, biased captions, and even fake news, as were the photos of the past. Despite what Frassanito calls the "overwhelming reality" of battlefield photos, photographers regularly created and enhanced scenes and stories to better project that which they wanted.[5] This was most often done at the time of creation by including props and people to reinforce a notion of war, death, or peace. Photographers placed and rearranged guns and ordnance for various treatments. People played dead for the camera, and, on at least one occasion, a man posed as a corpse next to an actual corpse.[6]

Moreover, authors, enthusiasts, and social media users frequently reinforce photographer manipulations and often create their own. *Civil War Times Illustrated* editor Frederick Ray documented that photographers moved one corpse at Gettysburg's Devil's Den to create a more dramatic photo. People have misinterpreted that fact to assume that photographers

---

5 Frassanito, *Gettysburg: A Journey in Time*, 16.

6 David Lowe and Philip Shiman, "Substitute for a Corpse," *Civil War Times*, December 2010, 40–42.

In terms of facial hair, Captain John Elder (left) and General Lafayette McLaws would compare favorably to any twentysomething today. *Library of Congress*

regularly dragged corpses around.[7] Yet, we only know of this one documented instance. Another photography misconception comes from Ken Burns's PBS series *The Civil War*, which gives the impression that the images on most or all Civil War negatives were burned away when they were used as glass for the nation's greenhouses. Burns has, in my experience, convinced an entire generation or more that the glass plates—what photo historians call "witness glass"—are simply gone. This is untrue. Bob Zeller demonstrates in his *The Blue and Gray in Black and White* that the negatives, or at least prints, of most of the key documentary photos have survived and are preserved in the Library of Congress, the National Archives, and other institutions.[8] The images used in greenhouse glass undoubtedly were common portraits, not the priceless plates showing U.S. Grant at Cold Harbor or Robert E. Lee in Richmond!

The most pervasive myths and mistakes about Civil War photography that appear in books and on social media come from ignorance or carelessness. Through his body of work, Frassanito has set up systems to help group

---

7 Frederic Ray, "The Case of the Rearranged Corpse," *Civil War Times Illustrated* 3, no. 6 (October 1961): 19. Ray was the first to publish that the two bodies were the same, and Frassanito expanded upon the story in *Gettysburg: A Journey in Time*, 186–95 and in *Early Photography at Gettysburg* (Gettysburg, PA: Thomas Publications, 1995), 268–73.

8 Bob Zeller, *The Blue and Gray in Black and White* (Westport, CT: Praeger, 2005), 189–200.

images by photographer, date, and location, but he also helps readers separate fact from fiction. People who identify a man wearing a top hat in a June 1865 Manassas photograph as Abraham Lincoln simply don't know that the photo was taken after Lincoln's death, not to mention that Lincoln was not known to have ever visited the Manassas battlefield. People often see what they want to see in photographs, and when you combine this with the quick treatment that most things receive in mainstream culture, it's no surprise that people see every man in a forage cap as General Stonewall Jackson or every Yankee with an Imperial goatee as Col. Robert Gould Shaw!

Whether or not today's mainstream culture gets its history right, even the briefest glimpse at Civil War photographs presents public eyes with something familiar—a person's expression, a house or a tree that looks like one they've seen, or some contraption that we think we could make better today—something American or human that might make you stop scrolling, click, and subscribe.

I. The Confederate Flag in Popular Culture

by John M. Coski

NOTE: This article was originally written in 2017. Parts of the essay are derived from The Confederate Battle Flag: America's Most Embattled Emblem *(Cambridge, MA: Belknap Press of Harvard University Press, 2006) and are used with permission.*

On June 17, 2015, a 21-year-old white man with an affinity for white supremacist groups and for the Confederate flag murdered nine African-American worshippers at Mother Emanuel African Methodist Episcopal Church in Charleston, South Carolina. Within weeks, South Carolina officials ended display of the Confederate flag on the grounds of the state capital, and major global retailers, including WalMart and Amazon, announced that they would cease selling Confederate flags and flag trinkets.[1]

---

[1] Here and throughout this essay, "Confederate flag" and "Confederate battle flag" refer to the familiar star-studded diagonal blue cross emblazoned on a red field, regardless of size, shape, and other details. For details about Confederate flags, see John M. Coski, *The Confederate Battle Flag: America's Most Embattled Emblem* (Cambridge, MA: Belknap Press of Harvard University Press, 2005), chap. 1; and Devereaux Cannon, *The Flags of the Confederacy: An Illustrated History* (Memphis: St. Luke Press, 1988).

It wasn't just politicians and national retailers but also bastions of white Southern identity who distanced themselves from the flag in the wake of the Charleston murders. Warner Brothers, creators of the enormously popular *Dukes of Hazzard* television show, ceased selling replicas of the "General Lee"—the 1969 Dodge Charger with the Confederate battle flag on its roof. NASCAR issued an official press release reiterating its desire to make its stock car racing events as "fan-friendly" as possible. "This will include the request to refrain from displaying the Confederate Flag at our facilities and NASCAR events."[2] Five years later, in the wake of the nationwide protests in reaction to the murder of George Floyd in Minneapolis, NASCAR issued a statement formally prohibiting the Confederate flag "from all NASCAR events and properties."[3]

Stung by such apostasy and resentful of the unprecedented hostility to a symbol now branded as irredeemably racist, the flag's defenders rallied around it, sending sales soaring and promising aggressive public display of the flag along the nation's highways.[4] The Charleston murders and the reaction against the Confederate flag was the *zeitgeist* in which this essay was written.[5]

The murders generated the most extensive and intensive hostility yet displayed toward the Confederate flag, but that hostility was hardly unprecedented. For nearly half a century, most headlines pertaining to the Confederate flag have involved efforts to define it as a symbol of hate and to remove it from the American public landscape versus countervailing efforts to preserve it as a symbol of Southern heritage.

What gets lost in the battles over the display of the Confederate flag is that, in order for it to be removed from the public landscape, first it had

---

2 Daniel Kreps, "Warner Bros. Bans 'Dukes of Hazzard' Car with Confederate Flag," *Rolling Stone*, June 24, 2015; "Statement from NASCAR Industry Members on Confederate Flag," July 2, 2015, Official NASCAR release, NASCAR.com.

3 www.nascar.com/news-media/2020/06/10/nascar-statement-on-confederate-flag/.

4 Hilary Stout, "Confederate Flag Sales Soar as Retailers Pull Stock," *New York Times*, June 23, 2015, https://www.nytimes.com/2015/06/24/business/amazon-big-retailers-remove-confederate-flag-merchandise.html.

5 Public protests against Confederate monuments in the wake of the murder of George Floyd in 2020 further marginalized the Confederate flag's place in popular culture, as noted elsewhere.

A replica of the General Lee sits in front of a *Dukes of Hazzard* museum in Luray, Virginia. The museum is owned and operated by Ben Jones who played Cooter on the show. *Chris Mackowski*

to be placed on that landscape. Before governments could decide that the offices, roofs, and plazas of public buildings were not appropriate places to display a flag that many believe to be a symbol of racism, government bodies and officials had placed them there purposefully. Before retailers could pull flags and flag trinkets from their shelves and websites, such items must have been popular enough to be manufactured, marketed, and sold. Before schools, organizations, and businesses could decide that Confederate flags don't belong on their signs and logos, those schools, organizations, and businesses had designed signs and adopted logos bearing the flag. In short, the popular culture and wider symbolic landscape to which the events of 2015 delivered a coup de grâce were relics of an earlier era that not only tolerated, but promoted, the display of the Confederate flag.

The heyday of the Confederate flag in American popular culture was relatively short, from the early 1950s into the 1980s. It was an era that many people today would find incredible and abhorrent. It was also an era that Americans before World War II—especially white Southerners—found incredible and abhorrent. But for radically different reasons. The Confederate flag's emergence as a pop culture icon met stiff resistance—from the most dedicated defenders of Southern heritage.

"The attention of members of our organization has been called to the fact that in certain demonstrations of college groups and some political groups at times the Confederate Flag or insignia has been displayed with seeming disregard of its significance," began a November 1949 report from a committee of the United Daughters of the Confederacy (UDC) investigating "legislation to protect the Confederate flag from misuse." The committee conceded that the misuse might occur "purely in the exuberance of youth or with no intent to disrespect" but recommended developing model legislation to be submitted to state legislatures.[6]

What had happened that prompted the UDC to issue formal rules and lobby for legislation curbing "misuse" of the flag more than 50 years after the Confederate heritage organization was founded? The answer to this obvious question testified to a fundamental change in the flag's place in American life and culture during the World War II era.

When the UDC's president general in 1948 issued an "urgent call" to curb misuse of the flag, she described the flag "as a sacred symbol to be used only by Sons and Daughters of the Confederacy."[7] Indeed, for most of the 75 years between the demise of the Confederacy and World War II, Confederate heritage organizations—the United Confederate Veterans (UCV), the Sons of Confederate Veterans (SCV), and the UDC—effectively owned the Confederate flags and defined their meaning. The UCV used the square battle flag pattern in its official logo and bequeathed it to the SCV for the same purpose, while the UDC adopted (and continues to use) the Confederacy's first national flag—the flag to which properly belongs the name "Stars and Bars." The heritage organizations used Confederate flags, especially the familiar red flag with the star-studded blue diagonal cross, in their meetings and rituals, Memorial Day observations, and monument

---

6 *Minutes of the Fifty-Sixth Annual Convention of the United Daughters of the Confederacy, 1949*, 186–87.

7 *Minutes of the Fifty-Fifth Annual Convention of the United Daughters of the Confederacy, 1948*, 68–69.

dedications. Between the 1890s and the 1930s, the Confederate flag was an important icon in the white Southern civil religion.

For that reason, it was virtually absent from popular culture except in the portrayal of Confederate history. Popular novels of the Civil War, from late nineteenth-century boys' adventure stories to the novels by Southern writers Ellen Glasgow and Margaret Mitchell, captured the Confederate battle flag's visceral connection to the thinly clad soldiers in gray who carried it. Popular films followed suit. Colonel Ben Cameron dramatically rammed a battle flag down the barrel of a Federal cannon during the dramatic battle sequence in D. W. Griffith's 1915 epic film, *The Birth of a Nation*. The celebrated panning shot in David O. Selznick's 1939 *Gone with the Wind* showing acres of wounded soldiers sprawled around the Atlanta railroad depot stops on a Confederate battle flag flapping high over the grim scene.

There were early twentieth-century portents of wider use of the Confederate flag in popular culture. It began appearing in advertisements as a symbol of the South and of Southern identity divorced from the historical context of the Confederacy. More significantly, the flag gained a foothold at southern colleges and universities as part of campus social life. Students at Clemson University raised the flag in 1904 and rioted when officials tried to remove it; University of Alabama students reportedly decorated Tuscaloosa light poles with Confederate flags after the Crimson Tide defeated the University of Washington in the 1926 Rose Bowl.[8]

The presence of Confederate flags on southern campuses probably owed to the Kappa Alpha Order (KA), a fraternity that began as a Confederate memorial organization. It was founded at Washington College in Lexington, Virginia, when Robert E. Lee became president in 1865. Not surprisingly, as the generations passed, KA became more fraternity than memorial organization, and the trappings of Confederate heritage grew less sacrosanct. KA chapters began holding "Old South" balls and parades as early as the 1920s. By the early 1940s (possibly decades earlier), Confederate flags had become part of the ritual of KA social events.[9]

---

[8] "College Boys and the Confederate Flag," *National Tribune*, April 21, 1904; President Patrick Hues Mell to Adjutant General, War Department, March 23, 1904, University Archives, Clemson University Libraries; Andrew Doyle, "Turning the Tide: College Football and Southern Progressivism," *Southern Cultures* 3 (Fall 1997): 42.

[9] See Coski, *Confederate Battle Flag*, 89–90.

Young southern men embraced the Confederate flag not only on college campuses but also in military service. A few stories of Confederate flag use emerged during the "Great War," but it was during World War II—at home and in the European and Pacific theaters—that Confederate flags garnered widespread attention. "What is the explanation for this display of these flags of the Confederacy?" asked the *Baltimore Evening Sun.* "Offhand, one might dismiss it as youthful high jinks, the natural ebullience of certain southerners in the army," but the editors speculated that the southerners were remembering and summoning the South's martial traditions. "And so, just to emphasize and particularize their own region, they hoist a Confederate flag. It seems a harmless and rather amusing gesture," the editors concluded. Other newspaper accounts echoed this attitude, though the military brass typically turned a jaundiced eye toward Confederate flags on American ships and bases and even in combat when they brought media attention.[10]

From the military forces and the fraternity houses the Confederate flag made its way onto the football field. The University of Mississippi became the school most closely associated with the Confederate flag, but it was the University of Virginia that first drew widespread attention. As early as the 1940 season, UVA fans cheered on their team with Confederate flags. The practice made national headlines in October 1947, when a *Time* magazine article implied a relationship between the flag waving and visiting Harvard's African-American tackle, Chester Pierce. Stung by the publicity, the university asked fans to leave their flags at home when the team went to Philadelphia to play the University of Pennsylvania in November. Instead, "the largest concentration of southerners in Pennsylvania since Gettysburg" crossed the Mason-Dixon Line with hundreds of flags.[11]

The Confederate battle flag had gained a foothold in American popular culture before 1948. This was important because the events of 1948 linked Confederate flag waving with white Southern resistance to integration and with the increasingly angry defense of white supremacy. If the Confederate flag's intrinsic association with the slaveholding Confederacy were not

10 "Flags of the Confederacy," reprinted in *Richmond Times-Dispatch*, July 3, 1944. See Coski, *Confederate Battle Flag*, 91–94.

11 *Time*, October 20, 1947, p. 25; "Virginia Victory," reprinted in *Richmond Times-Dispatch*, October 16, 1947.

enough to make it a controversial, racially charged symbol, its white supremacist use tainted even the most seemingly innocent pop culture use.

Perhaps the most important image ever taken of the Confederate flag was the widely syndicated photo of the July 17, 1948, States' Rights Party convention in the Birmingham, Alabama, City Auditorium. The convention met after southern delegates bolted the Democratic Party convention after it adopted a platform endorsing civil rights. The States' Rights Party (which headline writers dubbed "Dixiecrats") and its presidential candidate, J. Strom Thurmond, of South Carolina, championed racial segregation. Amid the cheering crowd were several Confederate battle flags held high by young men—convention delegates from more than a dozen southern colleges and universities—who had been waving flags on campuses and in military service for the last decade. Indeed, the University of Alabama's convention delegates returned from Birmingham to Tuscaloosa and "brought Confederate and Alabama flags out of mothballs" to fly on fraternity houses. The university's KA chapter passed a resolution condemning "the recent encroachment by the antagonistic North upon Southern culture and ideals," declaring that "from this day on the Confederate flag shall fly from the hights [sic] of the Kappa Alpha mansion" and calling for "ye men of Lee" to "Don your colors and put asunder this menace which threatens our age-old tradition."[12]

Those were the "demonstrations of college groups and some political groups" that elicited formal protest from the UDC. The election brought the surprising triumph of Harry S. Truman—and his party's civil rights agenda—and the defeat of the Dixiecrats. But neither the states' rights rebellion nor the Confederate flag faded away.

In 1950–51, the flag that began life as a battle flag of the Confederacy's most successful army emerged as a national popular culture symbol. The national media reported on the "flag fad" with amazement and amusement. "The fad that began slowly last year reached mammoth proportions in the July 4th parade at Daytona Beach, Fla.," reported *Newsweek* in September 1951. "Rebel flags were flown from planes at the air races in Detroit, carried by Shriners in their New York jamboree, and flaunted at the Atlantic City

---

12 Jim Harland, "Confederate Flags Fly Again on Capstone Fraternity," *Crimson-White* [University of Alabama], July 20, 1948; Kappa Alpha quoted in Chris Springer, "The Rebel Flag: The Confederate Flag and Its Image in America from 1865 to the Present" (B.A. Thesis, Brown University, 1990), 21. See Coski, *Confederate Battle Flag*, chap. 5.

Beauty pageant." Companies manufacturing and selling flags reported insatiable demand, much of it coming from north of the Mason-Dixon Line. "Everywhere along the Atlantic seaboard from New York to Miami and westward to the Mississippi watershed pert little banners wave in the breeze from car antennae, souvenir stands, bicycles or in the hands of youngsters, teenagers and grownups," John Long wrote in a *New York Times Magazine* feature story.[13]

"Why fly it now?" Long wondered aloud. "Why do cars of the northern states which defeated the Confederacy display it? Is there some deep underlying significance or political undertone or sectional significance to the movement? The answer, of course, is Certainly not. Although it may be difficult to explain to an outsider, America has a word for it: *fad*." Other observers agreed. "Don't ask me why," quipped a Birmingham, Alabama, flag seller. "Sometimes it's little green lizards, sometimes it's birds-on-a-stick. Now it's Confederate flags." Even an article in *The Crisis*, the magazine of the National Association for the Advancement of Colored Peoples (NAACP), concluded "that the waving of the Confederate battle flag is just a fad like carrying foxtails on cars, or the increasing use of skull and crossbones on flags, T-shirts, caps, and cuff links."[14]

Other African-American voices dissented from this conclusion, especially when the flag began appearing among American military forces.[15] The "flag fad" coincided with the Korean War. As in World War II, the new conflict brought reports of American troops displaying Confederate flags on ships and at bases home and abroad. Fort Jackson, South Carolina, was home to National Guard units from Alabama and Mississippi that made the Confederate flag their de facto symbol in 1951, marching with it on parade and wearing it on uniforms and accoutrements.[16] Because the United States

---

13 "Those Rebel Flags," *Newsweek*, September 24, 1951, 24; John Long, "Conquest by Bunting," *New York Times Magazine*, October 14, 1951, 52; Georgiana M. Root, "Stars and Bars Flying from Korea to Boston in Furious Flag Fad," *Wall Street Journal*, September 1, 1951; Coski, *Confederate Battle Flag*, chap. 6.

14 Long, "Conquest by Bunting," p. 52; Ruth Danehower Wilson, "Confederate Flag Wavers," *The Crisis* April 1952, 240.

15 See especially the *Pittsburgh Courier*, September 29, 1951.

16 Coski, *Confederate Battle Flag*, 112–15.

led a coalition operating under the aegis of the United Nations, its troops did not raise the Stars and Stripes in Korea; this left a symbolic vacuum that the men filled with unofficial flags. So prominent were Confederate flags that a soldier from New York proposed raising a New York City flag over his base "to give the Confederate emblem some healthy competition." New York City obligingly sent 100 city flags to servicemen in Asia. Other New Yorkers embraced the Confederate flag, noting that the United States was, after all, fighting to defend *South* Korea.[17]

Rather than sharing in the light-hearted spirit, the editors of the African-American newspaper the *Pittsburgh Courier* considered the Confederate flag an "emblem of disunity" and warned that its reappearance was "not a good omen for a nation which is pleading for unity in the face of world communism." The *Courier* also considered the Confederate flag "an odious symbol of slavery and servitude of Negroes in the South." The *Courier*, the *Chicago Defender*, and the *Afro-American* (published in Baltimore and Richmond) cautioned against allowing the trivial material culture aspects of the "flag craze" to distract attention from its sinister ideological significance.

The flag fad made strange bedfellows of the African-American press and Confederate heritage organizations. They all deplored the Confederate flag's emergence into popular culture, but for different reasons. The UDC continued its campaign against widespread use of the flag. The Advisory Council of KA accepted responsibility for the fraternity's role in "popularizing" the flag's display and requested that its members cease displaying it on neckties, caps, and automobile window stickers, which it characterized as "cheap, tawdry and vulgar exhibitions."

Despite protests from keepers of the Confederate flame, "cheap, tawdry, and vulgar exhibitions" only increased during the 1950s and 1960s. Those exhibitions not only took the form of commercialism but also widespread use by the Ku Klux Klan and ordinary white Southerners as an explicit symbol of resistance to racial integration, especially after the 1954 U.S. Supreme Court decision in *Brown v. Board of Education*. The white supremacist use of the flag vindicated the warnings of the African-American press and

---

17 "Marine 100th New Yorker in Korea to Fly a City Flag," *New York Times*, March 23, 1952; Scott Blomeley to *New York Times Magazine*, November 4, 1951; Henry H. Sampson, Jr., to John M. Coski, December 1, 1998; George J. Ellis to John M. Coski, November 11, 1998.

prompted white liberals to denounce the "slack-jawed youth" who defamed the honored banner.

It was in the 1950s and 1960s that the Confederate flag became part of America's pop culture vernacular as a symbol of things southern. The Confederate flag became a fixture of roadside America. Products, businesses, organizations, schools, and local governments associated with the South or with "Dixie" adopted Confederate flag iconography—something that seemed as natural in those decades as it had been unthinkable before 1948.

It also was in the era from the late 1940s to the early 1960s that pop culture stereotypes involving the Confederate flag evolved. Aside from politically charged stereotypes such as the flag-waving Klansman, most of the types spoke to a "rebel" identity. By the early 1960s, the flag had become a totem of motorcycle riders, long-distance truck drivers, and rural "rednecks," regardless of regional origin. Each of those stock types cultivated an image of fierce independence and individualism.

The rebel image and fierce individualism were central to another bastion of white Southern culture that became closely associated with the Confederate flag almost from the starting gun. NASCAR—the National Association of Stock Car Auto Racing—was organized in February 1948, a few months before the Dixiecrat convention. Opening in 1950, the new raceway in Darlington, South Carolina, immediately embraced the Confederate flag as a de facto logo for the Southern 500 and, beginning in 1957, for the Rebel 300 (later the Rebel 500). Although NASCAR was never entirely a southern phenomenon, the archetypical driver was southern in accent and in style, and the sport contributed to an identity for the Confederate flag that transcended region.[18]

Hollywood and television reflected the Confederate flag's new pop culture presence. *Operation Pacific*, a film released in January 1951, captured the high profile that the Confederate flag then held in the American military forces. Set in the Pacific theater of World War II and starring John Wayne and Patricia Neal, the film included a scene in which crew members reverently present to submarine commander Wayne a Confederate flag found among the possessions of a southernborn sailor. In contrast, an

18 See Coski, *Confederate Battle Flag*, 126–27.

episode of the Bugs Bunny cartoon, "Southern Fried Rabbit" (released in May 1953), featured offensive stereotypes of white and Black southerners and, incidentally, a Confederate flag standing guard with an unreconstructed Yosemite Sam at the Mason-Dixon Line. *Lover Come Back*, a March 1962 Rock Hudson, Doris Day, Tony Randall screwball comedy also starred Edie Adams as showgirl "Rebel Davis," whom Randall hired to entertain and win over a southern-born client. At one point in her charm offensive, Adams strips down to Confederate flag bustier.

Its varied use in film and television revealed that the Confederate flag had become familiar in contexts other than straight Civil War history and could serve as symbolic shorthand for other things—most notably white Southern identity.

Responsible for the fad that launched the Confederate flag into American popular culture, young people continued to be among its primary users. Ignoring their organization's 1951 appeal to cease irresponsible use of the flag, KA chapters all over the South ramped up the ritual of "Old South" events with parades, elaborate costumes, "secession" ceremonies, and flags aplenty. The University of Mississippi made the flag its all-but-official school symbol in the 1950s. Beginning in 1948, the band carried a huge flag onto the football field at halftime; the school's majorettes and "Rebelettes" marched with flags, and flags appeared on yearbooks and football game programs.[19]

The flag became a fixture at secondary schools, which were expanding in number to accommodate the "Baby Boom" generation. Testimony to how such things had become part of the American vernacular, many new schools chose "Rebels" as their nicknames and, inevitably, "Dixie" as their fight song, the Confederate flag or "Johnny Reb" as their school symbols. Not all of those schools were in the South. When the Thornton Fractional School District in suburban Chicago split into northern and southern districts in

---

19 *Ole Miss,1950*, 16–17; *Ole Miss, 1953*, cover, Homecoming and football section, 138; *Ole Miss, 1955*, 192; *Ole Miss, 1957*, 26–27; *Ole Miss, 1958*, 149; Kevin Pierce Thornton, "Symbolism at Ole Miss and the Crisis of Southern Identity," *South Atlantic Quarterly* 86 (Summer 1987): 254–68.

1958, the southern district embraced Confederate iconography. So did the new Southside High School in Muncie, Indiana, in 1962.[20]

Predictably, the observation of the Civil War Centennial brought a renewed avalanche of commercial products bearing the Confederate flag. Formed in 1957, the U.S. Civil War Centennial Commission resolved to hold a commemoration "free from stains of commercialism or vulgarity." A committee issued "Aids to Advertisers," offering lists of Dos and Don'ts, including an admonition not to "debase flags, symbols, or insignia by misusing them for commercial purposes."[21]

State governments joined the campaign to punish "desecration" of the Confederate flag.

In February 1958, the South Carolina legislature adopted a concurrent resolution denouncing Martex Corporation executive William D. Hartman as "an unworthy American" because of his role in producing a line of "Dixie beach towels" bearing the Confederate flag. The resolution denounced the towels as "a veiled attack, parading in the garb of legitimate advertisement, on the valor, courage and sacrifice of the Men in Gray who followed the immortal Robert E. Lee in defense of what was then, and is now, a burning question among all of the States of this Union—'What rights are reserved to the States?'" An SCV officer from Mississippi noted that his state had on the books a law protecting the Confederate flag from "desecration" (a law passed in 1916 during an era in which Mississippi and all other states passed laws protecting the Stars and Stripes). Prompted by the SCV, South Carolina passed its own act within days. The law incorporated standard language of other flag desecration acts, declaring it a crime to create, display, sell, or give away "an article of merchandise or a receptacle of merchandise upon which shall have been printed, painted, attached or otherwise placed a representation of any such flag, standard, color, or ensign, to advertise, call attention to, decorate, mark, or distinguish the article or substance on which placed." By the beginning of the Centennial, Florida, Louisiana, and

---

20 Donna Kiesling, "Confederate Flag Flap Still Flying at School," *Chicago Tribune*, August 19, 1993; Bonnie Miller Ruben, "Thornton Raises New Flag, but Not All Salute," *Chicago Tribune*, February 11, 1994; *Banks v. Muncie Community Schools*, 433F. 2d, 296–99.

21 "Aids to Advertisers," Committee on Advertising, Civil War Centennial Commission, 1961, CWCC Subject Files, National Archives and Records Administration, RG 79, Entry 32, Box 45.

Georgia had passed similar legislation.²²

The guidelines and laws had no measurable effect. "The enterprise of manufacturing Confederate flags and other secessionist paraphernalia, never in a languishing state, threatens to become a major industry before taps sounds the end of Appomattox day in 1965," warned historian John Hope Franklin in 1962. Items bearing Confederate flags and the increasingly popular "Forget Hell" slogan provided a pop culture rebuff to those who would stem the tide of flag-themed commercialism. In 1966, a South Carolina legislator decried the "cheapening" of the Confederate flag by use on towels and clothing, and tried in vain to strengthen the existing legislation.²³

Does it "cheapen" the Confederate flag to feature it on clothing? *Chris Mackowski*

---

22 "Those Confederate Beach Towels," *Richmond Times-Dispatch*, March 3, 1958; William D. Workman Jr., "Group Seeking Ban on 'Dixie Towels,'" February 26, 1958 and "Opposition to 'Dixie Towel' Growing," February 27, 1958, clippings in clipping book 8, William Workman Papers, South Caroliniana Library, University of South Carolina; T. W. Crigler Jr., to the Honorable Richard K. Jackson, March 2, 1958, and Richard K. Jackson to William D. Workman Jr., March 6, 1958, in Vertical Files (Flags, Confederate), South Caroliniana Library, University of South Carolina; *Acts and Joint Resolutions of the General Assembly of the State of South Carolina Regular Session, 1958* (Columbia: State Budget and Control Board, 1958), 1676–77.

23 John Hope Franklin, "A Century of Civil War Observance," *Journal of Negro History* 47, no. 2 (April 1962): 104; William E. Mahoney, "Pickens County's Sen. Morris Deplores 'Cheapening' Abuse of Confederate Flag," *The State* [Columbia, SC], December 2, 1965.

Ultimately, it was not the "cheapening" of the flag but its increasing use by white supremacists in the ongoing civil rights battles that transformed its place in American culture. Immediately upon the flag's expanded use in popular culture and in the American military, the African-American press had warned against its darker connotations. The subsequent decade proved them prescient. The flag's symbolic accompaniment to segregationist gatherings in New Orleans, Birmingham, Montgomery, and the University of Mississippi fixed it in the national consciousness as a symbol of racism.[24]

The backlash was not long in coming. As early as 1964, groups in San Francisco protested a public display of the Confederate flag.[25] A spate of lawsuits succeeded in banishing the flag from newly integrated public schools, especially where plaintiffs could demonstrate that the flag had been used as a symbol of resistance to integration.

Achieving status as a controversial symbol that liberal activists and Federal courts linked with racism did not prevent proliferation of the Confederate flag as a popular culture symbol. In fact, some of the most enduring and influential pop cultural associations developed *after* the flag began appearing in the headlines as a racist symbol. For several decades, rival interpretations coexisted in America's mass media.

Several 1970s country artists and southern rock bands, most notably Hank Williams Jr., Alabama, and Lynyrd Skynyrd, proudly embraced the Confederate flag along with a "redneck" image. The latter group's 1974 song "Sweet Home Alabama," with a pugnacious reply to singer Neil Young's 1970 song "Southern Man," became and remains a white Southern anthem. Williams coupled a tough, slightly uncouth image with a flag-toting, pro-Southern belligerence, most notably in his 1988 "If the South Woulda Won." More recent artists, such as Tom Petty and the Heartbreakers, Confederate Railroad, and the Detroit-born white rapper "Kid Rock," continued the southern music flag tradition into the 1990s and the new century.[26]

---

24 See Coski, *Confederate Battle Flag*, chap. 7.

25 *San Francisco Chronicle*, June 17, 1964; July 24, 1964.

26 See Coski, *Confederate Battle Flag*, 174; Jim Cullen, *The Civil War in Popular Culture: A Reusable Past* (Washington, DC: Smithsonian Institution Press, 1995), chap. 4; Brian McCollum, "Kid Rock: Confederate Flag Was Dropped Years before Protest," *Detroit Free Press*, July 16, 2015.

The most significant pop culture embrace of the Confederate flag and a positive image of white Southerners did not come out of Alabama but out of Hollywood. Warner Brothers and CBS television in 1979 brought to the small screen a wildly popular show featuring rural southerner good guys who drove a car bearing a Confederate flag painted on its roof. *The Dukes of Hazzard* was one of television's top-rated programs between 1979 and 1985, ranked third in the TV ratings in 1980–81, with 46 million viewers. The show catapulted its three principal human stars to celebrity and sex-symbol status, but the real star of the show was the muscle car 1969 Dodge Charger named the "General Lee." The producers considered the car a bona fide star of the show; appearing in approximately 30–35 percent of the show and responsible for $100 million in annual sales of toys, party goods, musical instruments, towels, and other retail products bearing the Confederate flag, the car accounted for more than half of the 60,000 fan letters that the show received each month. So profitable was the "General Lee" and its flag that the show's producer, Warner Communications, aggressively (and successfully) protected its trademark in federal court, winning at least two cases against manufacturers of copycat toy cars.[27]

After ceasing production in 1984, the show long enjoyed a cult following, living on in reruns and in the form of a 2005 feature film and a 2007 TV movie. A small fleet of full-size "General Lee"1969 Dodge Chargers made guest appearances at special events throughout the South.

Within three years after *The Dukes of Hazzard* went off the air, the Confederate flag became a high-profile object of controversy. The NAACP launched a concerted campaign to remove the flag from the state flags of Georgia and Mississippi and the Alabama and South Carolina capital buildings. As those and other controversies played out, national news bureaus based in Atlanta acquainted Americans with the binary argument of the Confederate flag as a symbol of "heritage" or "hate."[28]

The appearance of the flag in a pair of 1994 Academy Award–winning films provides a barometer of how it had become a darker, more negative

---

27 *Warner Brothers, Inc. v. Gay Toys, Inc.*, 724 F. 2d. 327(1983), 331–32; *Processed Plastic Co. v. Warner Brothers Communications* 675 F. 2d 852 (1982), 854; Tony Schwarz, "The Attraction of Hazzard," *New York Times*, April 25, 1981.

28 See Coski, *Confederate Battle Flag*, chap. 12.

symbol since the 1950s. In Paramount's *Forrest Gump*, "slack-jawed" redneck types in a beat-up truck (not the good-old boys of *The Dukes of Hazzard*) harassed and chased adolescent Forrest. The camera lingers on a small Confederate flag adorning the truck's front grille (a credible prop for a scene set in the early 1960s), linking the flag with the redneck's malevolent character. In Miramax's *Pulp Fiction*, the gangland boss and the boxer who double-crossed him waged a brutal fight along the streets of Los Angeles before rolling into a pawnshop. The camera briefly freezes on a Confederate flag on the wall, intimating that something bad was going to happen. Indeed, the redneck storeowners subdued the fighting men, took them to a secluded basement, and prepared them for a sadistic homosexual rape.

Before the end of the twentieth century, the flag's racist and darker associations brought a cultural backlash that mirrored the political backlash. Sensitive to criticism from civil rights activists, businesses and organizations that had embraced Confederate iconography in earlier decades distanced themselves from the flag. The Boy Scouts of America in 1991 announced that it would no longer allow the battle flag at official functions. American motorcycle manufacturer Harley-Davidson, which in 1977 had released a limited "Confederate Edition" motorcycle featuring gray paint and battle flag decals, in 1994 forbade the sale of products bearing the Confederate flag. Stung by criticism, the Milwaukee-based Harley-Davidson soon modified the policy to allow local dealers to decide whether or not to sell battle flag merchandise. Even NASCAR steered clear of the battle flag. As stock car racing became a mainstream and enormously successful commercial sport, race officials quietly ended the official use of Confederate symbols. NASCAR, in 1993, barred a car sponsored by the Sons of Confederate Veterans bearing the organization's battle flag logo.[29]

The trend continued into the new millennium. Spurred by several high-profile incidents involving racist gestures and the flag, the Kappa Alpha Order, which, since 1951, had issued several pronouncements discouraging

---

29 Letters of Jim Zeirke in *Civil War News*, October 1994, 3, and *Bugle Call* [monthly newsletter of the Lieutenant General Leonidas Polk Camp 1446, SCV], October 1994, and in *Civil War News*, January 1995, 4; Rebecca Bailey, "Race Car Officials Ban SCV Logo," *Civil War News*, December 1994, 9.

gratuitous flag use, in 2001 forbade chapters from using the flag.[30] In 2012, members of the southern rock band Lynyrd Skynyrd conceded that they had been disassociating itself from the flag because of its use by racist groups. Gary Rossington, the last original member of the band, complained that the Ku Klux Klan and skinheads "kidnapped" the flag and made it "look bad," and explained that they did not want to be perceived as agreeing with "any of the race stuff or any of the bad things." In the face of the predictable backlash from Skynyrd's fans, Rossington posted a "clarification" on the band's home page. The band still uses the Confederate flag on stage and considers it a symbol of "Heritage not Hate," he explained.[31]

The growing popular disapproval of the Confederate flag's racist heritage not only banished it from the public landscape. It also led to a kind of countercultural use of the flag. Just as manufacturers have emblazoned death's heads and other grotesque symbols over the Confederate flag to enhance its "rebel" iconography, so have others manipulated the flag's colors to make their own statements. Most notably, young African Americans combined the design of the Confederate battle flag with the red, green, and black of the Pan-African flag. In 1999, Nu South Apparel, a company based in Charleston, South Carolina, produced a line of clothing based on that hybrid design and an idea: "For the sons and daughters of former slaves. For the sons and daughters of former slave owners. Threads that connect us. Words that free us."[32] In 2002, artist John Sims launched a "Recoloration Project" that featured the Confederate flag in Pan-African colors in order to dramatize the inextricable links between Southern heritage, the slave trade, and racism.[33]

---

30 Press release from Kappa Alpha Order, January 31, 2001, courtesy of Kappa Alpha; *Kappa Alpha Journal*, Spring 2001, 4–5, 7, 16–21.

31 Alison Fensterstock, "Even Lynyrd Skynyrd Wanted to Stop Flying the Confederate Flag," *Times-Picayune* [New Orleans], June 26, 2015.

32 Vernon Chadwick, "Papa's Got a Brand New Flag: Confederate Symbolism and the Funky New South," *Southern Reader*, November–December 1991, 27; Mike Smith, "Banner Combines Confederate Flag, Colors of Black Liberation," *Atlanta Journal Constitution*, April 22, 1994; John T. Edge, "Living (and Dining) in the Nu South," *Oxford American*, January–February 1999, 76–77; Andy Steiner, "Dixie Rising," *Utne Reader*, July–August 1999, 22–24.

33 See johnsimsprojects.com.

Kanye West was the most prominent rap musician who appropriated the Confederate flag to make a statement about American race relations. He raised ire in the music world when he appeared wearing Confederate flag patches on his clothing. "The Confederate flag represented slavery in a way," he explained to a radio station in 2013. "That's my abstract take on what I know about it, right? So I wrote that song, 'New Slaves.' So I took the Confederate flag and made it my own flag. It's my flag now. Now what you gonna do?"[34]

Within two years of the tempest in a teacup surrounding West's controversial flag stance, association with the Confederate flag became a kiss of death for mainstream cultural figures. The June 2015 Charleston murders and, more specifically, the revelation about the murderer's affinity for the flag was the most significant moment in the Confederate flag's history since the 1948 "Dixiecrat" convention. Genuine revulsion against the act and political opportunism—an opportunity to renounce an increasingly troublesome symbol for the most noble of reasons—broke the dam of resistance to removing the flag from public display. The unequivocal statements from NASCAR, the producers of *The Dukes of Hazzard*, and the policies of Wal-Mart and Amazon seemed to have marked a passing of Confederate flag pop culture and material culture.

Predictably, however, the effort to relegate the Confederate flag to pariah status evoked spirited backlash. The democratization and decentralization of commerce and of broadcast communications in twenty-first-century America ensure that those who cling to the Confederate flag will be able to obtain it and display it. Beyond the network of "flagger" groups that have raised on private property large Confederate flags visible from interstate highways and other public places, a cottage industry of large and small businesses has emerged to sell flag clothing and merchandise.

Chief among these businesses in 2017 is Dixie Outfitters. Based in Odum, Georgia, Dixie Outfitters was founded in 1997 with the explicit intent of defending the flag and other icons of (white) Southern heritage and fulfilling the still-significant market for them. As others have scorned

---

34 Elliott C. McLaughlin, "Kanye West Co-opts Confederate Flag: Publicity Stunt or Way to Prompt Debate?" November 6, 2013, CNN.com; Soraya Nadia McDonald, "Kanye West Once Wore the Confederate Flag: What Does He Think about It Now?" *Washington Post*, June 21, 2015.

the Confederate flag, Dixie Outfitters dedicated its business not only to flag products but to resources that teach "true history" about the Confederacy and the South. The company's mission statement explains that "various groups have distorted the real meaning of the Confederate Flag for their own purposes." In reality, the flag "represents all Southern, and even Northern, Confederates regardless of race or religion and is the symbol of less government, less taxes, and the right of people to govern themselves. It is flown in memory and honor of our Confederate ancestors and veterans who willingly shed their blood for Southern independence."[35]

Merchants such as Dixie Outfitters will continue to exist and thrive as long as there is demand for Confederate flag products, which seems almost certain. People with Confederate ancestors will continue to revere the flag as a symbol of Southern heritage, and contrarians will embrace it to buck the establishment. More telling than this simple economic equation is the overt attitude with which Dixie Outfitters and the Georgia-based Ruffin Flag Company peddle their wares. To purchase and fly a Confederate flag, or to wear a tee-shirt with a Confederate flag emblem coupled perhaps with a Labrador Retriever or a silhouette of a motorcycle rider or an assault rifle is to make a statement or a gesture of defiance—a statement of conservative values and militant patriotism in defiance of "political correctness." This manifestation of the flag's "rebel" identity will no doubt thrive, but it will have the effect of further marginalizing the flag from the American mainstream.[36]

Long gone are the days when *The Crisis*, *Business Week*, and the *New York Times* could conclude that young people flying "pert little banners" meant nothing more than another fad. Or was the early 1950s flag fad and the decades of the ostensibly innocent Confederate flag that the fad ushered into American pop culture just an illusion? Was there ever a time that the Confederate flag's place in American pop culture was truly innocent? Judging by the motives of individuals who decided to put a Confederate flag

---

35 Alan Levinovitz, "If This Flag Offends You: Dixie Outfitters and the Meaning of Southern Heritage," *Los Angeles Review of Books*, September 9, 2013; dixieoutfitters.com.

36 An innovative and insightful quantitative analysis of U.S. Patent and Trademark Office data tracks the marginalization of the Confederate flag as a marketing tool. James I. Bowie, "The Confederate Flag Is Going Out of Business," *The Eye* (*Slate*'s design blog), July 30, 2015.

on a car antenna or to wave a flag at a football game because others were doing it or because it seemed the thing to do, there was an air of innocence. Judging, however, on the collective level, there was never a time after 1948 that the Confederate flag was completely innocent of political or ideological content. Once the flag fell into the hands of those who used it as a gesture of defiance against racial integration and in support of white supremacy, it became difficult to discern whether a Confederate flag stood for something benign or malignant. It seems unfortunate that the flag's emergence into American pop culture coincided with the civil rights struggle, but the historian cannot discount the possibility that those two phenomena were more than coincidental.

Today, the dwindling number of people who display the Confederate flag do so in defiance of a consensus among mainstream media and arbiters of popular culture that the flag is tainted with slavery and racism. Before 1948, those who displayed the flag for purposes not historical or commemorative did so in defiance of cultural arbiters who believed it to be a revered symbol. Ironically, today's anti-flag consensus has helped turn back the clock and reined in what the United Daughters of the Confederacy called "misuse" of the flag. Raleigh *News & Observer* editor Jonathan Daniels in 1965 bemoaned that the flag was "often just confetti in careless hands."[37] Many of those "careless hands" were intent on nothing but expressions of regional pride, individual hell-raising, or "youthful hijinks." But it was the "careless hands" that found it a useful symbol to send a message of hate—and the finger that pulled a trigger in Charleston, South Carolina—that have shaped the flag's place in contemporary American popular culture.

---

37 Quoted in "The Ever-Ever Land," in *The South Today: 100 Years after Appomattox*, ed. Willie Morris (New York: Harper & Row, 1965), 124.

1. The Gray Ghost on TV Made Me a Civil Warrior

by Stephen Davis

You never know what turns on a Civil War buff, a friend once observed, and he was so right. The Rolling Stones's late drummer Charlie Watts was well known as a big Civil War nut, but what got him? I wish I knew.

In the past century, at least a handful of experiential touchstones are obvious. Albert Castel recalled that seeing the film *Gone with the Wind* at the age of fourteen turned him on to the Civil War. Because of the popularity of her novel, Jim Cullen has called Margaret Mitchell "the most influential historian of the twentieth century." David Selznick's film adaptation of the novel is legendary, of course. At its premiere in Atlanta in December 1939, "people wept at the scene in which thousands of Confederate soldiers lie wounded in an Atlanta square," writes Bruce Chadwick; they "roared their approval when Scarlett shoots a Yankee soldier and clapped their hands and sang whenever any ragtag band in the movie struck up 'Dixie.'" Moreover, the film's effect upon viewers continues. "There have been few other well-made Civil War films," acknowledge James Lee McDonough and James Pickett Jones, historians of the war, "and none with a fraction of *GWTW*'s impact."[1]

---

1 Albert Castel, *Decision in the West: The Atlanta Campaign of 1864* (Lawrence: University Press of Kansas, 1992): xi; Jim Cullen, *The Civil War in Popular Culture: A Reusable Past* (Washington: Smithsonian Institution, 1995), 103; Bruce Chadwick, *The Reel Civil War: Mythmaking in American Film* (New York: Vintage, 2001), 185; James Lee McDonough and James Pickett Jones, *War So Terrible: Sherman and Atlanta* (New York: W. W. Norton, 1987), 351.

I can only guess that the future literature will document the profound impression that Civil War films in our own lifetime have made upon millions of viewers. Scholars have dissected Edward Zwick's *Glory* (1989) for its factual correctness, leading Brian Steel Wills to observe, "Most historians concur that the motion picture falls short of the mark for accuracy." I think the nitpickers are missing the point. Leaving the movie theater after watching *Glory*, I still remember what I told my wife: that a century and a quarter after the war, I had been transported back to a time when participants understood and felt the *sublimity* of war, and even the sublimity of *death* in war. (Thank you, Matthew Broderick.)

Then there is Ken Burns's documentary *The Civil War.* Aired on public television in 1990, it garnered the largest audience in the network's history. Years from now, I suspect historians of American popular culture will be able to document people saying, "I was turned on to the Civil War by Ken Burns's TV series." For now, we must settle for such observations as Robert Brent Toplin's: "The extraordinary reception demonstrated that a single television series could stimulate millions of people in the United States and the world to think seriously about the experiences of the past."

But wait: you can GOOGLE. "Thanks a lot, Ken Burns," wrote Prof. James M. Lundberg of Illinois's Lake Forest College in 2011. "Because of you, my Civil War lecture is always packed."[2]

I call Civil War buffs "Civil Warriors," and many of us can remember our conversion experiences—"Saul of Tarsus" moments, I sometimes term them. You can go way back. Douglas Southall Freeman, the son of a Confederate soldier growing up in Richmond, would probably have turned to the war in any event, but it was witnessing Mahone's brigade veterans reenact the battle of the Crater in November 1903 that caused him to conclude, "If someone doesn't write the story of these men, it will be lost forever."[3]

---

2 Brian Steel Wills, *Gone With the Glory: The Civil War in Cinema* (Lanham MD: Rowman and Littlefield, 2007), 143; Gary W. Gallagher, *Causes Won, Lost, & Forgotten: How Hollywood and Popular Art Shape What We Know about the Civil War* (Chapel Hill: University of North Carolina Press, 2008), 5; Robert Brent Toplin, ed., *Ken Burns's "The Civil War": Historians Respond* (New York: Oxford University Press, 1996), xxvi; James M. Lundberg, "Thanks a lot, Ken Burns," www.slate.com/articles/arts/culturebox/2011.

3 David E. Johnson, *Douglas Southall Freeman* (Gretna LA: Pelican, 2002), 54–56.

More recent writers have had their conversion moments. Tony Horwitz explains that as a boy, it was his father's reading aloud from Francis Trevelyan Miller's *Photographic History of the Civil War*, and staring at "the man-boys of Mathew Brady who stared back across the century separating their lives from mine." For historian William Garrett Piston, it was growing up during the Civil War Centennial. Piston was eight years old in the spring of 1961. "Every newspaper and magazine was flooded with pictures," he recalled. "We traded bubblegum cards. Every restaurant's placemat had a Civil War theme and every packet of Dixie Crystal sugar on the table told a Civil War story on the back. I earned a badge in Cub Scouts for my Civil War scrap book, which included the texts of articles by Bruce Catton clipped from the newspaper."[4]

For others, the experience of an important battlefield has been the transformative experience. Writing about iconic Gettysburg, Jim Weeks remembers that his visit there as a kid brought about "a transformation in me akin to religious conversion."[5]

One of the neat things you can do these days is to talk to reenactors about their "trigger moments," as Gordon Jones of the Atlanta History Center calls them. Dr. Jones interviewed a lot of reenactors during the 125th anniversary reenactment of the battle of Chickamauga in September 1988, as well as at other events. For one reenactor, Jerry, the trigger moment came when he was a lad of nine; during a family vacation he visited his first battlefields at Gettysburg and Petersburg. To cap it all, Jerry's family drove to Richmond and saw the James Stewart Civil War film, *Shenandoah* (1965). "That whole vacation really sold me on the whole thing," Jerry remembered.

Another reenactor declared that his trigger moments came when he visited his grandmother in North Carolina, and she took him on her knee and sang "Dixie" as well as "Stonewall Jackson's Way." Jones heard other buffs reflect on books as their instigators. For a reenactor from England, it was Bruce Catton's *Glory Road* (1952), which he picked up as a patient in a hospital.

---

4 Tony Horwitz, *Confederates in the Attic: Dispatches from the Unfinished Civil War* (New York: Vintage, 1998), 3–5; Robert J. Cook, *Troubled Commemoration: The American Civil War Centennial, 1961–1965* (Baton Rouge: Louisiana State University Press, 2007), 264–65.

5 Christopher Bates, "'Oh, I'm a Good Ol' Rebel': Reenactment, Racism, and the Lost Cause," in Lawrence A. Kreiser Jr. and Randal Allred, eds., *The Civil War in Popular Culture: Memory and Meaning* (Lexington: University Press of Kentucky, 2014), 192; Jim Weeks, *Gettysburg: Memory, Market, and an American Shrine* (Princeton, NJ: Princeton University Press, 2003), 1.

"Unbelievable," he exclaimed. "I got to read more about this! And at home now" he added, "I got every single damned book that Catton ever wrote." At one reenactment, Jones talked to Bob, a Pennsylvania minister, who pointed to the *American Heritage Picture History of the Civil War* that turned him on as a kid. Bob remembered poring over David Greenspan's colorful illustrations of battles, each one packed with hundreds of tiny Rebels and Yankees fighting each other. "Wow!" Bob squealed. "These are great!"

Reenactments themselves can be trigger moments. A South Carolina reenactor in his thirties told Jones how a living history event moved him so much that "I've been doing it ever since."

In an echo of Tony Horwitz's encounters with Civil War photography, another reenactor at an event in New York—a Canadian, no less—told Gordon: "You know how this whole thing started? I saw a picture of Grant, leaning against a tree and I saw this scrubby little guy in the old coat and he looked like a real drinker. Never heard about him before and I say, 'I love that guy, he is something. What the hell is this, you know?' So I got to reading books. I started from that one point until I got a library of books that could kill a horse."[6]

Thinking about my own Civil War epiphany as a kid, I can relate to David Greenspan's paintings in the *American Heritage* history, to *Gone with the Wind* (Max Steiner's glorious musical score!), and to Civil War illustrations (Santa brought me Fletcher Pratt's *Civil War in Pictures* [1955]). I also recall the books that hooked me as a kid—Margaret Mitchell Elementary School's library had a copy of MacKinlay Kantor's *Gettysburg* (1952). "*Ja*, the Rebels Eat Babies," Kantor's first chapter title, is a phrase that has haunted me ever since.

But as I try to retrace my own Civil War trigger experience as a fourth grader, when I shifted from dinosaurs to the American Civil War, I believe to this day that it was a weekly television show that aired during 1957–58: *The Gray Ghost*.

Rewatching episodes of *The Gray Ghost* is a time-trip return to 1950s America and its TV culture. Before we take the trip, it's useful to look at what was happening in the country back then.

---

6 Gordon L. Jones, "'Gut History': Civil War Reenacting and the Making of an American Past" (PhD diss., Emory University, 2007), 19–24.

At the start of the decade, just one in ten households in the United States had a television. By 1960, it was just the reverse: 90 percent of American homes had a TV. Americans were clearly buying a lot of sets in the '50s, despite their cost of nearly $300. Two-thirds of the nation's television broadcast stations popped up in 1953. The next year C. A. Swanson & Sons brought out their "TV Dinners": turkey, peas, and mashed potatoes in an easy-to-heat aluminum tray (disposable, too, so the missus was spared from having to do the dishes). Then came the TV tray. "Perfect for TV dining," read an ad from a leading manufacturer. "Choice of 8 colorful trays. Fits over the knees. Folds for storage."[7]

The Gray Ghost TV show presented the romanticized adventures of Confederate partisan ranger John Singelton Mosby. *Library of Congress*

In front of the trays and dinners, of course, were the shows. "With the exception of a brief and ill-fated craze for quiz shows inspired by *The $64,000 Question*," writes Eric Burns, the fifties was a decade of comedies and Westerns. *I Love Lucy* premiered in October 1951, and for the next six years ran as one of the three most popular shows on the air. In the broadcast year of October 1954–April 1955, seven of the top ten shows were comedies; during 1956–57, three of the top four were Westerns. *Hopalong Cassidy* had been America's first Western, on NBC in 1949. The next year, Hopalong (played by William Boyd) became the first TV character to be portrayed

---

7 Eric Burns, *Invasion of the Mind Snatchers: Television's Conquest of America in the Fifties* (Philadelphia: Temple University Press, 2010), 35, 37, 39–40, 62.

on a schoolkid's lunch box. *Davy Crockett*, premiering on Walt Disney's weekly hour-long show in December 1954, was not so much a Western as a frontier saga. But Fess Parker sold a lot of stuff: T-shirts, boots, pajamas, and, of course, coonskin caps (ten million of 'em).[8]

Comedies and Westerns (*Gunsmoke, Wagon Train*)—not to mention variety shows (Ed Sullivan), cop shows (*Dragnet*), kids' shows (*Mickey Mouse Club*), game shows (*The Price Is Right*)—all fulfilled the medium's ability to entertain Americans, to divert their attention from humdrum jobs or domestic stresses. "Reality was sure to be offensive to someone," Burns writes, and television wielded its power to divert audiences away from it.

Reality could be offensive to advertisers, too. Program sponsors back then exercised outsized influence in shaping the content of programming. "Advertisers would do their best to keep audiences happy," Burns adds, and that meant avoiding material that could make people uncomfortable—which would hurt sales. The American Gas Association, sponsor of *Playhouse Ninety*, agreed to support the dramatization of "Judgment at Nuremberg," before realizing that Nazis would speak of sending Jews to gas ovens. At the association's insistence, writers deleted the offensive word from the script, but not every instance was caught. Censors' last resort was their mute button. Viewers of the show, aired in April 1959, thus heard characters saying Jews would be executed in (pause) ovens. Few caught on to the backstory.[9]

Television the entertainment medium could alter reality, but not so TV the news medium. One of the most shocking stories of the decade involved the death of Emmett Till.

Till, a fourteen-year-old African American living in Chicago, was visiting relatives in Tallahatchie County, Mississippi, in August 1955. Shopping in a grocery store, Till encountered a white female clerk who later told her husband that Till had whistled at her. The husband, Roy Bryant, and his half brother, John Milam, drove to the shack of Moses Wright, Till's great-uncle. Despite Wright's pleas, they took Till off into the night, then beat and mutilated him before shooting him to death. They tied a weight around his neck with barbed wire and threw his body into the river.

---

8 Burns, *Invasion of the Mind Snatchers*, 91–93, 103–4.

9 Ibid., 81–82, 88–89, 106, 109–110.

Bryant and Milam were quickly arrested and tried the next month. An all-white jury acquitted them after less than an hour's deliberation.

All three networks covered the trial on their evening newscasts (which at the time ran only a quarter hour). This meant that the Till story would be given only a minute or so after the reporter's notes and film, flown from Mississippi to New York, were received and edited. Nevertheless, it was one of the first civil rights stories covered on American television.

John Chancellor, later the voice of NBC TV evening news, was covering the trial for network radio. After the verdict was announced, he began interviewing people about their reactions to it. When he began talking to a Black woman, some tough-looking white men approached threateningly. The woman hurried away, but Chancellor stood before them, holding out his microphone.

"I don't care what you're going to do to me," he told them, "but the whole world is going to know it." The toughs balked. Chancellor's microphone had become a weapon against menacing evil. He later called it "the technological equivalent of a crucifix."

Rod Serling, even then an accomplished writer for television, proposed for *The U.S. Steel Hour* a dramatization of the Till murder and the trial of the two white men. The sensational nationwide publicity assured high viewership, so the producers and sponsor went along . . . until Southern whites got word of the plan, voiced loud protest, and even called for a boycott of U.S. Steel. Ford Motor Company, dependent on Big Steel, asked CBS not to broadcast the show on its southern affiliates. The network refused.

But U.S. Steel balked and demanded a major rewrite of Serling's story. It wouldn't take place in Mississippi but New England; the murder victim would not be an African-American boy from Chicago but a white man from Europe. All things southern disappeared from the set, even bottles of Coca-Cola. A depressed Serling was forced to go along, and the radically revised "Noon on Doomsday" aired on *The U.S. Steel Hour* on April 25, 1956.[10]

The mid-1950s was indeed a time in the United States when tensions between whites and Blacks, and between the (white) South and the rest of the nation, ran high.

---

10 James T. Patterson, *Grand Expectations: The United States, 1945–74* (New York: Oxford University Press, 1996), 395–96; Burns, *Invasion of the Mind Snatchers*, 82–85, 224–25.

The cause was the U.S. Supreme Court decision, handed down unanimously on May 17, 1954, in the case of *Brown* v. *Board of Education*. Reversing a decision that it had itself handed down some sixty years earlier, the high court ruled that public schools that segregated students on the basis of race violated the Constitution's 14th Amendment, protection of equal rights for all citizens. But the court did not issue any timetable for desegregation of the nation's schools. A year later, it directed that federal district courts oversee the transition with "all deliberate speed."

That gave white supremacist politicians in the South all the time they needed to mount a campaign against the Supreme Court's decision. Neither Congress nor President Eisenhower was eager to speed desegregation in the South. The federal government stood by when, in February 1956, white rioters blocked implementation of a court order to desegregate the University of Alabama. Senator Harry F. Byrd of Virginia coined the term "massive resistance" for white Southerners' opposition to court-ordered desegregation. In March 1956, 101 of 128 U.S. senators and representatives from the eleven former states of the Confederacy signed a "Southern Manifesto," affirming their opposition to school integration. "Interposition" became the political term defining a state's authority to interpose its will between the federal judiciary and local school boards. By mid-1957, eight southern states had passed interposition laws; the other three (Texas, North Carolina, and Tennessee) had affirmed some form of opposition to the Brown decision.

Nevertheless, school desegregation occurred in cities such as Louisville, Baltimore, and St. Louis. In Little Rock, Arkansas, the local school board approved a plan for at least token desegregation: that of one senior high school in September 1957. Governor Orval Faubus, however, telling Arkansans he had a duty to enforce the state's interposition measure, called out the National Guard to block the action (which involved all of nine African-American students designated to join about 1,900 whites at Central High School). Crowds watched the guardsmen maintain segregation on September 3, as the nine Black children were advised to stay home. In the end, under order from a federal district judge, Faubus withdrew the guard. On the 23rd, desegregation began at Central under supervision by city police. But an angry white crowd gathered outside the school, forcing authorities to send the Black students home. At the request of Little Rock's mayor, President Eisenhower finally stepped in, sending troops of the 101st Airborne to maintain federal authority. The soldiers escorted the Black students to class and dispersed the mobs outside of Central. But the ugly incident had made Little Rock "the hub of southern resistance to racial desegregation," in the words of Numan Bartley, historian of "Massive Resistance."[11]

The fall of 1957, as it turned out, was the very time at which *The Gray Ghost* premiered on CBS television outlets across the nation.

The question is, why would a network and hypersensitive advertisers agree to broadcast a weekly action series that glorified a Confederate partisan ranger?

The quickest answer is to remind ourselves that in cultural history, there's always a lot of stuff going on. The 1950s in the United States was the heyday of the "Red Scare." A *Look* magazine article in June 1950, as the Korean War erupted, asked "How Prepared Are We If Russia Should Attack?" In 1953, Wisconsin Senator Joseph McCarthy's "investigations" into government agencies, universities, and Hollywood brought about widespread job dismissals and blacklists. The nation's weekly magazines ran helpful articles on how to build and equip a fallout shelter. Khrushchev brutally suppressed the Hungarian revolt in November 1956. Russians launched Sputnik nearly a year later.[12]

Through it all, and throughout the decade, there was still the American Civil War, especially on the silver screen. *The Red Badge of Courage* appeared in 1951, starring Audie Murphy. Three years later, Van Heflin led a band of intrepid Confederates to St. Albans, Vermont, in *The Raid*. Walt Disney released *The Great Locomotive Chase* in the spring of 1956. Following the appearance that year of Harold Sinclair's novel based on Grierson's Raid, John Ford directed his film adaptation, *The Horse Soldiers* (1959).[13]

---

11 Numan V. Bartley, *The Rise of Massive Resistance: Race and Politics in the South During the 1950's* (Baton Rouge: Louisiana State University Press, 1969), 58, 60, 64, 90, 117, 126, 131, 251, 253, 265–68; Randall Bennett Woods, *Quest for Identity: America Since 1945* (New York: Cambridge University Press, 2005), 93–95.

12 Michael Barson and Steven Heller, *Red Scared!: The Commie Menace in Propaganda and Popular Culture* (San Francisco: Chronicle Books, 2001) 71, 114, 133–35; Woods, *Quest for Identity,* 66–69.

13 Jack Spears, *The Civil War on the Screen and Other Essays* (Cranbury, NJ: A. S. Barnes, 1977), 221–22; Neil Longley York, *Fiction as Fact: "The Horse Soldiers" and Popular Memory* (Kent, OH: Kent State University Press, 2001), 55, 78–83.

In short, while Americans were battling Reds, looking for Commies, and confronting racism, they were still fighting the Civil War. It was as if Civil War–related popular entertainment could be created in a cultural bubble. Writing about Ford's *Horse Soldiers*, Gary Gallagher correctly claims, "The civil rights ferment of the 1950s apparently had minimal effect on the screenwriters' sensibility." Brian Steel Wills also sees in Ford's Civil War movie nothing of the racial tensions roiling American society at the time. *The Horse Soldiers* reflects, he writes, "the homogenization moviegoers expected of the America of the 1950s."[14]

Nothing homogenizes like the American West, as Hollywood had already learned through its many "Civil War Westerns," a popular genre of the 1950s. The Cold War era was a fit setting for a recurring storyline of the Civil War Western: Northerners and Southerners warring against each other could unite to fight a common enemy, the Indians (who happened to be red men). "Confederates and Federals often purge their sin of fighting between themselves in order to unite against some other adversary or adversaries," writes Melvyn Stokes, who notes that such a plot occurs in *The Outpost* (1940), *Rocky Mountain* (1950), and *Winchester 73* (1950).

This is what happens in *Two Flags West* (1950): Confederate cavalrymen languish in a Northern prison when they are offered the prospect of release if they will renounce their Rebel allegiance and go out to New Mexico Territory to fight Apaches (they do). Something similar occurs in *Escape from Fort Bravo* (1953). Confederate Captain John Marsh (John Forsythe) escapes from a Federal stockade in Arizona Territory, only to die fighting Indians alongside Union Captain Roper (William Holden).[15]

Thus, the marriage of the Civil War and the Hollywood Western was a very durable one by the late 1950s—which brings us back to *The Gray Ghost*.

Lindsley Parsons, who produced the series during its only year on the air, had already written the screenplay for at least eight Hollywood "B" Westerns when Virgil Carrington ("Pat") Jones's biography of *Ranger Mosby* was published in 1944. In carrying out his partisan warfare in the

---

14 Gallagher, *Causes Won*, 51; Wills, *Gone with the Glory*, 122.

15 Spears, *Civil War on the Screen*, 109; Melvyn Stokes, "The Civil War in the Movies," in Susan-Mary Grant and Peter J. Parrish, eds., *Legacy of Disunion: The Enduring Significance of the American Civil War* (Baton Rouge: Louisiana State University Press, 2003), 69; Wills, *Gone with the Glory*, 84, 167.

area of Loudoun, Fauquier, and Fairfax counties in northeast Virginia ("Mosby's Confederacy"), the cavalry raider "lived and operated with the freedom of an independent commander," Jones explains, "believing that the fierce hostility the Federals displayed toward him was more on account of the sleep he made them lose than the number he killed and captured."

Jones followed his biography a dozen years later with *Gray Ghosts and Rebel Raiders* (1956), a lively history of partisan warfare in Virginia. A number of chapters recount Mosby's exploits, including his famous capture of Union general Edwin Stoughton in March 1863.

Parsons, a Civil War buff, became aware of Jones's work and had a hunch that Mosby could make good TV—but in the Western genre. Parsons pitched the idea of a show to CBS executive Tom Moore, who later recalled, "He and I were talking about various kinds of folk heroes and this seemed like a good idea."

The year 1957 was a good year for Westerns on American television. *Have Gun—Will Travel* premiered that year, starring Richard Boone as Paladin. Also that year, *Maverick* debuted, with James Garner as Bret Maverick. *The Restless Gun* was another oater appearing in '57. Interestingly, the lead characters of all three shows had seen the Civil War; Paladin had served as a Union cavalry officer.[16]

"Neither Moore nor Parsons," write Ashdown and Caudill, "apparently considered that *The Gray Ghost* would be viewed as anything other than a Western action series." The problem, as it turned out, was that John Singleton Mosby was not a Western folk hero but very much a Southern one. Parsons did not foresee this would be a problem when he committed to producing *The Gray Ghost*. Indeed, he seems to have been aware that the Civil War's hundredth anniversary was approaching in a few years—in September 1957, Congress established a Civil War Centennial Commission

---

16 Paul Ashdown and Edward Caudill, *The Mosby Myth: A Confederate Hero in Life and Legend* (Wilmington, DE: Rowman and Littlefield, 2002), 180–81; Virgil Carrington Jones, *Ranger Mosby* (Chapel Hill: University of North Carolina Press, 1944), ix; Greg Biggs, "The Gray Ghost Story," *Blue & Gray* 11, no. 4 (April 1994): 31 (Parsons as Civil War buff); Larry James Gianokos, *Television Drama Series Programming: A Comprehensive Chronicle, 1947–59* (Metuchen, NJ: Scarecrow Press, 1980), 503, 512; Paul Ashdown, "Knights in Blue and Butternut: Television's Civil War," in David B. Sachsman, S. Kittrell Rushing, and Roy Morris Jr., eds., *Memory and Myth: The Civil War in Fiction and Film from Uncle Tom's Cabin to Cold Mountain* (West Lafayette, IN: Purdue University Press, 2007), 244.

to oversee the nationwide activities—and that he could tap into mounting popular interest in the subject.

Parsons embarked on his project, and landed Tod Andrews to play the title role. Andrews was 43 at the time. That made him more than a dozen years older than the real Gray Ghost had been when the war started. More important, Andrews, a New York native, did not have a southern accent, which led to a production decision. "We felt it would be best if I didn't try to affect a fake accent," he later said, "because it seems only to inflame Southerners." Andrews had a bit of experience with Westerns (a small part in *They Died with Their Boots On* [1941]). But he had to learn to ride horseback for the series. The clincher was that he actually resembled Mosby.[17]

In order to sell the proposed series to a national network, Parsons had to film a pilot episode. For his plot, he chose Mosby's most famous exploit, the capture of General Stoughton.

But the pilot needed a thoughtful introductory narrative—not so much to set the stage as to address big questions about America's Civil War. Who better than God and Abraham Lincoln to do this for American television audiences?

I'm not kidding. In the three-minute "Introduction" included in a DVD produced by Classic Reels & Broadcasts Company, the Lincoln monument in the nation's capital is the opening visual, as the narrator intones:

> The will of God prevails. In great contests each party claims to act in accordance with the will of God. Both may and one must be wrong. God cannot be for and against the same thing.
>
> At the same time in the present Civil War it is quite possible that God's purpose is something different from the purpose of either party. He could have either saved or destroyed the Union without a human contest.
>
> Yet the contest began, and having begun He could give the final victory to either side any day. Yet the contest proceeds.

---

17 Ashdown and Caudill, *The Mosby Myth*, 181–85; Richard F. Shepard, "'The Gray Ghost' Rides Again," *New York Times*, September 28, 1958, 16.

Then the message shifts as the face of Lincoln gives way to footage of Yanks and Rebs fighting:

> The Civil War—no period of American life can compare in heroic drama, violent deeds, bloody intrigue or majestic sweep of history than the mighty fight between the states. Life magazine pointed out the tremendous grip this conflict has always held on the nation's imagination.
>
> Says Life, the Civil War has produced more literature than any war in history. Last year alone over 100 volumes appeared, including the top bestseller Andersonville. In motion pictures the top grosser of all time is Gone with the Wind.[18]

Having aligned itself with providential will and having streamed into a nationwide popular phenomenon, the subject of the show is finally presented. "As in all times of great national stress, great heroes were born but none more colorful than John Singleton Mosby. Guerrilla warfare, a never-ending series of raids, fires, kidnappings, and train wrecks earned Mosby the name of the Gray Ghost. He fought masterfully in espionage and counterespionage, outwitting the enemy at every turn. He was a valiant fighting man but, first of all, an American." After the war, the narrator adds, he even helped President Grant "in binding the nation's wounds."[19]

Then came the actual episode, titled "Prisoner Exchange." The opening scene was used for the start of every show. With the Confederate battle flag floating faintly in the background, Mosby would gallop toward us, his horsemen riding in from each side to join him, as Andrews intones,

> We took our men from Texas, Virginia, Kentucky, the mountains, the backwoods and the plains. We put them under orders—

---

18 Biggs, "The Gray Ghost Story," 31; Ashdown and Caudill, *The Mosby Myth*, 187; *The Gray Ghost*, twelve episodes produced by Classic Reels & Broadcasts Company, Clarkesville, GA.

19 Ashdown and Caudill, *The Mosby Myth*, 184.

guerrilla fighting orders—and what we lacked in numbers, we
made up in speed and brains.

Both Reb and Yankee strangers, they called us Mosby's Rangers.
Both North and South, they knew our fame.

Gray Ghost is what they called me. John Mosby is my name.[20]

"Prisoner Exchange" follows Jones's narrative in *Gray Ghosts and Rebel Raiders*—up to a point.

The basic outlines of the story are well embedded in the Mosby literature.

Mosby, with 29 men, rode into the town of Fairfax Courthouse, 15 miles west of Washington, before dawn on March 9, 1863. They captured Federal guards and rounded up all the horses they could find. Then Mosby led five men into the house where Stoughton was sleeping.

Spanking the Yankee unceremoniously on his backside, he announced, "General, did you ever hear of Mosby?"

The bleary-eyed general answered, "Yes, have you caught him?"

"No," Mosby replied, "but he has caught you."

Mosby and his band rode off with Stoughton, 32 other prisoners, and 58 horses.

Union authorities suspected that Mosby had gotten information from a local Southern sympathizer, Antonia Ford. She was arrested a few days later and imprisoned in Washington for a few months, before being released and sent through the lines to Richmond. Miss Ford was undoubtedly a Southern sympathizer who fed information to General "Jeb" Stuart. But historian Jeffry Wert makes the point that she had nothing to do with Mosby's Fairfax raid.

Stoughton was also sent to Richmond—Libby Prison. There he languished until being exchanged in May.

After he learned of Mosby's achievement, President Lincoln is said to have remarked that he did not mind losing Stoughton so much as those horses: "I can make a much better Brigadier in five minutes, but the horses

---

20 Ibid., 187.

cost a hundred and twenty-five dollars apiece."[21]

Parsons took the story line by V. C. Jones, produced the pilot, then had Jones flown out to Los Angeles to view a rough cut. Jones caught at least one inaccuracy that was removed. But not everything was corrected. Antonia Ford—here, in the telecast, she is named Ansonia ("Sonia") Forde—sneaks to the Confederate camp and approaches Mosby's quarters, a tent. "Mosby never had a tent," Jones recalled years later, but the producer could not reshoot the scene, so it stayed. Jones may have noticed too that Andrews's character is referred to as *Major* Mosby. Technically, in early March 1863, Mosby was still a lieutenant in the Confederate cavalry; his promotion to major would come after the Fairfax raid. Mosby would hold that rank from March 26, 1863 to January 21, 1864 (when he was promoted to lieutenant colonel). But throughout Parsons's series, he would always be a *major*.[22]

But who wants to be a stickler when delightful embellishments abound?

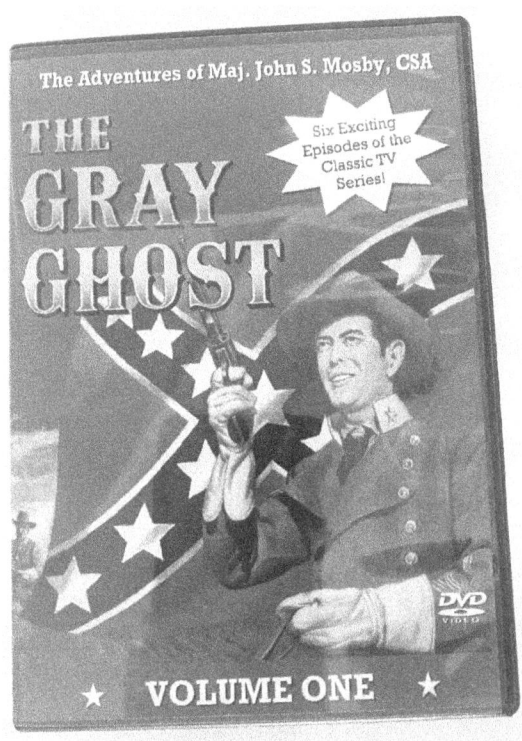

The first six of thirty-nine episodes of *The Gray Ghost* are collected in volume one of a DVD set. *Author's Collection*

---

21 Virgil Carrington Jones, *Gray Ghosts and Rebel Raiders* (New York: Henry Holt, 1956), 147–59; Jones, *Ranger Mosby*, 92–99; Jeffry D. Wert, *Mosby's Raiders* (New York: Simon and Schuster, 1990), 45–48; James A. Ramage, *Gray Ghost: The Life of Col. John Singleton Mosby* (Lexington: University Press of Kentucky, 1999), 68–71.

22 Biggs, "The Gray Ghost Story," 32; Ramage, *Gray Ghost*, 342; Wert, *Mosby's Rangers*, 46, 54, 138.

After Mosby hijacks a B&O train to get the valuable Union dispatches onboard, a Federal officer must report the news: "They don't call him the Gray Ghost for nothing, sir!"

An angry Stoughton splutters, "Yes, the man's a born guerrilla fighter."

Stoughton, suspecting Sonia's aid to Mosby, has her arrested and jailed in Fairfax. Rather than try to free her—which the Yankees expect him to do—Mosby instead takes his trusty aides Sam and Myles into the town before dawn.

True to the "original" story, Mosby awakens a sleeping General Stoughton.

"You mean you captured him?"

"No, but he's captured you. And if we get you out of here, we're going to exchange you for a good Southern lady."

To be sure, the exchange happens, Sonia for Stoughton. A headline from the Richmond *Courier* (the fourth fictional newspaper named in the show) blares, "Major Captures Stoughton To Exchange General with Ansonia Forde."

(One can almost see Pat Jones cringe.)

Afterward, Parsons retained Jones as historical advisor for the series. He reviewed scripts and coached Andrews, who traveled east and spent two weeks touring "Mosby's Confederacy." Parsons even looked ahead to a second year of production, assuring Jones, as Ashdown puts it, "that the first thirty-nine scripts would make use of some fiction, but that later scripts could adhere more to history."[23]

Yet historical accuracy would not be the producer's big problem for his proposed series: it was selling the series to the network. Parsons flew to New York and with Tom Moore pitched the show to the Columbia Broadcasting System. "CBS executives worried that it might seem inappropriate to have a Confederate raider humiliating the Union cavalry each week on television," Ramage writes, with understatement. "There was some apprehension that a favorable Confederate was not in keeping with the times," Moore recalled, adding that CBS had canceled *Amos 'n' Andy* in 1953 because of protests by the NAACP and other groups. Three different sponsors backed out

---

23 Biggs, "The Gray Ghost Story," 32; Ashdown, "Knights in Blue and Butternut," 246.

of supporting the show. "We tried to sell it to all the networks," Moore explained, "but they all had the same apprehension."

Richard F. Shepard of the *New York Times* got straight to the point: "To sponsor a Civil War theme at a moment in history when Federal troops were in Little Rock seemed as perspicacious an idea as one to serialize the life of Joseph Stalin as a situation comedy."

Then CBS's syndicated film division, CBS Television Sales, Inc., came to Parsons's rescue, offering the show to individual stations, which could then find their own sponsors. It worked. The division committed to 39 shows for the 1957–58 broadcast year.

After making the pilot, Parsons and his writers implemented a few changes. The opening music of the pilot, which includes "When Johnny Comes Marching Home," subsequently relies more on "The Yellow Rose of Texas," which recurs throughout the series. Sam, Mosby's aide, disappears from future episodes, allowing Sergeant Myles Magruder to be Mosby's ubiquitous sidekick. (Myles, always with a chaw of tobacco in his mouth, grows a moustache after "Prisoner Exchange.")

But the biggest change involved Mosby's uniform. In the pilot, he is dressed in an officer's regulation uniform. His gray coat, with upright collar and double row of buttons, drops well below his belt. His gray trousers have light seam lines (yellow?—it's hard to tell the exact tint on black-and-white TV). When the major reappears in the show's second episode, "The Humanitarian," however, his clothing is dramatically different. His uniform is no longer gray but much lighter (off-white, maybe?). His coat and pants are formfitting, almost tight. The coat falls only to the belt. Gone is the major's black neckwear of the pilot; now Mosby wears some white fluffy scarf. In such episodes as "Navy Man," the foppish white scarf broadens, covering the major's entire neck.

You guessed it: Major Mosby has been turned into a dandy.

Why the costume change? I don't see it addressed in the limited literature of *The Gray Ghost*—maybe others haven't watched the pilot against the other episodes. My guess is that to soothe jittery stations and sponsors, particularly in the non–South, Parsons and his team decided to visually set Major Mosby apart from his men, to make him look somehow *un*-Confederate. Look closely, and I think you can see that they reshot the opening scene, too; Mosby, being joined by his horsemen, no longer wears his gray uniform of "Prisoner Exchange" but his new, whiter one.

The Gray Ghost began airing in the fall of '57 on stations across the country. In New York City, it first appeared on Thursday, October 10 (9:30 p.m., WPIX-TV). But the rollout was not uniform. In Atlanta, when I was growing up as a lad of ten, the CBS affiliate, WAGA-TV, began broadcasting the show on Wednesday evening, November 13. The *Atlanta Constitution*, the city's morning paper, carried a big advertisement that day. "POWERFUL NEW TV SERIES," it blared; "AUTHENTIC TALES OF THE CONFEDERACY." Under a photo of Andrews, the ad announced,

> Re-live thrilling adventures of the old Confederacy. See action, drama, heart-break. Those gallant by-gone days recaptured! See "the Gray Ghost" . . . the breath-taking story of Colonel John S. Mosby, leader of Virginia's famous Confederate guerrilla raiders. Starring Tod Andrews, as Mosby, this series is the highlight of the television season. A real must on your viewing list!
>
> "Brought to you by Colonial Stores."

From then on, it ran on Wednesday evenings, at 7 p.m. on Atlanta's Channel 5 for a full 52 weeks, with the last episode shown by WAGA on November 5, 1958. They obviously aired some reruns, which means that somewhere along the way I probably saw all 39 episodes (although, after all these years, I only remember how Andrews's Mosby looked and that Sergeant Magruder always had that chaw in his jaw).

In a lot of them we got to see Mosby's Rangers outwit the Yankees, ride off and fade away. "No use, Major," admits one perplexed Federal. "They know the country and we don't."[24]

Beating the Yankees worked its way into many a show. In "Humble Pie," Mosby's men tear up a railroad. In "Observation Post, " Miss Molly lures Federal guards away with her Southern fried chicken so Mosby and a few men can slip through and capture a Northern telegraph station. In

---

24 Ramage, *Gray Ghost*, 342; Ashdown, "Knights in Blue and Butternut," 246; Biggs, "The Gray Ghost Story," 32; Richard F. Shepard, "'The Gray Ghost' Rides Again," *New York Times*, September 28, 1958, 16; Ashdown and Caudill, *The Mosby Myth*, 208n14 (WPIX); *Atlanta Constitution*, November 13, 1957, p. 20; Stephen Davis, "Riding with Mosby on 1950s TV," *Blue & Gray* 19, no. 1 (October 2001): 31.

"Problem of Command," Mosby's men defeat a Federal party in an open field fight and force their surrender (Mosby graciously paroles them).

The Gray Ghost is all about outsmarting the Yankees, but just as often it is about Mosby offering kindness and assistance to others. "The Humanitarian," for example, features the major securing the help of a counrty doctor for one of his wounded men.

"Jimmy" illustrates the two sides that could work into a *Gray Ghost* episode. The show is number 9, airing in the fall of '57. In Boston, it was shown on Dec. 11, 1957.

First job for Mosby and his men is to whip the Yankees.

Mosby encounters Dawson, a duplicitous sutler who sells goods to both sides. After he discovers gunpowder in the sutler's wagon—intended for Federal purchase—Mosby commandeers the wagon and its contents. He knows Dawson will complain to the Yankees—which the sutler does, informing Union Captain Wallace of the stolen gunpowder.

Wallace guesses that Mosby will use it to obstruct the railroad that Sheridan is building at Manassas Gap. He sends a patrol to the railroad, there to wait for Mosby.

But instead, the Gray Ghost uses the powder for another purpose: to block the nearby Salem Road, which the Federals use to move their artillery.

Wallace and his men hear the explosion. "How does Mosby know these things?" the exasperated captain splutters. "He's made fools out of all of us again."

So that job is done. The rest of the show is about getting Jimmy squared away.

A "war orphan," with both parents dead, teenaged Jimmy has been adopted by Dawson and his wife. The sutler treats him cruelly, and Jimmy wants to run away—but can't.

Lured by the $10,000 reward for Mosby, Dawson promises Wallace he'll learn where the raiders are camped and bring back the information. Wallace gives the sutler a wagon and team for their search.

Nearing the suspected Rebels' camp, Dawson tells Jimmy to swim across a river and confirm. When Mosby and his men appear on the other side, Dawson flees.

Jimmy falters in the middle of the stream, and Major Mosby, boots and all, jumps in to save him.

Instead of gratitude, Jimmy voices anger at Mosby. His father had died fighting for the Union, and he wants to go back to "Mr. Dawson." "You're all outlaws!" he sneers. Mosby calmly replies, "Boy, it's just a question of what side you believe in."

The major offers to escort the lad back to Dawson's home and the foster mother. "We might even get to be friends on the way," Mosby tells him.

They arrive at the farm home. Mrs. Dawson, like Jimmy, also appears to have been mistreated. When Mosby asks if he can buy food and fodder, she refuses. "He'd beat me half to death," she pleads. But she thanks the major for his care of Jimmy.

Mosby tells the lad, "You're a good boy." "But I still hate Rebels," he answers.

Jimmy secretly asks his mother to help him keep Mosby at their house while Dawson brings Union troops. He says they could use that reward money, but the mom tells him her husband would selfishly only spend it on himself. "Mr. Dawson has been treating me cruel for years," she confesses.

Sure enough, Dawson brings a Federal patrol toward his farm. They spot the Rebels there. As a Union officer sends back for reinforcements, he instructs Dawson to go to the house and lure Mosby outside, where he'll "snipe him" with a Spencer rifle. "If I snipe Mosby, I'll do better than getting medals," he says.

True to his duplicitous self, Dawson walks into his house and pretends to be on Mosby's side, warning of Yankees outside.

The knowing major will have none of this deceit, and throws Dawson out. From afar the rifle-wielding Federal mistakenly shoots and kills him.

The Confederates fire and down the sniper, and the rest of the Yankees ride away.

With her cruel, selfish husband out of the way, Mrs. Dawson assures Mosby, "I'll make a good home for him, Major." "I'm sure of that," he replies.

At the end of the show, Major Mosby reviews with Sergeant Magruder their accomplishments. He doesn't mention having fooled the Yankees and blowing up their key roadway.

No: "Getting that lad squared away is a good day's work," the major pleasantly concludes.

So John Singleton Mosby is more than the Gray Ghost—he's kind of a Father Knows Best in light tights.

The "Angel of Loudoun" episode makes another point about the plotline: in Mosby's Confederacy, there's a lot of spying going on. After one of his attacks on the Federal supply wagons is foiled by the timely arrival of

Union cavalry, the major concludes there's a spy somewhere. He first thinks a kindly Virginia lady, "Miss Nellie," is the informer—especially after he learns she is Union Secretary of War Stanton's mother (how old must she be?!). But he concludes it's Grace, Nellie's housekeeper.

In "A Belle Rebel," a comely Edith ("Edie") Page, played by Angie Dickinson, slips Mosby secret information on the location of Union forces. But when the Pinkertons want to arrest her, Mosby slips behind enemy lines to whisk her out. He forces a Federal officer, Colonel Egan, to help get them back to safety. The Yankee, though, is not really a Yankee but an Irish immigrant ("soldier of fortune," Mosby calls him). Mosby coaxes Egan to switch sides. At the end of the show, he does, professing his admiration for the daring, romantic way of Mosby's warring: espionage, outwitting the enemy, beautiful spies.

My point here is to bring up another element of the television show: how it took us back to the old times in a way that many viewers would probably not catch. To be sure, Mosby's actual exploits involved guerrilla warfare, which in itself involves securing information about enemy forces. But I think it goes a bit deeper. In American Civil War drama, the image of the spy can be traced at least as far back as R. H. Crozier's novel, *The Confederate Spy* (1871). "The office of a spy is both disagreeable and dangerous," Crozier writes, "for detection is certain death, and an ignominious one at that." Faced with that fate, espionage required courage indeed. In the postwar decades, when Civil War melodrama became the stuff of theater and stage, spy dramas became hits. William Gillette's play, *Held by the Enemy* (1886), is considered the first major Civil War drama, with a plot that emphasizes the spy's courage. "It is significant that of the five best plays of the Civil War, four should have a spy for the leading character," writes Arthur Hobson Quinn. Gillette followed his hit up with *Secret Service* (1895), whose theme again was the heroism of the spy. *Secret Service* strikes such resonant chords that in 1977, the Phoenix Repertory Company of New York staged a dramatization of the play, shown on no less than the Public Broadcasting System (with Hal Holbrook as narrator!).[25]

---

25 R. H Crozier, *The Confederate Spy: A Story of the War of 1861* (Louisville, KY: J. P. Morton, 1871), 115; Rebecca Washington Smith, *The Civil War and Its Aftermath in American Fiction, 1861–1899* (Chicago: University of Chicago Libr., 1937), 34; Arthur Hobson Quinn, *A History of the American Drama from the Civil War to the Present Day* (New York: F. S. Crofts and Co., 1943), 218, 260.

One does not have to be a sleuth to see that in the course of the series, plenty of fictions are thrown in. The whole landscape is unreal; it was all shot in southern California. At the start of "Navy Man," one sees a treeless row of hills on the horizon—a topographic impossibility in northeast Virginia. Scripts refer a lot to General Lee and General Stuart, but fictional ones are thrown in, too: a Union general named Bannersby is featured in "Humble Pie." Then there are the clumsy "B" moments. Rewatching such episodes as "Observation Post," one is struck by just how silly is the fake beard of Gen. "Jeb" Stuart (played by Sherwood Price in seven episodes). But back in '50s television, who cared?

On the other hand, the gentle touch of V. C. Jones can be seen when the major refers to Upperville and Middleburg, towns very much within "Mosby's Confederacy." Yet Pat must have cringed when, in "Belle Rebel," Mosby engages a Federal officer in a prolonged saber fight—and wins. (Jones later commented that he advised the writers that Mosby disliked swords and didn't wear one.)[26]

If *The Gray Ghost* can be considered as a "B" Western on TV, it follows that almost all of the supporting cast is of a "B" rank—meaning, unknown today. Exceptions are seen with actors who gained a bit of fame later in television. In "Observation Post," Confederate Major Heros von Borcke is played by John Banner, Sergeant Shultz of *Hogan's Heroes* (1965–71). Angie Dickinson (Edie the spy) later had her own show, *Police Woman* (1974–78).

I've watched as many episodes of *The Gray Ghost* as I can find, and there's one very important observation I must make: nary an African American is to be seen. It seems that while the show was in production, a group of Black actors visited screenwriter Jack DeWitt. "A delegation came to me and said they didn't want blacks depicted as servants," DeWitt remembered. "I told them that if we used them we would use them as they were during the war. When they didn't accept that I told them we wouldn't use them at all." As a result, the entire season of *The Gray Ghost* is as lily-white as Mosby's scarf.

---

26 Biggs, "The Gray Ghost Story," 32.

With these pluses and minuses, nobody could have predicted that the show would be so popular. In August 1958, well into its season, *The Gray Ghost* was being shown in 190 American cities by 144 stations to some 21 million viewers. And they lived in both North and South. The show consistently was in the top three of Boston, "making mincemeat," according to *TV Guide*, "of such well-established shows as *The U.S. Steel Hour*." It also did well ("for some as yet unstudied reason," shrugged the *New York Times*) in the Northwest, hovering at the top of ratings in Seattle.

Naturally, the show was most popular in the South. "All of us disappointed and dyed-in-the-wool Confederates have lived from one week to the next just to see 'The Gray Ghost,'" observed the *Raleigh Times*. "Somehow, we got a heady, if belated, pleasure in watching Mosby's band outsmart the bluecoats on every turn," the *Walton Tribune* of Monroe, Georgia, commented. According to a survey of 22 television markets conducted in June 1958, *The Gray Ghost* was the third most popular syndicated show in the country.

In the spring of 1958, Andrews made a publicity tour of southern cities, dressed up in his dandy costume. Bands played "Dixie"; crowds cheered, and "they greeted me as if I were Robert E. Lee reincarnated," Andrews remarked. Youngsters especially loved the show. "Kids—all kids—are fanatics," Andrews declared. "They want to hold my hat, shoot my gun, anything." This juvenile delirium led to the merchandising of Gray Ghost stuff. Colonial grocery stores sponsored the show in eastern North Carolina. A Colonial ad in the local newspaper of Hertford advertised round steak for 59 cents a pound and grapefruit, ten for 45 cents, but in a little square it read, "HEY KIDS!": a "Gray Ghost cap" (kepi) was on sale for only 49 cents. If you wanted a hat like the major wore, it'd cost 89 cents—what a deal!

Mosby's exploits even spawned a comic book, published by Dell in 1958. Again, V. C. Jones would have cringed: "He has a tent and fights on horseback with a saber," as Ramage observes.[27]

---

27 Ashdown, "Knights in Blue and Butternut," 247; "This Rebel's from New York," *TV Guide*, August 30, 1958 (copy courtesy of Greg Biggs, Clarksville, TN); Paul Ashdown, "Confederates on Television: The Cavalier Myth and the Death of 'The Gray Ghost,'" *Studies in Popular Culture* 2, no. 1 (Spring 1979): 15; Shepard, "'The Gray Ghost' Rides Again"; "Why No 'Gray Ghost,'" *Newsweek*, August 4, 1958 (copy courtesy of Greg Biggs); Colonial Stores advertisement, *Perquimans Weekly* (Hertford, NC), January 31, 1958 (copy courtesy of Greg Biggs); Ramage, *Gray Ghost*, 343.

Then the balloon burst. Things in Little Rock had not improved in the 1957–58 school year. In January 1958, Governor Faubus brazenly declared that the Supreme Court's Brown decision was not legally binding. On August 19, Faubus instructed the Little Rock School Board to announce plans to prevent integration; the next day, President Eisenhower vowed to enforce court decisions. That month, the United States Supreme Court convened in a special session to sort things out. On September 12, the justices ordered Little Rock to conduct a program of gradual integration. Yet southern political leaders continued to resist. "By the end of 1958," writes Bartley, "every Southern state except Tennessee had enacted school-closing laws"—authorizing the closing of public schools faced with integration.

In this highly charged atmosphere, little wonder that sponsors of *The Gray Ghost* dropped out before a second season could be produced. CBS Television Sales insisted upon 85 percent of stations to renew commitments for broadcasting a show, and Major Mosby did not make the cut. The show was canceled after its first and only season.

In *TV Guide*, Major Mosby was pictured standing resolutely beside a Civil War cannon, over the caption, "How come we lost?" Parsons blamed cancellation of the series on a federal district court judge's decision on Little Rock desegregation, but there were other factors. "Some of the blacks said *The Gray Ghost* glorified the whites and white supremacy," Parsons later said. *Variety* speculated that southern newspapers might have inflamed the situation, with their hot-blooded editorials praising Mosby for his victories over the Yankees.

Regardless of the cause, the show was done. Stations could still present reruns, but no new episodes would be produced. One may fairly conclude that Parsons's problem was that he was seeking to introduce a weekly series glorifying a Confederate folk hero at a time when racial tension in America ran high, advertisers held enormous sway with networks, and producers and sponsors worried about offending viewers. "The Gray Ghost," writes Robert J. Cook, "was so pro-Southern that it met stiff resistance from national advertisers concerned about its lack of appeal to nonsoutherners."

Thus *The Gray Ghost* rode off into, well, history.

With Major Mosby gone, the major networks returned in the fall of 1958 to its tried-and-true genre, the Western. Premiering that season were *The Rifleman*, *Bronco*, *Mackenzie's Raiders*, and *The Rough Riders*. All were set out in the *real* West, and all featured *former* Union or Confederate veterans.

In all these shows, the Civil War was very much over. *The Rebel* followed the next year, with Nick Adams as Johnny Yuma. "*The Rebel*," notes Paul Ashdown, "was in some ways both a 'rebel' of the 1950s and a ghost of the defeated Confederate army."[28]

I remember watching *The Rebel*, hoping to see something about the war. But after watching Major Mosby, Johnny Yuma was a disappointment.

But I had caught the bug, and I have been a Civil Warrior ever since—thanks, I believe, to a one-year run of a television show.

"It's a strange war when a man has the honor of shaking hands with his enemy," Major Mosby at one point says.

But even a strange war can make for exciting TV. And when I was a kid, that was all that mattered.

---

28 Bartley, *Massive Resistance*, 273–74, 288; "Why No 'Gray Ghost'"; Biggs, "The Gray Ghost Story," 32; Ashdown and Caudill, *The Mosby Myth*, 190–91; Cook, *Troubled Commemoration*, 229; Ashdown, "Knights in Blue and Butternut," 244–45.

1. Telling History vs. Making Art

by Chris Mackowski

In 2012, as part of my doctoral studies, I spent time focusing on Civil War-related literature, a term I defined broadly to include fiction, creative nonfiction, and film. One of the papers that resulted from that research turned into a ten-part blog series I published on Emerging Civil War in October 2012, "Telling History vs. Making Art." The following essay is adapted from that blog series.

"No harm's done to history by making it something someone would want to read."[1] So proclaimed two-time Pulitzer Prize-winning historian David McCullough, who made a career writing accessible, entertaining histories. It's an idea that has fundamentally guided my own historical writings.

I know some historians who would disagree with McCullough, who in fact seem to almost intentionally ignore the idea that good prose should be readable. Once prose becomes readable, after all, it's only a slippery slope away from being engaging, and once prose becomes engaging, it might then

---

1 David McCullough, "In the Course of Human Events," 2003 Jefferson Lecture, National Endowment for the Humanities. Web. Accessed 19 August 2012.

slide down into the blurry abyss of entertainment. In that murky realm, even angels may fear to tread—unless they be *Killer Angels*.

As a former battlefield guide at Fredericksburg & Spotsylvania National Military Park (FSNMP), I would frequently speak with folks who had come to the battlefields because they had read *The Killer Angels,* which in turn inspired them to see a Civil War battlefield. Michael Shaara's novel is about the battle of Gettysburg and has nothing to do with any of the battlefields at FSNMP (Fredericksburg, Chancellorsville, Wilderness, and Spotsylvania), but I was always grateful that the novel—or perhaps its film version, *Gettysburg*—stimulated someone's interest enough to bring them through the front door.

The Killer Angels has been one of the most important books in getting modern audiences interested in the Civil War. *Chris Mackowski*

Yet some colleagues roll their eyes or grumble the word "novelist" under the breath as an epitaph. *The Killer Angels'* Pulitzer Prize has often carried little weight with them. "I am a historian," wrote D. Scott Hartwig, a former National Park Service historian at Gettysburg National Military Park. "Consequently, I originally looked down upon Shaara's work. After all, it was fiction."[2]

Yet creative works undeniably teach Americans about the Civil War, says historian Gary Gallagher—"to a lamentable degree in the minds of many academic historians."[3] History, some suggest, should be left to the historians.

On one hand, art excites the public imagination; on the other, it can implant misconceptions or factual inaccuracies even as it tries to articulate larger truths. In fact, it may be within that balance between fact and truth—

---

2 D. Scott Hartwig, *A Killer Angels Companion* (Gettysburg, PA: Thomas Publications, 1996), v.

3 Gary Gallagher, *Causes Won, Lost, & Forgotten: How Hollywood and Popular Art Shape What We Know About the Civil War* (Chapel Hill: University of North Carolina Press, 2008), 9.

and the expectations that historians, artists, and readers/viewers have toward them—that the tension originates. That the public often bases its expectations on collective memories complicates matters further because such memories are often romanticized constructs at odds with what historians know to be true. The artist, meanwhile, must be guided by the conventions of his/her craft, such as pacing, narrative arc, etc.

Filmmaker Ken Burns once articulated the telling of history as "a tension between Art and Science":

> The *Science* of History would enumerate the myriad details equally, without discrimination; the telephone book at its worst. The *Art* of History has produced *Gone with the Wind*, and worse, *The Birth of a Nation*, and . . . mini-series dramas which try to convince us that it was not brother against brother, but heaving bosom against heaving bosom.
>
> Good history has always struck a balance between these two polarities, never allowing formal considerations to overwhelm and capsize the truth of events, nor allowing dry recitation of fact to render its meaning unintelligible or worse—boring.

Burns warns against "a kind of castor oil of dry dates and facts and events of little meaning, something we knew was good for us, but hardly good tasting."[4]

"Whatever else it is, history ought to be a good yarn," said journalist-turned-historian Bruce Catton, whose narratives on the Civil War have reached vast audiences since the war's Centennial. Catton's critics have retorted that, whatever else it is, history ought to be *accurate*. "Catton's knack for knowing a good story when he saw one did not always extend to recognizing a story too good to be true," one has said.[5] I've heard Shelby Foote criticized for the same thing.

The Civil War has already become so mythologized that many such too-good-to-be-true stories remain widely accepted as truth even if little

---

4 Burns, 160.

5 Thomas Desjardin, *These Honored Dead: How the Story of Gettysburg Shaped American Memory* (Cambridge, MA: DaCapo Press, 2003), 189.

evidence exists to actually support them—or, worse, even if evidence exists to refute them. The chasm between public memory and generally accepted scholarship remains wide.[6]

Into that breach marches art. Film or book, fiction or creative nonfiction—it matters little. As a few examples will demonstrate, the territory is dangerous, and as historian Leon Litwack points out, the stakes are high:

> Over the past century, the power of historians and filmmakers to influence the public, to reflect and shape attitudes and popular prejudices, has been amply demonstrated, often with tragic consequences. Rummaging through the past, filmmakers did not simply reinforce prevailing racial, ethnic, and patriotic biases; they helped to create and perpetuate them.[7]

Robert Penn Warren, whose fiction and poetry frequently concerned itself with the war and its legacy, and who "continually struggled to find a proper balance between history as fact and fiction as art," understood those dangers.[8] "[I]f, without historical realism and self-criticism, we look back on the War," Warren warned, "we are merely compounding the old inherited delusions which our weaknesses crave."

Presented in full Technicolor and with a stunning score, *Gone with the Wind* probably offers the best example of "old inherited delusions," soaked as it is in magnolias and moonlight. "*Gone with the Wind* had done more to keep the Civil War alive, and to mold its memory, than any history book or event since Appomattox," wrote Tony Horwitz in a chapter devoted to the movie's legacy.[9] I'll defer to Sarah Kay Bierle's essay in this volume

---

6 Tony Horwtiz offered a fantastic exploration of the lingering Confederate perspective in *Confederates in the Attic*—one of my favorite books.

7 Leon Litwack, "Telling the Story: The Historian, the Filmmaker, and the Civil War," *Ken Burns'* The Civil War*: Historians Respond*, Robert Brent Toplin, ed. (New York: Oxford University Press, 1996).

8 Howard Jones, "Introduction," *The Legacy of the Civil War* by Robert Penn Warren. (Lincoln, NE: University of Nebraska Press, 1998), ix.

9 Tony Horwitz, *Confederates in the Attic: Dispatches from the Unfinished Civil War* (New York: Random House, 1998), 296.

for more on that.¹⁰ *Birth of a Nation,* likewise cinematically stunning in its time, dressed up delusions even darker than *Wind*'s with groundbreaking innovations that literally redefined moviemaking. There, I'll defer to Sheritta Bitikofer's essay in this volume.

For our purposes in this essay, I'll begin instead with the *The Killer Angels.*

Killer Angels, Real and Fictional

The Killer Angels tells the story of the men who led the fight at Gettysburg. "It was not an attempt to document the history of the event, nor was it a biography of the characters who fought there," author Jeff Shaara explained of his father's work in the foreword to his own novel, *Gods and Generals.*¹¹

"I have not consciously changed any fact," the elder Shaara wrote in *The Killer Angels*' "note to the reader":

> I have condensed some of the action, for the sake of clarity, and eliminated some minor characters, for brevity; but though I have often had to choose between conflicting viewpoints, I have not knowingly violated the action. I have changed some of the language. It was a naïve and sentimental time, and men spoke in windy phrases. I thought it necessary to update some of the words so that the religiosity and naïveté of the time, which were genuine, would not seem too quaint to the modern ear. . . . The interpretation of character is my own.¹²

It's worth noting that Shaara faces many of the same issues a Civil War historian faces when constructing a battle narrative: What actions and which troops get more or less attention? Which competing accounts are more

---

10 For my take on *Gone with the Wind*, see part three of the blog series this essay is based on, "Telling History vs. Making Art: "Frankly, My Dear. . . ." 23 October 2012. https://emergingcivilwar.com/2012/10/23/telling-history-vs-making-art-frankly-my-dear/.

11 Jeff Shaara, *Gods and Generals* (New York: Ballantine Books, 1996), x.

12 Michael Shaara, *The Killer Angels* (New York: Ballantine Books, 1974), xiii.

credible? How far should an editor go in correcting the poor grammar and erratic spelling and capitalization of soldiers and eyewitnesses? How do you determine a person's motivation?

Most, if not all, of these issues are driven by the primary source material—how much is available, when was it written, what were the agendas of the writers, and so on. The methods for attacking such questions are different for historian and novelist, but the core issues remain the same. "Both types of writers seek truth, but the historian operates within the limits of the documents, and the novelist works within what is 'historically possible'—whether 'psychological fact, historical fact, sociological fact,'" explains historian Howard Jones.[13]

Shaara clearly outlined the aesthetic reasons that guided his choices: clarity, brevity, relevance. He'll tinker with action, he says, but won't tinker with the larger plot. After all, the plot—the battle—is clearly predetermined for him by the facts. He will, however, interpret character, which is less determinate than plot because characterization gets built on opinion as well as fact, and Shaara had plenty of opinions to draw on.

Alas, in the Lost Cause tradition, opinions about Lee are so universally positive that he's become known over time as "The Marble Man." Not everyone shared that opinion, though. Ulysses S. Grant, in his *Personal Memoirs*, described Lee as "a good man, a fair commander, who had everything in his favor . . . a man who needed sunshine." But he also believed Lee was treated like a demi-god.[14] The Lost Cause tradition still treats him as so. Michael Shaara generally stuck with that interpretation. "He is a man in control," Shaara wrote. "He is the most beloved man in either army."[15]

Where Shaara deviates significantly from Lost Cause tradition, though, is his choice to make Longstreet a hero of the novel. Lost Cause advocates, particularly Confederate generals Jubal Early and Fitzhugh Lee, scapegoated Longstreet (and others) for the Southern defeat at Gettysburg—all in an

---

13 Jones, ix.

14 Joan Waugh, "Ulysses S. Grant, Historian," *The Memory of the Civil War in American Culture* (Chapel Hill: University of North Carolina Press, 20040, 20.

15 Michael Shaara, xvi.

attempt to absolve Lee and preserve his Marble Man status.[16] Longstreet didn't help his own case after the war by becoming a Republican, accepting various government jobs, and criticizing Lee. History has not been kind to Lee's "Old Warhorse."[17] Shaara's sympathetic treatment of him in *The Killer Angels* almost single-handedly resurrected public interest in Longstreet's controversial career.[18]

On the Federal side, Shaara focuses on cavalryman John Buford and, most significantly, Col. Joshua Lawrence Chamberlain of the 20th Maine Infantry. Posted at the far-left flank of the Union army on a piece of topographically important ground, Chamberlain's men had to beat back a series of Confederate attacks on July 2, 1863. "You cannot withdraw," Chamberlain's commander, Col. Strong Vincent, tells him in the novel. "Under any conditions. If you go, the line is flanked. If you go, they'll go right up the hilltop and take us in the rear. You must defend this place to the last."[19] No documentary evidence exists to suggest Vincent said these words, but a novelist can create dialogue in a way a historian cannot.

The action as depicted in the novel and, later, in the movie *Gettysburg*, and as recounted in Ken Burns's *The Civil War*, has become the stuff of legend—in fact, "far more legend than history," says historian Tom Desjardin. "Shaara's novelized version of Chamberlain's day at Gettysburg exceeds by any measure the historical fact of the event."[20]

But Desjardin points out that Shaara isn't attempting to provide an exact chronicle of Chamberlain's day. "Novels are not bound by fact," he says.

---

16 Dick Ewell, like Longstreet, has been roundly blamed for the loss at Gettysburg because of his failure to take Cemetery Hill on the afternoon of July 1, 1863. It is perhaps the most second-guessed decision of the war. Shaara squarely comes down on the side of Ewell's critics, which results in one of my favorite scenes in the novel when General Isaac Trimble rages to Lee about Ewell's weakness (pp. 140-2). Although I love the scene, I actually side with Ewell, who made a smart choice. (See the cover story Kris White and I authored for the August 2010 issue of *Civil War Times*, "Richard Ewell at Gettysburg": http://www.historynet.com/richard-ewell-at-gettysburg.htm.)

17 Hartwig, 34. As of this publication, several recent bios have continued the upward trend of Longstreet's rehabilitation.

18 Desjardin, 182.

19 Michael Shaara, 210.

20 Desjardin, 146. His chapter "Constructing the Consummate Gettysburg Hero" outlines the curious growth of the Chamberlain myth.

"They have an emotive quality that only fiction can provide and often must provide in order to succeed."[21]

That success, suggests Hartwig, becomes a double-edged sword. "Shaara's story is told so well, his character portrayals are so believable, that the unknowing reader might believe what they are reading *is* history," he writes.[22] Hartwig had to discard initial prejudices against the book as a historian—"or tried very hard to," he admits:

> and found that there was more to this novel than met the eye. It held deeper meaning than simply to tell the story of the Battle of Gettysburg, and it was beautifully written. . . . Still, the number of people who read this novel and came away thinking they had read a history of the battle, annoyed me.[23]

The blurry line between fact and fiction in *The Killer Angels* is best exemplified by Buster Kilrain, a fictitious sergeant in the 20th Maine who serves as Shaara's personal voice.[24] The fictitious Kilrain interacts with the historically real characters because Shaara needs him, as a literary device, to do so. If Chamberlain is the American hero in the classical style, Kilrain contrasts against him as the modern everyman, too cynical for his own good yet someone who can still see the value in Chamberlain's goodness and appreciate it. Shaara's myth-building uses Kilrain's voice to help sculpt Chamberlain's heroic stature:

> You are damned good at everything I've seen you do, a lovely soldier, an honest man, and got a good heart on you too, which is rare in clever men. . . . The strange and marvelous thing about you, Colonel darlin', is that you believe in mankind, even preachers,

---

21 Ibid.

22 Hartwig, 1.

23 Hartwig, v.

24 For more on Kilrain, see "Steve Earle, 'Dixieland,' and the Irresistible Charm of Buster Kilrain" in this volume.

whereas when you've got my great experience you will have learned that good men are rare, much rarer than you think.[25]

In service to his myth-making, Shaara isn't afraid to subvert facts. For instance, on the third day of the battle of Gettysburg, he repositions the 20th Maine squarely behind the Union center along Cemetery Ridge. "[A] lovely spot," a lieutenant tells Chamberlain as the regiment gets ready to move. "Safest place on the battlefield. Right smack dab in the center of the line. Very quiet there."[26] Most readers know the area won't be quiet for long, so not only does Shaara create a touch of irony that serves as a foreboding end-of-chapter cliffhanger, it positions his hero to witness the climactic Pickett's Charge. "We're right in the path," Chamberlain thinks as the Confederates hit. "Would not have missed this for anything, not anything in the world."[27]

"This is pure fiction," says Hartwig.[28] In reality, the 20th Maine was positioned some three-quarters of a mile away from the battle—but because Shaara literally is creating "pure fiction," the move to Cemetery Ridge serves several artistic functions and contributes to the myth of his noble hero.

Shaara's son, Jeff, has not inserted himself as a Kilrain-style literary device into his own Civil War books the way his father did, but he otherwise takes similar liberties with his characters. "If you have read any of my books, you know that these stories are driven not by events, but by characters," he writes in the introduction to his Shiloh novel *A Blaze of Glory*. "For me, the points of view of the characters in this story are more appealing than the blow-by-blow facts and figures that are the necessary products of history textbooks. . . . [M]y goal is not to offer a complete detailed history of the event. If that's what you seek, then by all means, read Shelby Foote or Jim McPherson. I hope that when all is said and done, you will accept that what I am trying to offer you is a good story."[29]

---

25   Michael Shaara, 178-179.

26   Ibid., 282.

27   Ibid., 311.

28   Hartwig, 22.

29   Jeff Shaara, *A Blaze of Glory: A Novel of the Battle of Shiloh* (New York: Ballantine Books, 2012), xi-xii.

Nonetheless, Shaara engages in "painstaking (and voluminous)" research, making "a strenuous effort to be historically accurate, to get the facts straight."[30] From there, Shaara-the-artist can go where the facts take him, which is "often inside the thoughts of these characters."[31] Without a paper trail of some sort to follow, historians can't go there. The novelist has access to a kind of truth the historian does not.

Shaara dedicated his first novel, *Gods and Generals*, to "those who learned their American history in often impersonal textbooks."[32] His story, by contrast, is far more personal. Factual verisimilitude is not the point; emotional truth is.

When his readers walk into the Stonewall Jackson Death Site, I'm delighted that Shaara's book has inspired them to stop. From that point on, the onus rests on me and my colleagues to be sure they leave with the facts straight—and I hope we can tell them a good story, too, while we're at it.

The Civil War's Great Storyteller

No written work embodies the tension between art and history more fully than Shelby Foote's mammoth three-volume *The Civil War: A Narrative*. Few people realize Foote was a novelist before he became the "warm and folksy raconteur" of anecdotal Civil War history; his novel *Shiloh* sits almost forgotten in the shadow of his magnum opus.[33]

"Well, I am a novelist, and what is more I agree with D.H. Lawrence's estimate of the novel as 'the one bright book of life . . .'" Foote said in his author's note at the end of the first volume, *Fort Sumter to Perryville:*

> The point I would make is that the novelist and the historian are seeking the same thing: the truth—not a different truth: the same truth—only they reach it, or try to reach it, by different

---

30 Ibid., xii.

31 Ibid.

32 Shaara, *Gods and Generals*, x.

33 Horwitz, 151.

> routes. Whether the event took place in a world now gone to dust, preserved by documents and evaluated by scholarship, or in the imagination, preserved by memory and distilled by the creative process, they both want to tell us how it was: to recreate it, by their separate methods, and make it live again in the world around them.
>
> This has been my aim, as well, only I have combined the two. Accepting the historian's standards without his paraphernalia, I have employed the novelist's methods without his license. Instead of inventing characters and incidents, I searched them out—and having found them, I took them as they were.[34]

Although he listed his primary and secondary sources at the end of each volume, he made the intentional choice to leave out footnotes along the way, "believing that they would detract from the book's narrative quality by intermittently shattering the illusion that the observer is not so much reading a book as sharing an experience."[35]

Foote's lack of footnotes, in particular, has drawn the scorn of historians, as has his anecdotal style (and, frankly, his success—illustrating again the gap between public and professional perspectives).[36] People even harped on him for taking so long to complete the trilogy. "[I]n response to complaints that it took me five times longer to write the war than the participants took to fight it, I would point out that there were a good many more of them than there was of me," he wrote at the end.[37]

More serious criticism was leveled at him for focusing too much on military matters and for downplaying the role of slavery. "Shelby Foote is an engaging battlefield guide, a master of the anecdote, and a gifted and charming storyteller, but he is not a good historian," groused Leon Litwack.[38]

---

34 Shelby Foote, *The Civil War: A Narrative, Volume I: Fort Sumter to Perryville* (New York: Random House, 1958), 815.

35 Ibid.

36 See Horwitz, 151; Chapman, 177-178, 192-194, 218-220.

37 Shelby Foote, *The Civil War: A Narrative, Volume III: Red River to Appomattox* (New York: Random House, 1975), Endnote.

38 Litwack, 127.

The author kneels by Shelby Foote's headstone in Memphis's Elmwood Cemetery. Foote and his wife rest in the plots where Confederate cavalryman Nathan Bedford Forrest and his wife were originally buried before being moved to rest under a monument in downtown Memphis (which has since been moved). In Ken Burns's documentary *The Civil War*, Foote, an admirer of his fellow Memphisian, famously described Forrest as one of two authentic geniuses produced by the war (Lincoln being the other). *Curt Fields*

Trends and tensions within the field of history itself actually leave *any* historian open to that kind of criticism. I've heard historians dismiss each other as "too military" or "too Southern" or "too focused on a particular site and not enough on the big-picture." As a field, military history continues to take an intellectually unfashionable back seat to social history. Despite that emphasis on social history among academic historians, though, military histories "remain the most popular works Civil War historians produce for a general audience."[39] What the public wants and what scholars choose to study remain two separate spheres. It's no wonder the two groups come to a creative work as readers/viewers with vastly different expectations.

What gets forgotten in any discussion of Foote's lack of footnotes, for instance, is the beauty of his language, the smooth skill of his pacing, and the adroit weave of his complex narrative structure. Look at the way these two sentences, 113 words in all, unwrap as they go:

---

39 Barton Meyers, "The Future of Civil War Era Studies: Military History," *The Journal of the Civil War Era*. Web. Accessed 18 August 2012. <http://journalofthecivilwarera.com/forum-the-future-of-civil-war-era-studies/the-future-of-civil-war-era-studies-military-history>.

> A mile to the right of the point where the cluster of spires and gables showed above the ridge, and facing the road the led northward along it to Hagerstown, a squat, whitewashed building was set at the forward edge of a grove of trees wearing their full late-summer foliage; the autumnal equinox was still a week away. The sunlit brick structure, dazzling white against its leafy backdrop, was a church, but it was a Dunker church and therefore had no steeple; the Dunkers believed that steeples represented vanity, and they were as much opposed to vanity as they were to war, including the one that was about to move into their churchyard.[40]

Foote uses labyrinthine phrasing and careful punctuation—a style strongly influenced by Faulkner—to build his image of the church, revealing detail after vivid detail. He cleverly links "opposition to vanity" to "opposition to war," allowing him to work in additional information in a creative way. Then, his final phrase, "about to move into their churchyard," lets him return from his momentary snapshot of description back to the forward movement of the narrative.

He structures Volume I with a long section introducing Jefferson Davis followed by a long section introducing Abraham Lincoln, whom he then uses as a springboard into a discussion of the large strategic picture. He draws the volume to a close in reverse fashion, first using Davis's viewpoint to sum up the Confederate perspective as 1862 draws to a close, then uses Lincoln's perspective to sum up the Union perspective. He starts the book with Davis resigning his seat in the U.S. Senate to open a new chapter in his public life; he ends the book by returning to Capitol Hill for Lincoln's address to Congress: "Then came the end [literally as Foote ends the book], the turn of a page that opened a new chapter."[41] The parallels between beginning and end are subtle and masterful. When he finally wraps up his Volume III, Foote does so by returning to Davis again—this time as "the embodied history of the South" in his last days—thus using him to bookend the entire

---

40 Foote, *Vol. I*, 682. I've written several blog posts at Emerging Civil War that explore Foote's language in depth.

41 Foote, *Vol. I*, 810.

narrative in tidy fashion.[42] *The Civil War: A Narrative*—all three volumes and 1.3 million words of it—represents an amazing creative achievement.

In the end, those naysayers who criticized Foote's lack of proper historiographical technique won out: the Pulitzer committee passed him over, as did the National Book Award committee. It left Foote "bitter and angry."[43] The day would come, though—some fifteen years later, through the efforts of Ken Burns—when "Shelby Foote" and "The Civil War" would be synonymous for nearly every adult in America.

Communicating "The Incommunicable Experience of War"

"We have shared the incommunicable experience of war," Oliver Wendell Holmes says at the beginning of Ken Burns's documentary *The Civil War*. Burns could not have picked a more appropriate quote to start his film with, not just because it set a particular tone for the entire eleven-hour documentary but because it would describe the viewing experience of the documentary itself. For a week, some forty million Americans tuned in to public televisions to watch Burns's film—a shared media experience so profound that one book says, "For a generation of Americans, this documentary *is* the Civil War."[44]

Holmes' words were appropriate, too, because the war remained largely incommunicable. "Ken Burns encountered thousands of 'facts' about the war in the form of pictures, letters, statistics, maps, and other kinds of evidence," points out historian Robert Brent Toplin. "He could easily have turned his eleven-hour documentary into a 100-hour or 200-hour film, and still he would have to leave out much interesting material."[45]

That pragmatic reality didn't prevent critics from pouncing on Burns for all the things they felt he should have included (more emphasis on social

---

42 Foote, *Vol. III*, 1055.

43 Chapman, 223.

44 From the text on the back cover of Robert Brent Toplin's *Ken Burns's* The Civil War: *Historians Respond*.

45 Robert Brent Toplin, "*The Civil War* as an Interpretation of History," *Ken Burns's* The Civil War: *Historians Respond*. Robert Brent Toplin, ed. (New York: Oxford University Press, 1996), 21.

How much of the Civil War can you tell in a finite space and time? A civic group in Franklin, Tennessee, called The Fuller Story used art to address that question. In October 2021, in an effort "to provide proactive solutions on the national controversy surrounding Confederate monuments," with a focus "on what could be put up as opposed to what could be taken down," the group capped off a $150,000-effort to install a statue honoring USCT in the town square. The statue faces a Confederate monument that stands in the center of the square. Each monument tells part of Williamson County's fuller story in the war. *Chris Mackowski*

history, for instance) as well as for the things he included (too much traditional focus on battles and leaders, for instance).[46] "[D]espite the abundance of images and resources at the command of the filmmakers, that social upheaval is never played out with the same depth, the same sensitivity, the same emotional and dramatic intensity as the military engagements," contended Litwack.[47] He also criticized what he saw as the oversimplified conclusion Burns came to at the film's end. "The nation had been reborn, and it is this rebirth that Ken Burns chooses to celebrate in *The Civil War*," he said, calling it the "most appalling and revealing shortcoming" of the film.[48]

Historian Eric Foner agreed. "In choosing to stress the preservation of the American nation state as the war's most enduring consequence, Burns privileges a merely national concern over the great human drama

---

46   Toplin, vi.

47   Litwack, 128.

48   Litwack, 135, 134.

of emancipation," Foner said.[49] Others accused Burns of embracing the Lost Cause. Some "saw only capitulation to an 'old' narrative pro-southern version of history," Burns lamented.[50]

Part of the controversy—where it existed—might relate back to expectations, Burns suggested. "Had they forgotten the difference between literary scholarship and the demands of a popular medium?" he wondered.[51]

The film's principle writer, Geoffrey C. Ward, admitted that "it was only the special demands of documentary filmmaking that kept us from doing still more" in the film than they did.[52] "Time imposes crippling restraints," he said before outlining other issues, as well: "Before anything else, film demands something to look at. . . . And, just as sadly, there is precious little written evidence of the sort we would have needed to fill our script."[53] He also pointed out that "Television is better at narrative than analysis, better at evoking emotions than expounding complex ideas."[54]

The ability to evoke emotion easily stands out as *The Civil War*'s greatest strength: From its opening shot of a canon silhouetted against a fire-orange sky and the use of the Oliver Wendell Holmes quote and the haunting Appalachian violin of Jay Unger's haunting "Ashokan Farewell," Burns strives first and foremost to set an emotional tone.[55]

Even historian Leon Litwack, in all his criticism of the film as a piece of history, seemed taken with it as a piece of art:

---

49 Eric Foner, "Ken Burns and the Romance of Reunion," *Ken Burns's* The Civil War: *Historians Respond*, 105-6.

50 Ken Burns, "Four O'Clock in the Morning Courage," *Ken Burns's* The Civil War: *Historians Respond*, 172.

51 Burns, 173.

52 Ward, 146.

53 Ward, 148, 146, 147.

54 Ward, 148. At least public television made an attempt at analysis. As Gary Gallagher suggests, no one in Hollywood, would insist that a historical film "reflect the insights of the best recent scholarship—at least not anyone who hopes to attract and satisfy paying customers" (Gallagher, 9).

55 For more on The Civil War's beautiful theme song, see Dan Welch's excellent essay, "Not from This Century: A Longing Melody from a Modern Time—'Ashokan Farewell,'" in *Entertaining History: The Civil War in Literature, Film, and Song* (Carbondale, IL: Southern Illinois University Press, 2020).

Skillfully crafted, technically innovative, evocative and emotionally seductive, the television series made effective use of letters, diaries and journals, archival photographs, paintings, broadsides, newsreel footage, eyewitness accounts, and an often mesmerizing musical score.[56]

Sullivan Ballou
Library of Congress

The best example of his use of such primary-source material is the stirring narration of a letter written by Maj. Sullivan Ballou of the 2nd Rhode Island Infantry, killed during the battle of First Manassas. A week before the battle, Ballou wrote home to his wife, and Burns quotes the letter to a background of historical photos and beautiful modern battlefield landscapes, closing out the film's first episode. It is exquisite art. What most people don't realize is that Burns trimmed the letter by almost fifty percent—from 868 words down to 451—in order to maximize its poignancy on screen. Such editing, though, doesn't mean Burns's art compromised his history. Historians, too, quote selectively from primary sources when constructing narratives and arguments; Burns is using the same technique to the same end.

Burns's most common primary source materials are the hundreds of photographs he shows. Here, Toplin lauds Burns's "extraordinary filmmaking achievement in dealing with unequal source materials." Photos for the Union side of the story were much more abundant than for the Southern side of the story because, after the first year of the war, "photographic activity in the South dropped dramatically"—yet Burns crafted a balanced story from what he had to work with.[57]

56 Litwack, 126.

57 Toplin, 34-5.

The molasses-smooth authority of narrator David McCullough (who has himself taken flack for being too popular as a historian) shines throughout, punctuated by interview clips from a variety of experts, including historian Barbara Fields, who argued eloquently about the war's higher purpose of emancipation, and the yarn-spinning Southern gentleman Shelby Foote (whom Burns subsequently called "an American treasure").[58]

Not that every swing Burns took was a home run. His choice to encumber Ed Bearrs with a suitcoat and tie and confine him to a chair was widely seen among my National Park Service colleagues as a huge disservice to Ed. As the NPS's

Often mistaken as a Civil War-era song, "Ashokan Farewell" was written by Jay Ungar and performed by Ungar and Molly Mason in 1982 and popularized by Ken Burns's *The Civil War*. The song has since become a staple around reenactment campfires and at Civil War gatherings. *Jay Ungar and Molly Mason*

former chief historian, Ed was regarded throughout the agency as one of the best battlefield interpreters in the business because of his forceful style and animated storytelling. Up until his 2020 death at age 97, Ed still led dozens of sold-out bus tours a year. The Burns documentary did nothing to capture his charisma.

The film also contains a few factual errors. "The most spectacular must be the fact that we managed to get wrong both the date of Lincoln's assassination and his age at the time of his death," admits Ward. "Both

---

58 Burns's description of Foote appears as a cover blurb on the back of Chapman's Foote biography.

errors are mine alone. . . . And, unbelievably, through repeated screenings for our distinguished advisers and for ourselves, no one involved seems ever to have noticed either error." For such sins of commission, Ward says they deserved to be chastened.[59]

But for sins of interpretation—especially after the five-year collaborative process the many drafts of the script went through with panels of historians—Burns deserves some slack. Because his film was so public and so successful, criticism creates an impression of controversy when, in fact, any historian could face questions about his/her interpretation.

"[B]ecause of our medium, with all its inherent strengths and weaknesses, because of the almost Aristotelian demands of structure and pacing, our film, not theirs, *looked this way*," Burns finally said.[60] In other words, it was *Ken Burns's* Civil War; critics were welcome to go construct their own version of the story any way they'd like.

The result of Burns's achievement was a sublime intersection of history and art that used the strengths of both to tell a story so big it is, indeed, incommunicable. "[S]tory," Burns has said, "is a central part of the word 'history.'"[61] His *Civil War* remains a true story beautifully told.

Fictions Told Until They Are Believed To Be True

"Wars produce many stories of fiction, some of which are told until they are believed to be true," Ulysses S. Grant said in his *Personal Memoirs*.[62]

Grant was specifically referring to a fiction "based on a slight foundation of fact" from Appomattox Court House, where Robert E. Lee's army surrendered. The formal surrender took place in the home of Wilmer McLean in the heart of the small village, but a legend grew that the surrender actually took place beneath an apple tree. "Like many other stories," Grant

---

59 Ward, 143.

60 Burns, 172.

61 Quoted in Chapman, 259.

62 Ulysses S. Grant, *Personal Memoirs of Ulysses S. Grant* (Library of America, 1990), 732. I cite this edition of Grant's memoirs because it's my desktop reference version.

said, "it would be very good if it was only true."⁶³ Like a modern game of telephone, where a story evolves in the telling from one person to another, a kernel of fact grew into something totally beyond itself and subsequently became accepted as truth.

"The truth of an account is measured by the conviction the writer builds in the reader's mind," Paul Ashdown reminds us.⁶⁴ Facts evolve into fictions, and through repetition, become accepted as truths.

In Grant's mind, facts were "verifiable, quantifiable, recoverable, objective, and rational," says historian Joan Waugh, and they "could be retrieved from memory, conversations, written reports, letters, maps, telegrams, and diaries."⁶⁵ He believed so much in the objective power of facts that he employed a small team of fact-checkers to help him as he worked on his memoirs. However, Grant also worried about writers and historians who relied too much on those primary sources. Such writers, he believed, "reach conclusions which appear sound . . . but which are unsound in this, that they know only the dispatches, and nothing of the conversation and other incidents that might have a material effect upon the truth."⁶⁶ This echoes the challenge of a historical novelist who must go beyond the documentary evidence into realms beyond.

Ulysses S. Grant at work on his memoirs on the porch of a cottage atop Mt. McGregor in upstate New York.
Library of Congress

---

63 Ibid., 735.

64 Paul Ashdown, *A* Cold Mountain *Companion* (Gettysburg, PA: Thomas Publications, 2004), 21.

65 Joan Waugh, "Ulysses S. Grant, Historian," 20.

66 Grant quoted by Joan Waugh in "Ulysses S. Grant, Historian," 21.

Truth, says Waugh, derives from facts but is not dependent on them. "Truth was subjective and morally based," she says. "Truth had a higher meaning. Truth was based in the facts but ultimately not answerable to them. Today, professional historians call truth 'Interpretation.'"[67]

"It is not enough for historians and filmmakers to impart the facts," says historian Leon Litwack. "It is incumbent upon them to make people feel those facts, to make them see and feel those facts in ways that may be genuinely disturbing."[68] Artists know this already.

Grant set about writing his memoirs out of financial need, but he also did so because he was genuinely disturbed by the way facts were being interpreted by the growing Lost Cause school of thought. The war was about saving the Union, and "[T]he cause of the great War of the Rebellion against the United States [was] slavery," he believed.[69] He wanted to ensure no doubts about that cause—or characterization—remained.

"Thus, the *Personal Memoirs* were written both to advance a larger truth, that of Union moral superiority, and to remind America of Grant's contribution to the victory that remade America into 'a nation of great power and intelligence,'" Waugh says.[70] Grant's final battle was a war of words over the interpretation of facts and an attempt to advocate a particular truth.[71]

In the *Memoirs*, Grant was telling *his* truth. Indeed, by explicitly calling them memoirs, the dying war hero freed himself from the rigid conventions of a historian and gave himself the latitude to tell the story as he saw and understood it. Memoirs, by their very nature, are subjective. Grant could emphasize some aspects and ignore others depending on what was important

---

67 Waugh, 21.

68 Litwack, 139.

69 Grant, 773.

70 Waugh, 8.

71 John Guare, author of *Six Degrees of Separation*, wrote a play about Grant's memoir writing. "When *A Few Stout Individuals* opened, the most common reaction I got was, 'Is this true? This can't be true. How do you make this stuff up? It's true?' I imagined some of it . . . but you bet it's all true, except for the tonic salesman, and I know even he existed." (John Guare, "Preface," *A Few Stout Individuals* (New York: Grove Press, 2003), xi.) See also, Chris Mackowski, *Grant's Last Battle: The Story Behind the Personal Memoirs of Ulysses S. Grant* (Savas Beatie, 2015).

to him.⁷² Historian Frank Varney cautions us to be skeptical, despite Grant's stature and position of authority. "Grant was not at all shy about castigating his personal enemies, about praising his friends, or even about inventing things that buttressed his particular—and sometimes peculiar—version of history," he writes.⁷³ This can be problematic because, arguably, no first-person account of the war has had more of an impact on history's understanding of that war. Because the book was written as memoir, though, readers should not accept it as straight-up history, even if it reads as such.

Grant's memoir serves as a useful cautionary tale for us. In the end, the writer of history faces the same fundamental problem as any other storyteller: What truth am I trying to tell, and how shall I tell it?

Fictions and Histories

"[H]istory and historical fiction," says historian Paul Ashdown, "are alternate ways of telling stories about the past."⁷⁴ In that context, Ulysses S. Grant spoke more truth than he realized when he said, "Wars produce many stories of fiction." Aside from yarn-spun anecdotes about apple-tree surrenders and lemon-sucking generals, war also produces "stories of fiction" in a literal way as a source of inspiration: "An Occurrence at Owl Creek Bridge," *The Red Badge of Courage, Gone with the Wind, Shiloh, The Killer Angels*. Both kinds of stories present themselves as true, and both may even be based on facts. "Fact and fiction comingle, reminding us that history, like news, is only a part of the story," says Ashdown.⁷⁵ Art can offer another part of that story.

---

72 For more on this, see my "Author's Note" in *Grant's Last Battle*, vi–vii.

73 Frank P. Varney, "Foreword," *Grant's Last Battle* by Chris Mackowski, viii. For an in-depth exploration, see Frank P. Varney, *Ulysses S. Grant and the Rewriting of History: How the Destruction of General William S. Rosecrans Influenced Our Understanding of the Civil War* (El Dorado Hills: Savas Beatie, 2013).

74 Ashdown, 8.

75 Ibid, 20.

Ashdown points specifically to Charles Frazier's National Book Award-winning novel *Cold Mountain*, based very loosely on the real story of William Pinkney Inman, an ancestor of Frazier's. Facts on Inman were scarce. All Frazier knew for certain about him "could be written on the back of a postcard."[76] "'Facts' could not begin to tell the real story," Frazier wrote in the book, "and you could tell such things on and on and yet no more get to the full truth of the war than you could get to the full truth of an old sow bear's life by following her sign through the woods."[77]

Starting with those few scant facts, though, and then tapping into other resources, Frazier began inventing a story. "By making use of folklore, yarn, legend, myth, and what we can know of history, Frazier shows that although we can never know all that happened, or why it happened, we can at least obliquely participate in a continuing story," Ashdown says.

Frazier's story grew beyond the facts, which he was willing to sacrifice in service to the larger truth. For instance, he chose to drop Inman's first and middle names. "The use of the last name throughout the book suggests . . . a mythic universalism," says Ashdown. "The point is not so much to detach Inman from the past as it is to detach him from William P. Inman and historicity."[78]

Coal Black Horse, about a 14-year-old boy's journey to manhood as he travels from western Virginia to get his father from the battlefield at Gettysburg, does something similar. Because author Robert Olmstead avoids almost all mention of specific places, his protagonist, Robey Childs, travels across a mythic landscape, which suits the novel well because of the slightly surreal quality of the characters. Facts would ground the world too much. Olmstead doesn't even mention Gettysburg by name until page 145—two-thirds of the way through the book's 218 pages—well after Robey has arrived on site and well after the battle.

Even in instances when Olmstead does use specific information, he often does so with a cloud of mystery. Robey's mother sets the boy's quest

---

76 Ashdown, 19.

77 Charles Frazier, *Cold Mountain* (New York: Vintage, 1997), 342.

78 Ibid, 23.

in motion when she declares, on the evening of May 10, 1863, "Thomas Jackson has died." Jackson did, indeed, die on that date, but in their remote location, Robey's mother would have had no way to hear that news so quickly—yet know it, she does just as she knows, "It is now over." She doesn't look at Robey as she says this but is instead "looking past him and some place beyond. . . . Her face was the composure of one who had experienced the irrevocable. It was a fact unalterable and it was as simple as that."[79]

The unalterable facts, while true, appear in a way that couldn't be. What's more, readers may not know the truth to them, anyway, unless they have a fondness for remembering Civil War dates. Readers may have heard of Jackson, but mostly likely because of his famous nickname, "Stonewall," which Robey's mother doesn't use. These layers of meta-haze make the facts almost irrelevant as facts even as they're vital for Olmstead's myth-building.[80]

Conversely, a writer can deluge a reader with facts, as Paulette Jiles does in *Enemy Women*, a novel about the Civil War's guerilla conflict in Missouri. Jiles quotes extensively from *Inside War: The Guerilla Conflict in Missouri, 1861-1865* by Michael J. Fellman, which she includes as epigrams before each chapter as a way to provide background information and context. While those facts allow her to avoid exposition of her own, they still disrupt the flow of her narrative and interfere with her authorial voice. Facts, at least as Jiles uses them, can become too much.

As a historical story gets further from the facts, the harder it is to take the work seriously as history, but the easier it is to accept purely in terms of entertainment value. Nowhere is this more evident in the burgeoning science fiction subgenre of "alternate history." Harry Turtledove's *Guns of the South*, for instance, which pays meticulous attention to accuracy with its discussion of firearms and aspects of daily life, is clearly "alternative history" because time travelers bring AK-47s to Robert E. Lee's army from Apartheid-era

---

[79] Robert Olmstead, Coal Black Horse (Chapel Hill, NC: Algonquin Books, 2007), 3.

[80] See Chris Mackowski, "A beautiful, despairing journey with a coal black horse," 27 July 2012, http://emergingcivilwar.com/2012/07/27/a-beautiful-despairing-journey-with-a-coal-black-horse/.

South Africa. I know historians who think the premise is ludicrous, but they never accuse the book of trying to dress itself up as history, either.

Other alternate histories of the war typically hinge on "what ifs" less outlandish: in Turtledove's *How Few Remain*, the Federal army never finds the "Lost Order" that outlines Lee's plans for invasion into Pennsylvania; in Newt Gingrich and William Forestchen's *Gettysburg*, Lee takes Longstreet's advice and swings southward to better ground after the first day of fighting in Gettysburg; Peter Tsouras's *Gettysburg* gives the battle a full reimagining while Douglas Gibboney's *Stonewall Jackson at Gettysburg* puts the legendary general in the thick of it; Kevin Wilmott's biting satiric film *C.S.A.* explores modern America if the entire country, not just the South, had legalized slavery. An author with no less prestige than MacKinlay Kantor, who won the Pulitzer Prize for his Civil War prison novel *Andersonville*, imagined *If the South Had Won the Civil War*, basing his plot twist on a horseback riding accident that kills Union General Ulysses S. Grant.

Gingrich calls alternate history "a way of breathing life back into the adventure, to reopen the book on page one," but he insists that in order for them to be of any value beyond mere escapism, "internal logic, consistency, and a rigid adherence to reality must still be maintained. Otherwise, we fall off the track and it becomes an exercise in fantasy." For instance, he says an aggressive George McClellan would've probably won Antietam, but McClellan was "driven far more by his fear of failure than by the dream of success." To write his character any other way "is a denial of everything we know about him and becomes an exercise in fantasy." Likewise, the "magic bullet" scenario—Grant dying in a horseback riding accident, Jackson surviving Chancellorsville, Lincoln's mother not dying of the milk sickness—is little more than an exercise in fantasy.[81] (It is worth noting that Grant, an excellent horseman, nonetheless had serious horseback riding accidents several times during the war—April 4, 1862, before Shiloh; September 4, 1863, in New Orleans; and October 23, 1863, riding into Chattanooga—and a carriage accident late in life, making Kantor's premise seem more firmly grounded in the possible and less a mere freak accident.)

---

81 Newt Gingrich, "Introduction," *Gettysburg: A Novel of the Civil War* (New York: Thomas Dunne Books, 2003).

I mention these alternate histories only as a way of probing the outer boundaries of history and fiction, where art clearly stands as art and central facts are clearly false. At the other end, I could likewise cite James McPherson's Pulitzer-winning *Battle Cry of Freedom* or Drew Gilpin Faust's *This Republic of Suffering* as examples that clearly stand in the realm of history and where facts are clearly true. One pole privileges story over fact, the other fact over story. Somewhere in between rest the examples I've discussed in this essay. All of them, fiction and nonfiction alike, strive to strike a balance between fact and story in the service of a particular truth.

"People interested in the Civil War become obsessed with facts and don't have much patience with fiction," Ashdown says.[82] They criticize art for being "unfactual" (just as artists criticize history for being "boring"). Before they insist on sacrificing art on the altar of fact, though, they'd do well to keep in mind the lesson Grant knew well: facts themselves are hard things to hold on to and can be interpreted into all sorts of happy and unhappy truths. Truths compete with truths.

"Today, professional historians call truth 'Interpretation,'" Waugh said—but what interpretations are true? What *kinds* of interpretations lead to the best kinds of truth? What truths are true?

What to do with facts, and how to interpret those facts into truths, are central issues for storytellers of all sorts, whether historians or novelists, documentarians or feature filmmakers. "Historical sense and poetic sense should not, in the end, be contradictory," Robert Penn Warren said, "for if poetry is the little myth we make, history is the big myth we live, and in our living, constantly remake."[83]

---

82 Ashdown, 7.

83 Warren quoted by Jones in "Introduction," ix.

Birth of a (Lost Cause) Nation

by Sheritta Bitikofer

Originally published as a blog post on Emerging Civil War on June 14, 2022

It's human nature for people to gravitate toward stories and media that line up with their perceptions of themselves, their communities, and their interpretation of history. Those stories then pass into popular consciousness, becoming part of the identity of the people, sending ripples through society, sometimes changing it almost irrevocably. One set of such stories was packaged up in the 1915 D. W. Griffith silent film *The Birth of a Nation*. The film and its extraordinary 120-piece orchestra accompaniment was celebrated as "astounding for its time."[1] Theaters across the country, including the South, showed the film, charging $2.00 admission—the price for a typical live performance.[2] President Woodrow Wilson—still in mourning for the late Mrs. Wilson—was invited to view the film in a private screening at the White

---

1 Kevin Brownlow, *The Parade's Gone By . . .* (Berkeley: University of California Press, 1968), 78.

2 Arthur Lennig, "Myth and Fact: The Reception of 'The Birth of a Nation,'" *Film History* 16, no. 2 (2004): 119.

House and believed the film was an authentic telling of history. Griffith, acclaimed for his innovative use of the close-up, editing shots, and dramatic storytelling, is best known for this three-hour film, which remains as controversial today as it was more than a hundred years ago.

For those who have not seen *The Birth of a Nation* (originally called *The Clansman*, after the book it was based on by Thomas Dixon), the story follows two families: the Camerons, who were ardent secessionists and resided in the fictional town of Piedmont, South Carolina, and the Stonemans from the North, who align

Ground-breaking as a piece of art yet problematic as a piece of "history," *The Birth of a Nation* has influenced generations of filmmakers and Lost Causers alike. *Library of Congress*

themselves with the radical Republicans. Ben Cameron (Henry B. Walthall) and Phil Stoneman (Elmer Clifton) were old boarding school friends, and each developed a romance with the younger sister of the other: Ben with Elsie Stoneman (Lillian Gish) and Phil with Margaret Cameron (Miriam Cooper). All the sons of each family enlisted at the outbreak of the Civil War. In two parts, the film covers the experiences of these two families during the war and in the following Reconstruction era.

The story is told primarily through the lens of the Southern Confederate narrative, giving far more screen time to events such as the volunteers going off to war, the destruction of Atlanta, and the degradation of Southern society. It's also evident within the first ten minutes that the aim of the film was to romanticize antebellum society, when Southern aristocracy ruled their communities and the Black population was enslaved (but allegedly happy and submissive). Federal soldiers are interpreted in the film as being cruel to Southerner civilians, and Confederates are shown as benevolent foes, as in the scene when Ben Cameron runs to the aid of a fallen Union soldier at Petersburg to give him a drink of water before making a final charge that ended with his wounding and capture at the hands of his old friend, Phil Stoneman.

Historical figures make notable appearances, such as Generals Robert E. Lee (Howard Gaye) and Ulysses S. Grant (Donald Crisp), Senator Charles Sumner (Sam De Grasse), and President Abraham Lincoln (Joseph Henabery). Lincoln was depicted not as a hated villain of the South but as an advocate for the former Confederates who returned home from the war when other politicians—like the patriarch of the Stoneman family (Ralph Lewis)—demanded retribution. Upon hearing of Lincoln's assassination, Ben Cameron lamented, "Our best friend is gone, what is to become of us now!"[3]

In terms of production design, *The Birth of a Nation* stands out for the technological innovations it makes to the film medium. As with most silent movies, the acting is over the top to fully convey the emotions characters experience. Few of the slides contain any kind of dialogue, leaving the audience to imagine the words of the players, while the slides only explained the context of the scene. The sequence of the siege of Petersburg alone is a stunning piece of set coordination, as countless extras charge and skirmish across a smoky, fiery battlefield, all viewed from a great height so the audience may understand the scale of a Civil War battle.

The film lacks historical accuracy, but the average moviegoer who knew next to nothing going into the theater may have come away learning something new, while also "learning" quite a few things that were (and remain) totally erroneous, yet which may have shaped their view of history. It's almost never safe to accept a film's interpretation of history verbatim, even if the film was based on true events, because the directors and writers may be more devoted to sensationalism and theatrical storytelling than to true history.

3 *Birth of a Nation*, directed by D. W. Griffith (David W. Griffith Corp., 1915), 1:29:45.

Still, *The Birth of a Nation* might always "be considered the film which gave the motion pictures its stature as an art form."[4] Griffith's trademark use of narrative filmmaking enthralled audiences who became invested in the characters and story. All twelve reels of its original cut featured 1,640 separate shots and titles, employing the use of dramatic close-ups and editing techniques, such as crosscut sequencing of parallel actions and the use of montages, which were unprecedented. The original orchestral score, composed by Joseph Carl Breil, was carefully synchronized to the film to avoid any melodies that might be incongruous to the scenes. With coordinated sound effects and distinct character themes spaced out between 214 separate cues, the intended music for *The Birth of a Nation* alone was impressive to moviegoers, who were used to a single piano or no sound at all in the theater.[5] The *Los Angeles Times* heralded it as "the greatest picture that was ever made and the biggest drama ever filmed."[6] All of these innovative techniques proved to revolutionize the moviemaking industry, and any producer that wanted to top Griffith had to continually work at the craft to make the next film bigger, better, and more engaging than *The Birth of a Nation*. Between 1915 and 1946, over 200 million Americans viewed this film, and its impact can never be understated in the movie industry.[7]

If Griffith had ended his film after the assassination of Abraham Lincoln, *The Birth of a Nation* might have received only as much criticism as *Gone with the Wind* did two decades later. However, the second part of the film, which covered the Reconstruction era, outraged the Black population, the people who had the most to lose from the shift in society that would come as a result of the film's showing. Within the first few minutes, the film establishes that Blacks were the villains of the story. The first text slide stated that the importation of enslaved Africans sowed the seeds of disunion in America, placing the blame for the war and the societal upheaval on the shoulders of the Blacks who were captured and deported against their wills.

---

4 Raymond A. Cook, "The Man Behind 'The Birth of a Nation,'" *North Carolina Historical Review* 39, no. 4 (1962): 519.

5 Lennig, "Myth and Fact: The Reception of 'The Birth of a Nation,'" 118.

6 *Los Angeles Times*, February 9, 1915.

7 Conrad Pitcher, "D. W. Griffith's Controversial Film, *The Birth of a Nation*," *OAH Magazine of History* 13, no. 3 (Spring 1999): 50.

In a way, this lines up with the use of disunion rhetoric as an accusation against Northern abolitionists for inspiring discontent, which culminated in the Union's dissolution and Southern secession.[8] But the few opening shots of early African enslavement was only the beginning of why *The Birth of a Nation* has remained so unshakably problematic for modern viewers.

Throughout *The Birth of a Nation*, Black and mixed-race characters—played by white actors in blackface—like Lydia (Mary Alden) and Silas Lynch (George Siegmann) were depicted as heinous, scheming, ignorant, destructive, carnal, and easily beguiled by Northern carpetbaggers and politicians. These traits aligned with the typical white supremacist view that Blacks and non-whites were inferior beings that deserved to be subjugated and that unleashing freedmen upon society would only end in the ruin of civilization itself. The only Black characters represented in a positive light were Mammy (Jennie Lee)—who is called the "faithful servant" in the opening credits—and her fellow male servant, who remained with the Cameron family throughout the film and even assisted in rescuing Dr. Cameron (Spottiswoode Aitken) from imprisonment. By painting this picture of Black submission as an admirable virtue, the film portrays the ideal place for freed Blacks in society and their relationship with whites.

The fate of Gus (Walter Long), the "renegade negro," is a case in point. After Congress passed a law that legalized interracial marriage in the movie, Southern whites were appalled and deeply concerned for the fate of its women, now surrounded by lustful freedmen. Flora Cameron (Mae Marsh) came under the special attention of Gus and, after a lengthy chase through the South Carolina countryside, Flora committed suicide by jumping off a cliff rather than be caught by a Black man. Her death drew the ire of the local Ku Klux Klan, which hunted down Gus and exacted vigilante justice to avenge the honor of the Southern woman—the rationale for much of the terrorist actions carried out by the KKK.

At the hour-and-a-half mark, the film featured several panels that might have been intended to assuage audiences from believing that the film was meant as propaganda. Griffith's infused message of peace over hatred and war—especially the Great War going on in Europe at the time—was a far

---

8 Elizabeth R. Varon, *Disunion! The Coming of the American Civil War, 1789–1859* (Chapel Hill: University of North Carolina Press, 2008), 84, 216.

more powerful theme, presented in the film's final scenes. It claimed that the film was meant to be a historical presentation of the war and "not meant to reflect on any race of people of today." However, it follows this with a nod to President Woodrow Wilson's *History of the American People*, which condemned the Reconstruction era as a means to "put the white South under the heel of the black South" and that the Ku Klux Klan was intended to "protect the Southern country."[9] Ben Cameron was painted as the leader of the Piedmont KKK, which "saved the South from the anarchy of black rule."[10] By the end of the film, it certainly appeared that way. The riotous Black mob in the streets of Piedmont were driven out by an army of white-clad, masked Klansmen, and Silas Lynch—who was ready to force Elsie Stoneman into marriage—was killed along with countless other Blacks who antagonized the Cameron family. The KKK appeared as the heroes who triumphed over Southern Reconstruction and induced the birth of a white supremacist nation.

D. W. Griffith and Thomas Dixon, the masterminds behind both the book and movie adaptation, were Southerners who grew up listening to stories told by their Confederate veteran relatives. Griffith's father, Jacob, served as a lieutenant colonel in the 1st Kentucky Cavalry, the same unit that escorted the fleeing Confederate government in April of 1865. Dixon's maternal uncle, Leroy McAfee, ended his military career as a colonel for the 49th North Carolina and was the inspiration for the protagonist in his nephew's 1905 play and novel, *The Clansman*. In addition to stories from the war, Dixon's father and uncle were members of the North Carolina Ku Klux Klan, allowing Dixon to witness the Klan's vigilante efforts firsthand throughout his childhood.[11] These stories shaped their worldview and colored their telling of this crucial period of American history.

Griffith denied being racist but firmly believed that he was telling the truth about the Southern experience in the latter half of the nineteenth century. On several text slides, he added "footnotes" to explain where he

---

9 *Birth of a Nation*, 1:30:02–37.

10 Ibid, 2:03:05.

11 Maxwell Bloomfield, "Dixon's *The Leopard's Spots*: A Study in Popular Racism," *American Quarterly* 16, no. 3 (1964): 387–401.

drew inspiration for certain scenes, such as the surrender at Appomattox, the assassination of Lincoln, or the "invasion" of the House of Representatives by free Blacks after the war. However, what remained was the overall theme that the South was victimized during and after the war, and the majority of the story is infused with Lost Cause propaganda. When one learns about the principles of early Reconstruction historian William Dunning—that Blacks were ignorant and unworthy of social advancement, Southerners were victimized during the Congressional Reconstruction period, and all whites suffered under Black suffrage until the rise of the "home rule" movement— the film's interpretation of history makes sense for the time in which it was made. Modern scholars and historians have since acknowledged the deep flaws in Dunning's interpretation, but far too late to be of any benefit to those who had to live through its acceptance and the waves that have resulted since.[12]

The KKK, which had all but died out toward the close of Reconstruction, resurged around the release of *The Birth of a Nation*, leading many to believe that the two events were directly linked or had at least indirectly influenced each other. Klan leaders admitted to using shots from the film, such as the massive ride of the Klansman to the aid of Piedmont, as a recruitment tool.[13]

Today, the film can be viewed as an unfiltered representation of white supremacist sentiment at the expense of Black Americans 50 years after the Civil War. Much of the early films of the era supported the stereotype of Black inferiority, making the portrayals in *The Birth of a Nation* congruous with contemporary trends in the movie industry. The release of the film also coincided with racial segregation institutionalized by the Wilson administration.[14] Many thought this regression of civil rights for African Americans would only worsen after the showing of *The Birth of a Nation*. Activists like Booker T. Washington, W. E. B. Dubois, and William Monroe Trotter vigorously demanded the censoring of the film

---

12 Eric Foner, *A Short History of Reconstruction: Updated Edition* (New York: Harper Perennial, 2015), xi–xii, 258.

13 The best overview of the influences of the film on the KKK is Maxim Simcovitch's "The Impact of Griffith's *Birth of a Nation* on the Modern Ku Klux Klan," originally published in the first issue of *Journal of Popular Film and Television* 1, no. 1 (1972): 45–54.

14 Caroline E. Light, *Stand Your Ground: A History of America's Love Affair with Lethal Self-Defense* (Boston: Beacon Press, 2017), 81.

for its misrepresentation of Black history.[15] The film and its depiction of Black people, critics believed, would reinforce racial prejudice in America and only damage the cause of racial equality that the National Association for the Advancement of Colored People aimed to advance. According to a Harvard University study that evaluated the reception of the film as it was viewed in various counties across the nation, "on average, lynchings . . . rose fivefold in a month after [the film] arrived."[16] To this criticism, Griffith wrote, "The public should not be afraid to accept the truth, even though it might not like it" and discredited the Black—and some white—voices that spoke against his film.[17]

As Vincent Brown, professor of African and African-American History at Harvard University, aptly put it, *The Birth of a Nation* was a form of "racist pornography" because it gave a physical manifestation to racist ideas and fantasies and justified racial violence to a nation particularly vulnerable to these images.[18] In a telling move, theater owners denied selling tickets to Black moviegoers who were curious about the film so as to avoid any outbreak of violence in the audience. A mass protest in Boston in April of 1915 demanded that the film not be shown, but since the president had personally approved of the film, protestors failed to sway public opinion on the matter.

Another film was produced in 1920, *Within Our Gates,* intended to undo some of the damage caused by *The Birth of a Nation*, reversing the narrative and showing audiences a Black family being unjustly lynched and a Black woman being raped by a white man. Ironically, this film was censored in many cities and could not overturn the tide of racial prejudice.

The Birth of a Nation became one of the most successful silent films of the age and set a precedent for movies to follow, such as *Gone with*

---

15   Richard Brody, "The Black Activist Who Fought against D. W. Griffith's 'The Birth of a Nation,'" *New Yorker*, February 5, 2017; David Copeland, *The Media's Role in Defining the Nation: The Active Voice* (New York: Peter Lang, 2010), 168.

16   "A Tarnished Silver Screen: How a Racist Film Helped the Ku Klux Klan Grow for Generations," *Economist*, March 27, 2021.

17   David Rylance, "Breech Birth: The Receptions to D. W. Griffith's *The Birth of a Nation*," *Australasian Journal of American Studies* 24, no. 2 (December 2005): 1–20, esp. 15.

18   *Birth of a Movement*, produced by Sam Pollard, Henry Louis Gates Jr., Julie Anderson (Northern Light Productions, 2017), 26:42.

the Wind, underpinning not only the Lost Cause spawned out of the Civil War but the racial prejudice that America continues to struggle with today. Though technologically impressive in 1915, the mark this film has left on pop culture and the media industry is far from positive. The harmful themes and ideas presented in the film gave consent to other writers and filmmakers to continue the trend in their own projects, receiving their own level of acclaim for their presentation of life during and following the Civil War. This only helped to reinforce racism and false conceptions of Civil War history to a national audience.

In recent decades, pop culture began to work to reverse and repair the damage of *Birth*. Other films and television series focused on the true story of slavery and postwar racism in America like *Glory* (1989), *Night John* (1996), *Rosewood* (1997), *12 Years a Slave* (2013), and *The Birth of a Nation* (2016)—which was far from a remake of the 1915 original because it focuses on the point of view of the enslaved during the Nat Turner uprising—just to name a few. In these films, the suffering of the enslaved on Southern plantations and the struggle against varying forms of racism, which were true to historical narrative, provides a fierce contrast to the images first presented in *The Birth of a Nation*.

The evolution of the reception of this film over the last century from a popular blockbuster and cinematic innovative masterpiece to something that is widely accepted as atrociously racist and what one Griffith scholar dubs "one of the ugliest artifacts of American popular art" is indicative of the ideological and cultural shift that has taken place within American society and our own self-awareness of a painful past.[19] Because of this shift in reception, the film should be studied by film students and historians alike. The racist ideas presented in the film are beyond dispute and will continue to be deeply problematic for viewers in the following decades, but put within the proper historical context and film historiography, much can still be learned from *The Birth of a Nation* about society and the movie industry in the early twentieth century.

---

19 Scott Simmons, *The Films of D. W. Griffith* (Cambridge: Cambridge University Press, 1993), 105.

A Fun Civil War Movie: The General

by Dwight S. Hughes

Originally published as a blog post at Emerging Civil War on January 23, 2020

We know the great Civil War movies, but how about one that is both great and really fun? *The General*, starring and directed by Buster Keaton, is a 1927 silent film (79 minutes). Keaton plays sad-sack little engineer, Johnny Gray, who loves two things: his big steam locomotive, the General, and the adorable Annabelle Lee.

War erupts. Johnny longs to enlist for the South and impress his girl. The recruiting officer rejects him as too valuable in his current position as locomotive engineer but does not tell anyone that. To Annabelle's disgust, a dejected Johnny is mistakenly branded a coward for not joining up.

Yankee spies steal the General and its train with the girl aboard and head north. Johnny sets off running after them single-handedly, straight through enemy lines, on a fanatical chase, doing almost everything wrong but getting it all right. After many harrowing adventures, he recovers the General and gets the girl, winning a battle in the process. Johnny is acclaimed a hero and presented with a lieutenant's uniform and sword.

The story is a takeoff on the Great Locomotive Chase, or Andrews's Raid. On April 12, 1862, Union civilian scout James J. Andrews led a group of army volunteers on a raid in northern Georgia on the Western and Atlantic Railroad (W&A), a vital link between Atlanta and Chattanooga. They commandeered the General at Big Shanty (now Kennesaw) and fled northward, sabotaging the line and cutting telegraph wires as they went.

Confederate forces pursued for 87 miles, first on foot and then on a succession of locomotives, including the Texas. The General ran low on fuel and came to a halt north of Ringold, where Andrews and his raiders attempted to flee through the woods. Confederates captured and executed some, including Andrews, while others escaped. Survivors were the first to be awarded the Medal of Honor by the U.S. Congress, but as a civilian scout, Andrews was not eligible.

Buster Keaton was reknowned for his broad physical comedy, which he acted out with stone-faced expressions. *Library of Congress*

A 1956 Walt Disney production, *The Great Locomotive Chase*, starring Fess Parker of *Davy Crockett* TV fame, is not a great film but is fairly accurate and good for kids. Both screenplays were based on the book of the same name by William Pittenger, the actual engineer involved.

Don't think a silent film won't hold your attention. *The General* was one of the most expensive films of its time. It features racing action, outlandish stunt work and sight gags, and an inventive storyline based on real events. Observe the working of real period locomotives, which are stars themselves. Acting in a silent film is also fun to watch—hammier than talkies, but then so much must be expressed by expression.

All the actors are good, but Keaton is superb in his signature style as the deadpan "Great Stone Face." He conveys more thoughts and emotion with his eyes and body than all but the very best actors. Watch his eyes as he stares out from the racing engine to see a loose boxcar that was behind him suddenly appear in front.

Or when he loads a giant flatcar mortar and aims it at the fleeing General, only to find the jarring of his speeding Texas has repointed it right at him. He's just a regular guy doing the best he can in extraordinary circumstances, and you're right there, cheering him on all the way. Keaton's acting seems more lasting than his more famous contemporaries, Charlie Chaplin and Harold Lloyd.

We are jaded by today's wowzie special effects, so keep in mind that every death-defying stunt Keaton performs with acrobatic skill and grace is wholly real. In one scene, for example, he sits on the cowcatcher of the Texas with a big railroad tie in his arms, tearing along just behind the General. Union men on the General throw another tie onto the tracks in front of him, and Keaton, with perfect aim and timing, knocks it away by throwing the one in his arms. You wonder how he did that and how many takes it took.

The final battle is dramatic. Hundreds of extras from the Oregon town near the filming site charge, shooting one way in Union uniforms and then the other direction in Confederate uniforms. The climactic scene is the fiery end of a real locomotive crossing a burning trestle, not faked and spectacularly staged. The broken hulk remained in place for years as a tourist attraction.

Rotten Tomatoes gives the movie a 92 and describes it this way: "Brilliantly filmed and fueled with classic physical comedy, *The General* captures Buster Keaton at his timeless best." With the advent of sound, Keaton's career stalled, and he struggled in obscurity before being rediscovered late in life. *The General* was not a financial success when released, but today it is regarded as a masterpiece. In 1989, it was selected by the Library of Congress to be among the first class of films in the National Film Registry for being "culturally, historically, or aesthetically significant."

Both the General and the Texas are 4-4-0 "American" type steam locomotives built in the 1850s. They are still around, now restored to near original configuration. The General is preserved at the Southern Museum of Civil War and Locomotive History in Kennesaw, Georgia, and is listed on the National Register of Historic Places. The Texas is at the Atlanta History Center.

The General (the movie) is available for streaming on Amazon Prime and in various DVD editions. I watched the Amazon version. I would have preferred a digitally remastered and enhanced copy, but the picture quality was good enough on a big screen, and it featured the original movie organ score, which I recommend. See customer comments under the streaming version on Amazon for more information on DVD editions. Some customers didn't like more recent orchestral scores on DVD. The Wikipedia entry has good background information.

If you fancy yourself a Civil War film connoisseur or just want a fun movie, *The General* is a must-see.

Gone with the Wind: Some Thoughts

by Sarah Kay Bierle

Adapted from a series, "Gone with the Wind: Some Thoughts," published June 21-25, 2020, at Emerging Civil War

Gone with the Wind hit the trending list on June 10, 2020, because HBO Max pulled it from their list of movies. Shortly after, news arrived that it would be returned sometime in the future with some disclaimers and maybe some historical context, which did occur several weeks later. In the meantime, some critics voiced their opinion that it should never come back. Many celebrities and newscasters added their voices for keeping or archiving the 1939 Hollywood classic, and, of course, the discussion turned political.

Through it all, several points came to mind:
- What would I tell the kids?
- How do we remember Hattie McDaniel and her challenging rise to fame?
- How did 1930s segregation create real rebels for respect and equality in Hollywood on *Gone with the Wind*'s sets?
- How have viewers' implied and imprinted feelings affected the memory around the movie?
- What about cinema art?

Starting with Question 1: What would I tell the kids about *Gone with the Wind*? I mean the children who are reaching "movie-watching age" ten, fifteen, or twenty years from now. I imagine my own kids or my nieces and nephews looking at the history books on my shelf and asking, "What's this about?"

I imagine telling them the synopsis of the story. Telling them about the making of a Hollywood epic, talking about the difference between a good story and historical facts. I will make it clear that this is a story. It is not a documentary. We will talk about racism and how that is evident in some scenes. We will also talk about Hattie McDaniel, the movie's opening night in Atlanta, and what life was like in the 1930s—for all Americans.

Yes, *Gone with the Wind* has some cringe-worthy, stereotypical, insensitive moments. But there was a memorable fight when the scriptwriters and African-American cast battled to reduce it to what eventually made it to the screen. What is offensive, and rightfully so, in the twenty-first century was a groundbreaking reduction of the racism originally intended for that movie. If we cover up the racism that did make it to the screen, will it be harder to remember the injustices?

Used properly, *Gone with the Wind* could be an effective way to look at the "happy plantation myth," Lost Cause ideas in early twentieth-century pop culture, and how Reconstruction was remembered and interpreted for a long time. I strongly believe that *Gone with the Wind* should not be used to teach Civil War history, but it can be used to teach historiography in a very powerful way.

If we shove this film into the dark recesses of the past, we lose a valuable—albeit painful—snapshot of how the Civil War, Reconstruction, and Black history were portrayed and interpreted in the 1930s. And we would lose an opportunity to teach and discuss. If we do not teach and discuss the awful and uncomfortable moments, how can we help the next generations recognize the subtle or blatant injustices and inequalities? And will it be easier to pretend they didn't happen?

If we forget those injustices and inequalities by removing an uncomfortable piece of bigscreen art, do we also risk losing a link to the history of the men and women who endured and battled against those injustices and the intense racism? Does their courage deserve a memory?

In a twist of fate, the 2020 *Gone with the Wind* controversy burst on June 10, Hattie McDaniel's birthday. McDaniel, who portrayed Mammy in the film, received an Academy Award for Best Supporting Actress and was the first African American to win an Oscar. She received that award for her

Gone with the Wind: Some Thoughts

The three strong women of *Gone with the Wind*: Hattie McDaniel, Olivia de Havilland, and Vivian Leigh. *Library of Congress*

skillful acting in *Gone with the Wind*. Does removing and vilifying *Gone with the Wind* take away something from McDaniel's achievement? Or does the removal somehow bring a sense of reparation or justice for the injustices she faced during her lifetime?

Born on June 10, 1893, McDaniel was the youngest of thirteen siblings. Both of her parents had been enslaved prior to the Civil War, and her father had served in the Union army. Seeking a new place to live after experiencing increasing segregation and threats, the McDaniel family settled in Colorado. Her father and several of her brothers went into show business, and as she grew up, McDaniel loved to perform, sing, and recite. Her professional career as an entertainer started with a minstrel show, and by the 1920s, she performed on radio shows and recorded some of her own songs and music.

In 1931, she joined some of her siblings in the Golden State, seeking roles in films and performing as "Hi-Hat-Hattie" on a radio program. By the mid-1930s, McDaniel's talent was noticed by the major studios. Fox Film Corporation offered her a contract, and she played in a Shirley Temple film. One of her first major feature roles was in *Show Boat* (1936), and McDaniel made friends with many Hollywood stars who recognized her talents and character. Roles for African-American women were limited in 1930s Hollywood, though, and McDaniel was often cast as a maid, servant, or slave.

Referencing the unfortunately limited roles, McDaniel declared to a Hollywood reporter, "I'd rather play a maid than be one." Though she made a choice to work within the studio systems and endured segregation and racism regularly, McDaniel made it clear that she had made decisions that she hoped would open doors for other African Americans to go farther in the growing entertainment world. She also took stands when she felt strongly about an issue and felt that she could change a director or studio effectively. In 1947, after her *Gone with the Wind* fame, McDaniel wrote an article for the *Hollywood Reporter*, stating, "I have never apologized for the roles I play. . . . Several times I have persuaded the directors to omit dialect from modern pictures. They readily agreed to the suggestion. I have been told that I have kept alive the stereotype of the Negro servant in the minds of theatre-goers."[1]

Indeed, press and reviewers praised her stereotypical portrayal of faithful Mammy in the myth of "happy Southern plantations," in language that is awkward to twenty-first-century readers but was supposed to be laudatory and liberal in the segregated world of the 1930s.

Though McDaniel saw herself as a groundbreaker, shattering a few glass ceilings along the way for other African-American women who would follow in her footsteps, others in the Black community did not find her Hollywood roles and life agreeable. *Gone with the Wind* put her in the hot seat from the beginning. The controversy predated McDaniel, starting with the publication of the best-selling novel in 1936 and the quick sale of the movie rights to David O. Selznick. The leaders of the National Association for the Advancement of Colored People (NAACP) led the charge against the book and movie, pointing out racist language and stereotypes. McDaniel actually convinced Selznick to drop several verbal slurs because she refused to say them or have them said to her.

Some sources claim that Clark Gable recommended Hattie McDaniel for the role of "Mammy" since he had worked with her on a previous film

---

1 Kat Eschner, "What Hattie McDaniel Said about Her Oscar-Winning Career Playing Racial Stereotypes," *Smithsonian Magazine*, June 9, 2017, https://www.smithsonianmag.com/smart-news/what-hattie-mcdaniel-said-about-her-oscar-winning-career-playing-racial-stereotypes-180963575/.

and recognized her acting talents. Initially, McDaniel did not expect to get the part, but she auditioned with enthusiasm. Once she had the role, McDaniel joined other Black actors and actresses on a segregated set. They threatened to walk out unless certain steps toward equality and appreciation for all talents were taken, including the removal of racial designated areas within the set and preparation areas.

McDaniel befriended many of the film's stars, including Vivien Leigh, who often went to lunch with her. She shared a laugh with Gable, who filled their glasses with scotch instead of colored water for one memorable "take." Olivia de Havilland recognized that McDaniel would probably win a major award for the scene where Mammy talks with Melanie about little Bonnie's death.

Though small breakthroughs had been made socially on the sets of *Gone with the Wind*, McDaniel and her fellow Black actors and actresses faced an unkind world when the movie finally premiered. They were forbidden to attend the opening night in Atlanta, Georgia. Even when McDaniel was nominated for an Academy Award, Selznick had to convince the event site to change their segregation rules to allow her attendance.

Following her success from *Gone with the Wind*, McDaniel starred in more films during the 1940s. She performed with the USO during World War II and toured to promote *Gone with the Wind*. Later, she became the first Black actor or actress to star in her own radio show, creating the comedy series called *Beulah* and making $2,000 per week for her performances. However, the show created controversy for continuing to use racially stereotypical scenarios. In 1952, McDaniel stepped away from entertaining; she had been struggling with health challenges and had been diagnosed with breast cancer. On October 26, 1952, at age 59, McDaniel died of cancer. She had requested to be buried in Hollywood Cemetery, but her final request was denied because of segregation, and she was buried in Rosedale Cemetery.

Through her life, Hattie McDaniel battled racism and segregation nearly everywhere she turned in the entertainment industry. She chose to push some boundaries and accepted others. Her talented acting in *Gone with the Wind* secured a historic moment when she won Hollywood's highest award for best supporting actress. While this acknowledgment of her skills should never be used as an excuse for the racism and segregation she endured, it does bring the question: Should we forget the movie that led to her groundbreaking achievement?

Fans of the movie often forget Margaret Mitchell's novel, on which it was based, won the Pulitzer Prize in fiction in 1939. *Library of Congress*

To some viewers during the movie's release in 1939 and 1940, *Gone with the Wind* was seen as a humbling and demeaning travesty in the Black community. Selznick, the movie's producer, saw it differently. Recognizing the racial and segregation debates gripping the United States and seeing those debates against the larger global backdrop of racism and genocide in Nazi Germany, he took deliberate measures to alter details from Margaret Mitchell's novel. For example, he refused to name or portray the Ku Klux Klan, turning Ashley, Frank, and the others into a revenge group (unnamed) that was going to defend Scarlett's honor. He also purposely changed the perpetrator of Scarlett's attack to an unruly white man and gave a freedman the role to rescue Scarlett.[2] Selznick debated with his scriptwriter, Sidney Howard, and insisted, "I, for one, have no desire to produce an anti-Negro film either. In our picture I think we have to be awfully careful that the Negroes come out decidedly on the right side of the ledger."[3]

Influenced by Franklin D. Roosevelt's administration and a new generation of Black activists, Hollywood had already been changing in the 1930s. Though film roles were limited and often stereotypical, more opportunities opened, and some movies offered strong, emotional roles for Black actors and actresses. The changes were small (and almost imperceptible to the twenty-first-century eye), but they happened. Selznick was part of that movement.

---

2 Thomas Cripps, "Winds of Change: *Gone with the Wind* and Racism as a National Issue," in *Recasting: "Gone with the Wind" in American Culture*, ed. Darden A. Pyron (Miami: University Presses of Florida, 1983), 137.

3 Ibid., 140.

On set, the African-American cast created their own boundaries and refused to be devalued or treated unfairly as they created cinematic art. The cast threatened to walk out unless the restrooms were desegregated; Clark Gable made a call to declare that if there weren't changes for equality, he would not play Rhett Butler.[4] Butterfly McQueen, who played Prissy, declared she would not continue a scene because Vivien Leigh was slapping her too hard. "I can't do it, she's hurting me. . . . I'm no stunt man, I'm an actress." Though the director got angry, McQueen held her ground, and Leigh apologized, apparently not realizing she had been hurting her.[5]

If change had arrived on the movie sets and friendships and mutual admiration of talents had been forged between white and Black cast, these Hollywood "rebels" faced a different world outside the studio. One of the most remarkable public displays of fond memories of the Old South—and a victorious display of Lost Cause-ism of the early twentieth century—came during the Atlanta premiere of *Gone with the Wind*, on December 15, 1939.

Due to Georgia's strict segregation policies—which the Atlanta civic leaders refused to bend or break at that time—the movie studio decided that Hattie McDaniel and the rest of the Black cast would not be allowed to attend the opening night. Privately, some of the film's white stars expressed displeasure—with Clark Gable again raising heavy protest—but they were trapped by a system that was unwilling to accept change.

Margaret Mitchell sent a letter to McDaniel during the festive December week in Atlanta, which read in part:

> Your very fine letter reached me just when the excitement about the Atlanta premiere of 'Gone with the Wind' is at its height. I am so glad you wrote to me and I thank you for your letter and all the nice things you said about my book. Thank you for wanting to play 'Mammy.' I take that as a compliment to the character. Of course I have seen many still pictures of you in this part and I am looking forward with the greatest interest to seeing you on the

---

4 Ibid., 140.

5 Ibid., 144.

screen.... Should you be in Atlanta at any time, please telephone me. I would like to see you and talk to you.⁶

She also sent a congratulatory telegram the morning after the Atlanta premiere.

A couple months later, Selznick, Gable, and other cast members broke a segregation rule for McDaniel to attend the Academy Awards and receive her Oscar in person. McDaniel spent part of the event at a table with her fellow cast members, though other parts of the evening were painfully segregated and uncomfortable.

Olivia de Havilland struggled that evening. She had hoped to win Best Supporting Actress, but the award was given to McDaniel. De Havilland later described that she was mad at God over losing the award, but then: "One morning I woke up in more ways than one, filled with delight that I lived in a world where God was certainly present, and where justice had indeed been done.... I suddenly felt very proud ... that I belonged to a profession which honored a black woman who merited this [the Academy Award], in a time when other groups had neither the honesty nor the courage to do the same sort of thing."⁷ She had begun to realize the significance of the moment in history.

While *Gone with the Wind* was groundbreaking in Hollywood history, audiences accepted the film as Civil War history, and it became a favorite classic. Over the years, I have noticed several trends among women who love the movie and fiercely defend it:

1. They thought it was an accurate portrayal of the past.
2. They admired Scarlett O'Hara's strength to overcome and survive.
3. They drew relationship lessons from the movie.
4. They had very fond memories of watching the film on TV with their moms or sisters.
5. Who cares about the history or the plot? It's THE DRESSES.
6. Forget all else ... it's CLARK GABLE.

---

6 Margaret Mitchell, edited by John Wiley, Jr., *The Scarlett Letters: The Making of the Film "Gone with the Wind"* (Guildford: Globe Pequot Press, 2014), 306.

7 Carlton Jackson, *Hattie: The Life of Hattie McDaniel* (Lanham, MD: Madison Books, 1990), 52–53, Kindle.

Gone with the Wind: Some Thoughts 105

A portrait of Vivian Leigh as Scarlett O'Hara hangs in the Margaret Mitchell House in Atlanta, reminding visitors how larger-than-life Scarlett was. *Sarah Kay Bierle*

Those warm fuzzy memories have become part of the "defense" of *Gone with the Wind*. "How dare anyone touch that movie?" echoes with "How dare you wreck my fond memories of movie nights with my sisters?" I believe there is a strong culture around the movie that does not necessarily intend to be offensive or insensitive, but that culture is so deeply entrenched in how it views the movie (and personal memories associated with it) that it is hard to see how others might be offended by stereotypes or racist moments.

Thoughts, feelings, memories, and maybe even life-changing moments have been associated with the four-hour marathon, imprinting an entirely "new" set of thoughts and emotions that are different from 1860s history and different from 1939 views. Will adding a streaming disclaimer and options to view some additional resources raise awareness of some of the historical challenges with the all-time favorite? Maybe. I hope so.

Now, admittedly, there is another side to this: What about wanting to look at *Gone with the Wind* as a historically accurate salute to a bygone era where "cavaliers and ladies took their last bow in a lost civilization"? Some people see *Gone with the Wind* as a depiction of their heritage and an accurate portrayal of history, and to some extent, that's what the 1930s filmmakers intended.

Privately, Margaret Mitchell felt disturbed by some of the liberties Hollywood took with her north Georgia plantation. Mitchell had done meticulous research with the resources available to her in Atlanta and had put forth a solid effort for historical fiction in her novel. Certainly, her views were influenced by her location and Lost Cause interpretations, but she did not have in mind a white-pillared, happy plantation for Tara. That came from the writing room, the back lots of Hollywood, and the American imagination.

The concern about racism and inaccurate depictions of the past are real and heavily connected to *Gone with the Wind*. How can we have constructive and kind conversations with our acquaintances about this classic movie? How can we find out why *Gone with the Wind* is so important (or so offensive) to some of our friends or family? We need to talk about it. The discussions and debates about this movie are happening, and they are really just a continuation of the eighty-year discussion. Nothing will be settled by landing a ton of bricks, heated arguments, or heavy history books. But it might work to listen first, figure out why this movie matters to a person, and then move the conversation from there. It's surprising how often the attachment to this movie is simply a long-time crush on Clark Gable or Vivien Leigh.

So, should we see *Gone with the Wind* as art? I argue: yes. A film that wins eight Academy Awards makes us take notice. It's still the highest grossing film of all time when adjusted for inflation. And it's in the top 100 most historic films of all time in the sense of movie history.

However, just because something is art doesn't mean it should be left running wild and unexplained in society and pop culture. But, if *Gone with the Wind* stays as a cultural reference or work of cinematic art, why shouldn't it have a label, a proverbial museum sign, or something that explains a little about the era when it was made and why it gives this version of Civil War "history" mixed with a tumultuous love story?

Just because something is or can be acknowledged as art does not mean it does not need to be explained. Personally, I think that's where we are with *Gone with the Wind*. It might be a good thing to see it as art that needs to be explained in context. Art without explanation can quickly become a propaganda piece.

Frankly, my dear, let's get back to 1860s history and leave the twentieth-century novel and movie as pieces of antiquated literature and cinematic art, keeping them around with some new contextual references. As we continue to pursue studies of primary sources in the antebellum, Civil War, and Reconstruction eras and seek a deeper understanding of what happened and how it has been influenced by memory, *Gone with the Wind* will hopefully fade as a *historical reference* for the Civil War and be seen as a *moment of cinema history* with its own set of complexities, struggles, and triumphs.

The Margaret Mitchell House still preserves the author's writing space. *Sarah Kay Bierle*

1. Charlton Heston's Civil War

by Brian Steel Wills

Storming past audiences as triumphant Judah Ben-Hur in the iconic chariot race, the actor Charlton Heston continued to display a powerful screen presence that would take him through classic historical roles as Moses, El Cid, Andrew Jackson, Charles "Chinese" Gordon, Michelangelo, and others in a long and productive career.[1] For Heston, whose interest in history and reading long predated his rise to international superstardom in the movies, the American Civil War was an important piece of the American experience that deserved a place on celluloid.

In *Major Dundee* (1965), Heston's Maj. Amos Dundee led a mixed band of Union, Confederate, and civilian forces against Apache raiders. "It has to be about the Civil War, I'm convinced," Heston said while preparing for the film.[2] Later, in his autobiography, he observed that while he found the title character compelling, "the possibility of at last making a film about the Civil

---

[1] For Heston see, Brian Steel Wills, *Running the Race: The "Public Face" of Charlton Heston* (El Dorado Hills: Savas Beatie, 2022). For films related to Heston and the Civil War, see, Brian Steel Wills, *Gone with the Glory: The Civil War in Cinema* (Lanham, Mass.: Rowman and Littlefield, 2007).

[2] "January 8, [1964], Los Angeles," Charlton Heston, *The Actor's Life: Journals 1956-1976* (New York: E.P. Dutton, 1976), 190.

War [was] enormously attractive." He insisted, "I wanted to be the first to make a film that really explores the Civil War."³ To a biographer, he maintained, "I was very interested, and remain interested, in making a film about the American Civil War."⁴ Although his movements as a young person had precluded his awareness of the conflict that had torn the nation asunder in the 1860s—"I never did get the Civil War; I missed it in Georgia, Michigan, and Ohio," he confessed—his wife Lydia Clarke Hestons's ancestors featured "any family's full share of the gravestones of the Civil War."⁵ Heston was well-aware that his Academy Award-winning performance as Ben-Hur

A charcoal sketch of Charlton Heston depicts him following his 1959 Academy Award for *Ben-Hur*—based on a novel written by Civil War Maj. Gen. Lew Wallace. Nicholas Volpe/Wikipedia Commons

drew from a former Civil War general's popular novel. As he embarked upon a 1957 television project that pitted him as the prosecutor in the trial of Andersonville's Henry Wirz, he later quipped, "considering the part I was to undertake some months later, I probably should've played the president of the court-martial, General Lew Wallace," author of *Ben-Hur*—although he insisted, in true actor's fashion, "The colonel was the better part, though."⁶

Throughout his career in films based on real-life events and personages, Charlton Heston's quest for an audience competed with his desire for historical verisimilitude. As he embarked on a film in which he portrayed an ex-Confederate officer attempting to return home after the war, Heston was less

---

3 Charlton Heston, *In the Arena: An Autobiography* (New York: Simon & Schuster, 1995), 317 and 326.

4 Michael Munn, *Charlton Heston: A Biography* (New York: St. Martin's Press, 1986) 126.

5 Heston, *In the Arena*, 32 and 45.

6 Ibid., 163.

interested in tackling the heftier questions of reconstruction and reconciliation than in going to work. From the "Paramount back lot," as filming opened on *Three Violent People* (1956), the actor noted gratefully, "Well, I'm making a living again." He concluded, "It's good to be back at it."[7]

However, being "back at it" meant also devoting himself to the role. He preferred to sketch a backstory that would provide motivation for the character and prided himself on researching thoroughly whatever existed on his subject, primary or secondary, that could give him a sense of the individual. He denied that he enjoyed "excellent research discipline," and occasionally miscalculated some details, but Heston was famous on sets for carrying stacks of books and other research materials. He considered the effort so significant that it became one of the pieces of advice he passed along to his son, Fraser. "I was finished with school," he observed candidly, "before I figured out that history is not only the most important subject, it's the only subject."[8]

Even when the filming occurred, the behavior of the cast and crew, on and off the sets, remained an uncertain factor to consider. An admittedly distracted Heston took a fall from a horse, "showing off for the girls, of course," while wife, Lydia, visited their location. "I turned out to have stretched, or smashed, or some damn thing, a cartilage in my left elbow. It's damn painful." Doctors insisted upon a couple of weeks to recover; Heston knew better. "I managed to smuggle my bum arm on the set, concealed beneath a serape I'm wearing in the fiesta scene," he later revealed. He worried that should the director learn about his mishap, "he'll start trying to shoot around me and I don't want that. Luckily the shots today required little action."[9] At no point did this incident appear to compromise or hinder the work or Heston's place in it.

On a broader scale, the actor understood the sense that not only could film shape popular understandings of the past, but that it satisfied more important needs. "Art fills the soul as surely as meat fills the belly," he observed before

---

7 "March 26, [1956]," Heston, *Actor's Life*, 3.

8 Munn, *Charlton Heston*, 22, 24; Roberta Plutzik, "Last of the Epic Heroes," *Horizon* (March 1980), 32.

9 "February 23 (Sunday), and February 24, [1964]," Heston, *Actor's Life*, 192-193.

a Congressional committee while representing the American Film Institute. "And if art fills the soul, then film is the bread and butter that is part of every meal our citizens take at the table."[10] He knew well that each project still required the full commitment, dedication and professionalism—values her cherished and nurtured for himself—to make the sustenance complete.

Of course, pictures of any kind required audiences to offset the high costs of production, particularly if the film or television production were to have the air of authenticity. Employing location shots could add to the scenic qualities and the historical value, but came at a high price when crews and animals had to be transported to the sites. For *Major Dundee,* remote Mexican locales meant Heston's Dundee could benefit from the small village venue and the people who inhabited it. "As an actor, I had to use this," he recalled, believing that the expressions of the residents to the arrival of his mounted command passing through allowed him to "tap into the reality of their reaction." Of the total experience, he would explain, "I've never made a film, I think, that moved so far and so often to find food for the cameras." This was still early in a career that would see location shoots in Spain, Italy, Hawaii, and Canada, but the actor's point remained valid in this instance.

The requirements for proper locations and other elements prompted considerable effort. For *Major Dundee*, Heston and his son traveled out to a ranch to inspect horses that trainers had prepared for the sights, sounds and other demands of film shoots. "It's even harder to get them to hit and hold the marks necessary for filming, especially when ridden by horsebackers of uncertain abilities, whose hands are likely to be too heavy or too light on the reins," he wrote. Still, the necessary mounts did not arrive on sets spontaneously. "These horses are moved by truck to the location, a process that takes some time [and money] when it's as far off as Mexico."[11]

---

10 Testimony, Hearings Before the Special Subcommittee on Arts and Humanities of the Committee on Labor and Public Welfare, United States Senate, Ninety-third Congress, Second Session on H.R. 17504, December 11, 1974 (Washington: Government Printing Office, 1975), 6, 14, 45.

11 Heston, *Actor's Life*, 191. For this film, the actor concluded, without mentioning himself, "Only Jim Coburn can horseback," although he was pleased that Richard Harris "looks loose on a horse, which is a plus. The others will get by, I expect." "January 28 [1964], ibid.

Obtaining an appropriate setting for *Major Dundee* strained even the most generous budget, and overruns threatened the Sam Peckinpah-directed motion picture. Even so, Heston might not have been able to complete the work without first coming to terms with the mercurial director's style. As tempers mounted, a confrontation of almost historical measure took place when Heston attempted to bring his troops into action while Peckinpah shouted instructions. The director berated his star as a "stupid prick" for failing to canter rather than trot, as he had insisted earlier, unleashing a fury in Heston that Amos Dundee would have exhibited. "Irrationally, a line I'd read in some Civil War memoir leaped into my mind," Heston remembered. "So I lifted my saber and stood in my stirrups and shouted, 'Kill 'em . . . ride 'em down.'" As the men raced toward the Chapman boom holding the camera, the director stood in place for a moment before leaping into the chair and ordering it up out of the way. Heston slid to a stop as he reached the device, which had hoisted Peckinpah safely out of reach. "I can't believe I would have actually ridden Sam down, let alone sabered him," Heston recalled when cooler circumstances prevailed, "but I was as angry as I can remember being in my life." He would ask if the canter had met with the director's approval and Peckinpah would grumble that it had. There was no point in explaining that concern over the fading light had gotten the better of Peckinpah or that he might indeed have issued conflicting instructions. "[N] either of us ever spoke of it to the other after, in our lives," Heston said.[12]

Then, facing the critical budget overruns that threatened to remove the director before he could finish the motion picture, Heston took the extraordinary step of contacting the studio executives to offer his salary as recompense. Operating under an old contract that provided a base salary, but none of the gross percentages his future contracts would allow, this meant that if the studio accepted, he would be working on this film for nothing. Heston thought that the producers would reject the gesture, and indeed, one of the people he spoke with indicated as much. Heston's agent, Herman "the Iceman" Citron, thought differently: "Chuck, when are you going to learn this business? They'll take the money." A suddenly contrite Heston had to wait to see what would happen. When the studio accepted, the actor faced a

---

12 Heston, *In the Arena*, 330-331.

spate of questions from the press as to whether his actions would set a trend. "Trend, hell!" he retorted. "It won't even start a trend with me!"[13]

The film proved, in the actor's assessment, "neither a disaster nor a smash; it was disappointing." Heston would always insist that he wanted as close to perfection in every role he undertook. "I ran *Dundee* not long ago," he explained near the end of his career. "There are many good things in it, mostly performances. Best of all, the troop looks like cavalrymen. Every one of us. Real horse soldiers. I'll settle for that."[14]

Charlton Heston admired strong leaders in history, particularly those who, like Winston Churchill and Abraham Lincoln, could mobilize their nations in the dark days of warfare through their rhetoric. Lincoln's words served as one of the more identifiable efforts the actor explored as he traveled at home or abroad to provide dramatic readings for audiences. His voice carried the narrative for renditions of Aaron Copland's *A Lincoln Portrait*, as well as for the Smithsonian's program on the American Civil War.

Charlton Heston's role in motion pictures and television productions continue to shape the popular views of historical subjects like the American Civil War. His work remains infused with his passion for history and his desire to obtain the best performance possible in every role on stage or screen. The quest for an audience, for relevance in the work in his profession, and for his fortitude in developing his skills for acting and promotion are hallmarks of this career.

13 Ibid., 329.

14 Ibid., 335.

1. Violence and Forgetting in the Crater

by Kevin M. Levin

In December 2003, moviegoers were treated to a vivid recreation of the battle of the Crater in Anthony Minghella's screen adaptation of Charles Frazier's bestselling work of fiction, *Cold Mountain*. Though references to the battle do not appear in Frazier's book, the vicious fighting that took place outside Petersburg, Virginia, on July 30, 1864, proved to be an effective introduction to the main character, Inman, played by Jude Law, who had grown disgruntled with the Confederate war effort and who would eventually desert from the army to make his way back to his lover, Ada (played by Nicole Kidman), still struggling to make ends meet in western North Carolina.

Most students of the Civil War were likely satisfied with the opening battle sequence, which accurately depicted the construction of a tunnel by men in the 48th Pennsylvania under a Confederate salient, followed by the early-morning detonation of explosives and the advance of Union soldiers of the Union IX Corps under the command of Ambrose Burnside. The movie follows their advance into the crater, and the close hand-to-hand fighting that ensued for close to eight hours, resulting in a decisive victory for General Robert E. Lee and his Army of Northern Virginia. The movie briefly acknowledged the presence of United States Colored Troops (USCTs) in the battle. At one point, a black Union soldier and a Native American in Confederate uniform confront one another amidst the violence in the crater, but as with all Hollywood movies set in the past there are also clear oversights.[1]

The size of the crater in *Cold Mountain* is much too large. The focus on the crater itself also distracts from the fact that most Union soldiers successfully maneuvered around the gaping hole and into adjacent Confederate earthworks. More problematic is the movie's failure to acknowledge the scope of the involvement of USCTs in the battle. Black soldiers made up an entire IX Corps division under the command of Brig. Gen. Edward Ferrero. Though they were the final unit to advance, following the initial explosion, these men managed to position themselves, along with their white comrades, into a position beyond the crater, where they were poised to make one final advance into the city of Petersburg itself. The timely arrival and counterattack of Confederate Brig. Gen. William Mahone's division around 9:00 a.m., proved to be a turning point in the battle.

The failure to accurately acknowledge the presence of USCTs in *Cold Mountain* is unfortunate given that at least one scene depicting the execution of a Black man by a Confederate soldier was deleted from the final cut. The scene, which takes place after the battle, involves a disgruntled Confederate soldier who notices a severely wounded Black soldier crawling on the ground. After picking up three empty rifles, the soldier finally shoots the Black man at point-blank range. While the scene would have proven a distraction from the broader goal of highlighting the popular perception of Confederate disenchantment with the war after their defeat at Gettysburg, it would have served as a reminder of a salient aspect of the battle that Lee's men highlighted in their diaries and letters home to loved ones in the days and weeks that followed.[2]

The fight at the Crater was the first time that Confederates in Virginia confronted an entire division of USCTs since President Abraham Lincoln

---

1 For a history of the battle, see Earl J. Hess, *Into the Crater: The Mine Attack at Petersburg* (Columbia: University of South Carolina Press, 2010 and A. Wilson Greene, *A Campaign of Giants: The Battle for Petersburg* (Chapel Hill: University of North Carolina Press, 2018), 419-516. On the memory of the battle, see Kevin M. Levin, *Remembering the Battle of the Crater: War as Murder* (Lexington: University Press of Kentucky, 2012).

2 The popular assumption that Confederate morale lagged during the summer of 1864 has been challenged by a number of historians. See, J. Tracy Power, *Lee's Miserables: Life in the Army of Northern Virginia from the Wilderness to Appomattox* (Chapel Hill: University of North Carolina Press, 1998); M. Keith Harris, "We Will Finish the War Here: Confederate Morale in the Petersburg Trenches, June and July 1864," in Gary W. Gallagher and Caroline E. Janney eds., *Cold Harbor to the Crater: The End of the Overland Campaign*, (Chapel Hill: University of North Carolina Press, 2015), 210-27.

signed the Emancipation Proclamation on January 1, 1863. In response to the recruitment of Black men into the Federal army, the Confederate government issued a proclamation declaring that in the event of capture they would be handed over to state authorities, where they risked being sold into slavery. White officers would be tried by military tribunals for inciting insurrection. But by the summer of 1864, the Confederate rank and file didn't need a proclamation from their government directing their response as to how to treat armed Black men in uniform.

Lee's men relished in the retelling of their experiences at the Crater fighting Ferrero's men. "Our men killed them with the bayonets and the but[t]s of their guns and every other way," wrote Laban Odon, who served in the 48th Georgia, "until they were lying eight or ten deep on top one enuther and the blood almost s[h]oe quarter deep." A South Carolinian who survived the initial explosion recalled that the sight of armed Black men "had the same affect upon our men that a red flag had upon a mad bull."[3]

Confederates openly admitted to massacring Black soldiers during and after the battle. One soldier admitted, "Some few negroes went to the rear as we could not kill them as fast as they passed us." Lieutenant Colonel William Pegram described scenes of the men under his command executing USCTs. "Every bombproof I saw had one or two dead negroes in them, who had skulked out of the fight, & been found & killed by our men. Black soldiers at the Crater and elsewhere were treated as slaves in rebellion.[4]

Rather than intensifying Confederate dissatisfaction with the war and leading to increased desertion, the experience of fighting Black men at the Crater served as a reminder of the consequences of defeat. Decades after the war, Confederate artillerist Edward Porter Alexander recalled, "The sympathy of the North for John Brown's memory was taken for proof of a desire that our slaves should rise in a servile insurrection & massacre throughout the South, & the enlistment of Negro troops was regarded as advertisement of that desire & encouragement of the idea to the Negro." Pegram spoke for many in the battle's immediate aftermath when he admitted, "I had been hoping that the enemy would bring some negroes against this army." And now that they had, "I am convinced . . . that it has

---

3 Levin, 27.

4 Levin, 27-28.

a splendid effect on our men." Though "it seems cruel to murder them in cold blood," the men who did it had "very good reason for doing so." The *Richmond Examiner* spoke for many on the home front in its encouragement to Mahone and his men:

> We beg him [Mahone], hereafter, when negroes are sent forward to murder the wounded, and come shouting 'no quarter,' shut your eyes, General, strengthen your stomach with a little brandy and water, and let the work, which God has entrusted to you and your brave men, go forward to its full completion; that is, until every negro has been slaughtered.—Make every salient you are called upon to defend, a Fort Pillow; butcher every negro that Grant sends against your brave troops, and permit them not to soil their hands with the capture of a single hero.[5]

The admission to massacring Black soldiers in their letters home is best understood as an extension of long-standing fears attached to the constant threat that enslaved people posed throughout the antebellum period going back as far as Nat Turner's Rebellion in 1831 and more recently at Harpers Ferry in 1859. The experience of fighting USCTs for the first time at the Crater served to remind Lee's men of exactly what was at stake in the war—nothing less than an overturning of the racial hierarchy of their antebellum world.

The racial violence at the Crater was compounded by the relatively small number of accounts of Black soldiers who refused to take Confederates prisoner during and after the battle. The men of the Fourth Division entered the battle shouted "Remember Fort Pillow"—a reference to the massacre of their comrades by Confederates under the command of Maj. Gen. Nathan Bedford Forrest at Fort Pillow, Tennessee, in April 1864. Some of Ferrero's men likely sought revenge as they engaged Confederates and likely feared for their lives in the event of their own capture.[6]

It should come as no surprise that a Hollywood movie released in 2003 and set during the Civil War failed to acknowledge the scale of racial violence witnessed at the Crater. With few exceptions, Hollywood steered

---

5 Levin, 30-31.

6 Hess, *Into the Crater*, 123-29.

clear of the divisive issue of racial violence in the Civil War for much of the twentieth century and instead embraced the Lost Cause's emphasis on "loyal slaves" in movies like *Gone with the Wind* and *Gods and Generals* or the theme of reconciliation in movies like *Gettysburg*.[7]

One of the few exceptions to hit theaters before *Cold Mountain* is the academy-award winning film *Glory*, released in 1989. The movie told the story of the 54th Massachusetts Volunteer Infantry—the first all-Black regiment raised in the North in 1863—and its young colonel, Robert Gould Shaw. In the final scene, the regiment leads a daring but ultimately failed assault against Battery Wagner outside Charleston, South Carolina, that cost the regiment roughly forty-percent casualties, including its commander, who was killed in battle. In documenting the bravery of the men in the regiment, the movie captured, as none had done before, the violent hand-to-hand combat that ensued once the regiment breached the walls of the fort.

Much had changed by the beginning of the Civil War sesquicentennial in 2011. The collective memory of the war, which had long embraced a Lost Cause and reunion narrative, had come to focus more and more on the tough questions surrounding slavery and emancipation.

In contrast with the Civil War Centennial celebrations of the early 1960s, the story of Black Union soldiers and a broader "emancipationist" narrative figured prominently in a wide range of educational programs, including lectures and battlefield tours organized by the National Park Service.[8]

The public's growing interest in emancipation was captured in Steven Spielberg's film *Lincoln,* released in 2012. Spielberg's story of Lincoln's efforts to convince Congress to pass a constitutional amendment ending slavery begins with a scene depicting the savage fighting at Jenkins's Ferry on April 30, 1864, along the Saline River in Arkansas. The brief scene depicts Black Union soldiers in the 2nd Colored Kansas Infantry and Confederates engaged in close-quarter fighting in the mud and hard rain. Men on both sides are brutally killed and wounded with bayonets, fists, and strangulation.

---

7 For an overview of how Hollywood has depicted the Civil War in film, see Gary W. Gallagher, *Causes Won, Lost, & Forgotten: How Hollywood and Popular Art Shape What We Know About the Civil War* (Chapel Hill: University of North Carolina Press, 2008).

8 Emmanuel Dabney, Beth Parnicza, and Kevin M. Levin, "Interpreting Race, Slavery, and United States Colored Troops at Civil War Battlefields," *Civil War History* (June 2016): 131-48.

Close-up shots of the men in the heat of battle points to the racial animus that animated everyone involved. The scene is followed by a rather unlikely encounter between Lincoln and two veterans of the battle, in which one of the men lectures the president on the true meaning of his "Gettysburg Address."

Nate Parker's *Birth of a Nation*—released in theaters in 2016—also embraced a thoroughly emancipationist narrative through the story of Nat Turner and the men and women he led in rebellion against slavery in Virginia in 1831. As Turner hangs from the gallows in the final scene, a young African-American boy looks on and is transformed into a Black Union soldier marching forward with his comrades in line of battle.

The movie was released shortly after the mass murder of nine African-American churchgoers by a white supremacist at the Mother Emmanuel AME Church in Charleston, South Carolina, in June 2015. Calls to remove Confederate flags from public spaces soon included demands that Confederate monuments also be removed or relocated—all part of a broader reckoning over the legacy of slavery and the long history of racial violence encouraged by the new "Black Lives Matter" movement. Hundreds of Confederate monuments would eventually be removed in towns and cities across the nation—a process that included violent incidents in a number of places, including Charlottesville, Virginia, in 2017, where a young woman was murdered during a rally of white nationalists hoping to prevent the removal of a monument of Robert E. Lee. This racial reckoning peaked in the summer of 2020, following the police murder of George Floyd in Minneapolis, Minnesota.

Throughout this period, movies like *Free State of Jones* (2016), *The North Star* (2018), and the television mini-series remake of *Roots* (2016) offered a stark and honest portrayal of the violence of slavery. United States Colored Troops continued to be highlighted in films during this period. Black soldiers appear at the end of the movie *Harriet* (2019) in a scene in which the famous conductor of the Underground Railroad leads the 2nd Regiment South Carolina in what became known as the Combahee River Raid on June 2, 1863.

If *Cold Mountain* fell short of fully accounting for the scale of racial violence on one Civil War battlefield, the release of *Emancipation* in 2022, starring Will Smith, fully confronts the subject head on. The film—based loosely on the life of a man known as "Whipped Peter," whose scarred

120   The Civil War and Pop Culture

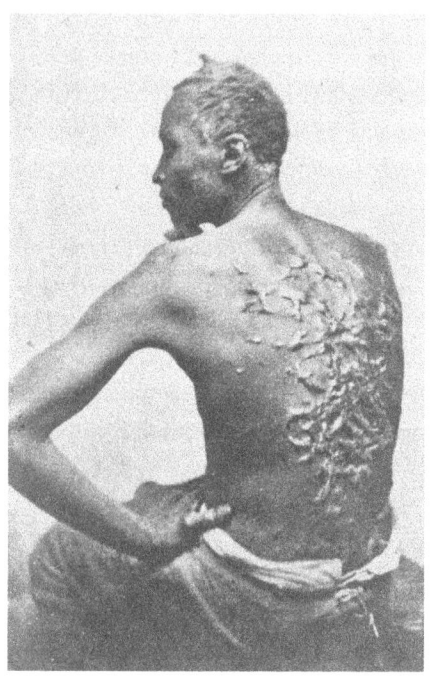

"Whipped Peter" has become one of the most iconic images of the war, even if his name remains unknown to most people. *Library of Congress*

back appeared in *Harper's Weekly* in 1863—follows an escaped slave impressed by the Confederate army to help build a military rail line. After a harrowing escape through the swamps of Louisiana and evading the pursuit of a sadistic Confederate officer, Peter finally reaches the Union army near Baton Rouge, where he promptly enlists in the all-Black 1st Louisiana Native Guard. In the movie's penultimate scene, Peter lines up with the rest of his regiment to take part in an assault against an enemy position at Port Hudson on May 27, 1863—one of the last Confederate strongholds along the Mississippi River.

The scene leaves little to the imagination as the regiment maneuvers through a hail of rifle and artillery fire to engage Confederates directly in close hand-to-hand combat. Though the battle is depicted inaccurately as a Union victory, it serves to bring this self-emancipation narrative full circle. The movie closes with Peter and the rest of his regiment liberating his former plantation and reuniting with his family.

The release of Civil War movies that feature Black soldiers since *Cold Mountain* (now twenty years ago) cannot be understood apart from a growing recognition among many that the United States has never fully reckoned with the legacy of slavery and the long history of racial violence. The message in all of these movies is clear: The fight of Black Union soldiers against racism and injustice during the Civil War is our fight today.

Glory: Rediscovering the USCT in Popular Culture

by Steward Henderson

The Academy Award–winning movie *Glory* is one of my favorites, and its tremendous impact led to the rediscovery of the United States Colored Troops (USCT). By the end of the war, almost 10 percent of the Union army consisted of USCT, yet their story remained largely forgotten until the movie came out.[1] I want to examine *Glory*'s role in popular culture, then tell some of the stories of the men who have been inspired by the movie to teach the country about the role of the USCT in the Civil War, through living history and reenacting.

Glory is the story of the 54th Massachusetts and its colonel, Robert Gould Shaw. Before the movie, many people in this country did not believe that African Americans fought for their freedom in the Civil War; after the movie, many people still think that the 54th Massachusetts was the only Black regiment in the Civil War. Before the movie, there were very few Black Civil War reenactors and living historians; after the movie, there are hundreds of Black reenactors and living historians, many represented by the United States Colored Troops Living History Association (USCTLHA) and the African American Civil War Memorial and Museum.

---

1 Approximately 2.1 or 2.2 million soldiers served in the Union army. The African American Civil War Museum lists 209,145 names on the monument and in its records. That equates to roughly 10 percent, including Hispanics and white officers.

Members of the modern 23rd USCT and 54th Massachusetts regiments at Emancipation Day festivities in Washington, D.C. on April 16, 2016. Steward Henderson stands in the front row, first on the left. *54thmass.org/Perspective Photography and Louis Carter*

Included among them are several companies of the 54th Massachusetts Volunteer Infantry, including Company B in the Washington, DC, area. Company B was founded by well-known historian Brian Pohanka, Sergeant Major Bill Gwaltney, and Captain Jack Thompson. They began as the 1st USCT, but when they acted in the movie *Glory*, they decided to become Company B of the 54th Massachusetts. Their website is 54thmass.org.

I have been involved with the 54th Massachusetts since 2012. I'm also a founding member of the 23rd USCT—a regiment important to me because it consisted of many former slaves from Spotsylvania County, Virginia, where I live. They came back as part of the Union army and were the first Black troops to fight Robert E. Lee's Army of Northern Virginia. That fight took place, ironically, back in Spotsylvania County, just a few miles from the apartment where I now live.

Since 2011, I have often lectured and written about the history of the USCT. When I first started, I inquired of my audiences if they had seen the movie *Glory*. When I was in the Washington, DC, area or in more northern areas, many people would raise their hands. However, in Fredericksburg, Virginia—where I'm now based—and in more central and southern parts of the state, not as many people raised their hands. Today, I still mention the movie somewhere in the text of my lectures, although I am amazed by how many people have not seen the movie south of Washington.

I first saw *Glory* in 1990, close to the time it was released. I was very much drawn to the movie because, as an African American, I was elated to see that Hollywood had finally produced a movie about Black Civil War heroes and provided America with a history it had ignored for so many years. As a Civil War buff at that time, I knew about the 54th Massachusetts, although I also knew the regiment depicted in the film was not representative of the real 54th. The men of the 54th came from all over the Northern states, and most were educated. "Only a small proportion had been slaves," according to Captain Luis F. Emilio, Company E, 54th Massachusetts Volunteer Infantry, as written in his book, *A Brave Black Regiment: History of the Fifty-Fourth Regiment of Massachusetts Volunteer Infantry 1863–1865*.[2] Rather, the movie seemed to show the experience of the average USCT unit—for example, the 23rd USCT.

Initially released on December 14, 1989, *Glory* was nominated for five Academy Awards and won three, including one for Denzel Washington as best supporting actor. The film also received a Golden Globe nomination for best film, and Washington again won best supporting actor. The movie also won a Grammy for its soundtrack, which I listen to whenever I write about the Civil War or go to a Civil War event—the music inspires me to be at my best.

Glory depicted Black men determined to prove they *were* men and that they would fight for their freedom. It showed their discipline under fire, and it demonstrated that they were just as brave as the other Union soldiers. In one of the movie's most poignant scenes, officers told the men that the Confederates would not treat them as prisoners of war, yet they remained in the army. In their first skirmish, they courageously proved they could defeat the Confederates and developed pride as a result. On the night before their climactic attack on Fort Wagner, they chanted a call-and-response, showing their solidarity with each other and the peace they'd made with the Lord. These men knew what they would face.

Many people even now, more than 30 years after *Glory's* release, still think there was only one Black regiment in the Civil War. Even people who

---

2 Luis F. Emilio, *A Brave Black Regiment: History of the Fifty-Fourth Regiment of Massachusetts Volunteer Infantry 1863–1865* (Boston: Boston Book Company, 1891), 21.

do realize there were more can only name this one regiment. Today, the living historians of the United States Colored Troops—as they march in parades, fight in reenactments, or participate in living history programs—are often referred to simply as the 54th Massachusetts. In many large events where we usually have several regimental flags with our unit designations, regardless of the units, many people come by us and say, "Give 'em hell, 54th!" This is a direct quote from the movie: as the regiment marched onto the beach prior to its final assault against Fort Wagner, the white regiments that were lined up in reserve urged them on.

The reason for this cultural amnesia is less complicated than you might expect. The United States government abandoned many African-American veterans when they were subjected to the violence of Southern whites when they returned home after the war.[3] The reunions of the veterans of the North and South from the 1880s, continuing through the Centennial of the Civil War, excluded most Black veterans. The history of Black Civil War soldiers and their contributions in the war were not taught in most of the schools in the country. Blacks were simply phased out of the memory of the war. By 1989, people had mostly forgotten them until *Glory* appeared in theaters.

A few books were written about the USCT and African-American contributions during the war; however, most were not widely publicized.[4] Fortunately, many of the USCT's reports were contained in the *Official*

---

3 For examples of violence against Black veterans, see chap. 18 of Noah Andre Trudeau's *Like Men of War* (1998); pp. 156–75 of Ira Berlin, Joseph Reidy, and Leslie Rowland's *Freedom's Soldiers* (1998); and Donald Shaffer's entire book *After the Glory: Struggles of Black Civil War Veterans* (2004).

4 For example: *The Negro in the American Rebellion: His Heroism and His Fidelity* (1867) by William Wells Brown (prominent abolitionist, lecturer, historian, author, playwright, and novelist); *The Black Phalanx: African-American Soldiers in the War of Independence, the War of 1812, & the Civil War* (1887) by Joseph T. Wilson (soldier in the 2nd Regiment, Louisiana Native Guard, and later in the 54th Massachusetts Volunteer Infantry and historian); *A History of the Negro Troops in The War of the Rebellion 1861–1865* (1888) by George Washington Williams (Civil War veteran, lawyer, minister, historian, and first African American to serve in the Ohio House of Representatives); *The Negro in the Civil War* (1953) by Benjamin Quarles (Professor Emeritus, Morgan State University); *The Sable Arm: Black Troops in the Union Army, 1861–1865* (1956) by Dudley Taylor Cornish (Professor Emeritus of American History, Pittsburg State University); *Marching Toward Freedom: Blacks in the Civil War 1861–1865* (1965) by James M. McPherson (retired Professor of History, Princeton University). The first three were written by Black men in the 1800s and have been used as source material in several of the books on the USCT in the twentieth and twenty-first centuries.

Records of the War of the Rebellion. *Glory* ignited research into the 54th Massachusetts and other USCT units.

Glory also inspired the establishment of the African American Civil War Monument, which was finally dedicated in Washington, D.C., in 1998. The centerpiece is a ten-foot-tall monument surrounded by a wall inscribed with the names of 209,145 soldiers. The list contains 201,000 Blacks, 7,000 white officers, and 1,145 Hispanics.

During this time, USCT living historians were in heavy demand to make appearances at many Civil War events. We remain in demand, too: the 23rd USCT has participated in more than 250 events in the past five years, including several appearances with the 54th Massachusetts.

I first saw the 54th Massachusetts, Company B in 1994, at an event at Fort Stevens, one of the Civil War forts that encircled Washington, DC. I next saw them at the 1998 dedication of the African American Civil War Monument in Washington, DC. I was interested in joining them, but at the time couldn't because of the responsibilities of my banking position. The next time I saw them was in Spotsylvania Court House at a reenactment of the battle of Spotsylvania Court House in 2011. By then, I had become the president of the 23rd USCT, and the 54th's president, Louis Carter, took me under his wing and related the responsibilities, the enjoyment, and the disappointments of being an African-American Civil War reenactor and living historian. "Carry yourself with dignity and respect while in and out of uniform," Lou impressed on me. "Represent the USCT with class."

In 2012, I became a member of the 54th Massachusetts, Company B and the USCTLHA, while maintaining my membership in the 23rd USCT. In fact, all of the area's USCT living historians often portray whatever USCT regiment is represented in an event. For example, the 23rd and 54th Massachusetts, Company B portrayed the 4th USCT in the 150th anniversary of the battle of New Market Heights.

Glory has had an impact on us all, so I asked several of my colleagues with the 54th Massachusetts, Company B about the effect the movie had on them.

One of the first men recruited for the new regiment was Walt Sanderson. I have often talked with Walt at various events, and I asked him how he got started with the 54th. "I was actually inspired to tell the African American story of military involvement in the Civil War before I was recruited to participate in the filming of Glory," he told me. He remembers walking to the library to pick up a copy of *Lay This Laurel*, by Lincoln Kirstein and Richard

Steward (left) stands with members of the modern 23rd USCT and 54th Massachusetts regiments at the opening dedication of the Museum of the Confederacy (now the American Civil War Museum) at Appomattox Court House. *54thmass.org/Perspective Photography and Louis Carter*

Benson, a book about the 54th Massachusetts memorial in Boston, where the regiment mustered in, when he was a teenager. "Interestingly enough," Walt said, "Kevin Jarre, who wrote the screenplay for *Glory*, commented that he read this book around the same time and thought that it would make a great movie. May he rest in peace; we were born only months apart."

Walt's father attended Robert Gould Shaw Junior High School in Washington, DC, and his grandfather made him memorize the Gettysburg Address when he was eight. "I read almost everything I could get my hands on about the CW as a child," he said.

In the early '80s, Walt worked with a reenactor with the 28th Massachusetts who attempted to put him in touch with the small—"I think four," Walt said—African-American cadre in the hobby who were based in Baltimore. "We didn't connect, but a couple of years later I heard Bill Gwaltney being interviewed on WHUR radio as he made the call for men of color to reenact," Walt recalled. "I remember him saying, 'There are 50,000 CW reenactors and only four of them are Black. Hollywood can work magic and they can make 200 look like a thousand, but four is just insufficient to make a movie about these brave men.' That's all it took for me to sign up."

Walt traveled with dozens of other reenactors to Jekyll Island, where much of the movie was filmed. "One of the most revealing interactions I had during the filming on Jekyll Island was a chance encounter with a woman at the campground where our tents were pitched," he told me. "Observing my uniform, she asked, 'What are you guys doing?' I responded, 'Making a movie about Black soldiers in the Civil War.' She replied, 'That's fiction, right?' I knew then that what we were doing was important. Many Americans had no idea of the size and scope of the impact African Americans had on the war that resulted in the extinction of chattel slavery and laid the foundation for racial equality in this nation." Walt went on to add, "I know I would have had this interest without a film, but I can't overemphasize the cultural impact of an Oscar-winning movie on awakening general public interest in a subject long ignored. Nearly 30 years after its release, *Glory* still provides recognition that would have been difficult to achieve otherwise. For its support in spurring this exposure, I am grateful for this film and humbled by my role in its creation."

One of my best friends and confidants in the 23rd USCT is Kevin Williams, our hospital steward and a past vice-president of the group. Kevin was in the navy, first as a hospital corpsman, then as an officer. "The movie opened my eyes to a hidden truth in the history of our nation," he told me when I asked him about *Glory*. "I was taught that Abraham Lincoln and white Northern people freed my people from slavery. *Glory* allowed me to experience what it must have been like to transform from nothing to an equal member of the human race."

That brought to mind Augustus Saint-Gauden's monument to Colonel Shaw and the 54th in Boston. "An angel of the Lord glides over them to symbolize God's hand in justice and freedom of the oppressed," Kevin explained. "Each time I put on their uniform and tell their story, the road to total justice is closer to completion."

Kevin drew a parallel between the 54th and his own "successful 24-year military career," which was "made possible by their success on the battlefield," he said. "The least I could do was ensure their sacrifice and glory was never forgotten."

Louis Carter, my mentor, missed the filming of *Glory*, but he and the 54th Massachusetts, Company B were featured in the documentary *The True Story of "Glory" Continues*, narrated by Morgan Freeman and included as part of a special two-DVD set of *Glory*. Ironically, Louis is the man we all now call "the Godfather of the USCT."

Originally from Richmond, Lou "was drawn to the Civil War." He read about it when he was young and saw the monuments around the city. He went to the battlefields in and around Richmond and Petersburg, including the Crater—the site of one of the war's most infamous USCT actions. He read about and went to New Market Heights, where 14 Blacks earned the Medal of Honor. However, the ground there was not saved, and he had to walk around in people's yards to see what was left of the battlefield. During his travels, Lou did not see any Black soldiers on the battlefields, although he saw white ones.

Later, after a stint in the Air Force, he served as the chief of the EMTs in the Washington, DC, Fire Department. Upset by the number of young men killed in the Black areas of the city, he started going to schools and speaking about the 54th Massachusetts Volunteer Infantry and the movie *Glory*. He wanted those young men to have respect for their history. He, in turn, gained a lot of respect on the streets because of this project, so when he came to a crime scene, he had the respect of the community at a time when it was dangerous for first responders.

When he decided to get into living history, Lou first considered reenacting with a Confederate group as a camp servant, but some of them told him about the USCT. Lou then found out about the 54th and caught up with them at Fort Washington, a week after *Glory*'s premiere at the Smithsonian Institution. Lou got involved—and then more and more involved. The regiment participated in reenactments at Fort Wagner and Olustee, marched in parades in Washington, D.C., and Boston, and filmed the documentary about the original 54th Massachusetts. They also helped clean up the Shaw memorial in Boston and dedicate the African American Civil War Monument in Washington, D.C.

Lou explained something that had nagged at me: why were they "Company B" even though they were the first regiment of the 54th Massachusetts reenactors? Well, he said, because they were from Washington, D.C., they thought Company A should be from Boston—and they even helped with the organization of that company. He also explained that they were traveling to so many places, participating in Civil War events, parades, and reenactments, that he encouraged African Americans in those areas to form their own regiments. As a result, Lou has mentored several USCT regiments and often serves as the go-between for the regiments and event organizers—hence his title "the Godfather." Lou also served as my best man at my Civil War marriage to my wife Malanna at Historic Salem Church, with the Reverend Hashmel Turner, the first recruit in the 23rd and its chaplain, serving as the minister.[5]

Within the USCT community, I have noticed a sincere dedication to teaching the true history of the African-American involvement in the Civil War. *Glory* provided the inspiration to perform this service as our duty to the public. Because of *Glory*, the Black USCT living history community has grown to about 400 soldiers, plus additional Civil War African-American civilians. We also now have the United States Colored Troops Living History Association (USCTLHA), many USCT regiments, the Women of the Civil War, Female RE-Enactors of Distinction (FREED); African American Ladies of the Civil War; Auxiliary Organization of the African American Civil War Museum; and, of course, the African American Civil War Memorial and Museum. We also thank the National Park Service, which not only helped with the recruiting for the movie but now, in its Civil War parks, has exhibits dedicated to African Americans in the Civil War.

Thank you, Hollywood, for producing *Glory*. We still celebrate its impact in popular culture because we still *live* it.

---

5 I would also like to pay tribute to my friends, the fallen members of the 23rd USCT and 54th Massachusetts Co. B, who have passed away since this essay was written: Kevin Williams, Mel Reid, Marcellus Williams, John Gourdin, Moses Humes, and Hari Jones, former curator of African American Civil War Memorial and Museum.

1. Reconsidering Gettysburg

by Tom McMillan

Adapted from a guest post first published on Emerging Civil War on January 5, 2019

I was at a movie theater in suburban Pittsburgh on an otherwise forgettable rainy Tuesday night in the fall of 1993.

"I left my spectacles over there," General Robert E. Lee of the Confederate army said to his ranking subordinate, James Longstreet, as they pored over a map of Pennsylvania, anxiously plotting strategy for their great invasion of the North. "What is the name of this town?"

I knew the answer but leaned forward anyway in anticipation.

"Gettysburg," Longstreet said.

In each person's life there are seemingly innocuous moments that affect you in ways you never imagined. That night—watching the movie *Gettysburg* in a darkened, old-fashioned theater full of strangers—was one of those for me.

I had always been a student of history and visited the Gettysburg battlefield with my parents when I was in grade school in the 1960s, but nothing had yet drawn me back to the small town in south central Pennsylvania or plunged me more deeply into study of the Civil War. Until then. "We may have an opportunity here," said the actor Martin Sheen, playing Lee, and it was as though he were speaking directly to me.

I got in my car three days later and drove to Gettysburg, contracting a Civil War "illness" that remains to this day. I have attended the anniversary days of the battle every year for more than a quarter century, served on the board of directors of the Friends of the National Park at Gettysburg, joined the marketing committee of the Gettysburg Foundation, and wrote two books on the battle, most recently *Armistead and Hancock: Behind the Gettysburg Legend of Two Friends at the Turning Point of the Civil War.* I was married in Gettysburg, and my wife and I even own a plot in the town's famous Evergreen Cemetery. That's about as all-in as you can be.

I dare say none of that would have happened had I not been in the theater that night watching Sheen and Tom Berenger, as Lee and Longstreet, making final arrangements to plot their insurrection, and the Union army's heroic actions to repel them.

The movie was that compelling, that dramatic . . . that impactful.

In the 29 years since then, director Ron Maxwell's epic *Gettysburg* has earned its rightful place in the pantheon of outstanding American war films. Coupled with Ken Burns's epic PBS series *The Civil War*, it touched off an astonishing surge of battlefield visitation and attracted a new generation of scholars to the nineteenth-century war that shaped the country's future. Previously obscure figures such as Joshua Chamberlain and John Buford of the Union army became as well known to modern students as Lee, Longstreet, and the star-crossed leader of Pickett's Charge, George Pickett. Certain lines from the script—"We should have gone to the right" and "All they had to do was roll rocks down on us"—became such a part of the Civil War lexicon that they are repeated even today by visitors on the craggy slopes of Little Round Top.

I wasn't the only one.

But I soon came to learn there was an unexpected "downside" to the public's newfound interest in Gettysburg. Many thousands of viewers took the movie as unvarnished fact—when, in fact, it was based on a historical novel, *Killer Angels*, with many fictionalized scenes. The novelist, Michael Shaara, altered certain details and created much of his own dialogue among soldiers to move the story along, doing it well enough to win the Pulitzer Prize for Fiction in 1975. Maxwell, in adapting Shaara's novel to the theater, couldn't possibly cover the entire three-day battle in four hours, so he picked and chose his subjects as a director must. He elevated Chamberlain,

Lewis Armistead, and John Bell Hood to icon status while virtually ignoring George Meade, the Union's commanding general, who appears on-screen for all of 60 seconds.

This all struck me for the first time in the summer of 1994, when a National Park Service ranger doing a tour of Little Round Top pronounced the site of the 20th Maine monument as "the place where the great Joshua Chamberlain saved the Union army and the entire United States." His words fairly dripped with sarcasm.

Students with the deepest knowledge of the battle seemed to struggle most with this new reality—appalled that such a complex battlefield narrative had been condensed to a few fascinating vignettes in the minds of many visitors. For instance, Chamberlain's stand against the 15th Alabama had merited only six pages in Edwin Coddington's 550-page *Gettysburg Campaign*, considered the best single-volume academic study of the battle, and yet it was hailed in the movie as the singular turning point of the second day's action. Other scenes and speeches were so riveting and believable that viewers took them for fact.

I realized this early on and dove deep into study of the battle and its aftermath, trying to untangle the myths and legends of the movie. What I found, at first, surprised me.

Among other things:

- Two emotional conversations between Longstreet and Armistead on the eve of battle never happened. The overwhelming drama of these scenes served a clear purpose for the movie, personalizing the friendship between Armistead and General Winfield Scott Hancock of the Union army—which became a key subplot—but they simply are not based in fact. The main reason I wanted to write my book about Armistead and Hancock was because their relationship was so heavily fictionalized in the novel and movie. Armistead and Hancock were certainly friends from the old army, having served together on the frontier and in the Mexican War, but they were not "almost brothers" as the movie contends. In addition, there is absolutely no evidence that they were talking about facing one another on the eve of battle at Gettysburg. (And yet I found the "real" story of their friendship to be unique and compelling.)

- Buster Kilrain, the crusty old sergeant of the 20th Maine, and one of the most popular characters in the movie, was a figment of Shaara's imagination. Names of soldiers from the 20th who were killed at Gettysburg are listed on the side of the regimental monument on Little Round Top. Many modern-day visitors often wonder why Kilrain's name does not appear.

- One tear-jerking line attributed to Armistead is especially misleading. In the movie version of a prewar conversation with Hancock, he blurts out, "Win, so help me, if I ever lift a hand against you, may God strike me dead!" However, according to a book written by Hancock's wife, who was present when the two men spoke in 1861, what Armistead actually said was, "I hope God will strike me dead if I am ever induced to leave my native soil." Using the correct (but far less emotional) quote would have changed the impact of the entire scene.

- Joshua Chamberlain's brother, Tom, wasn't the Union officer who spoke with Armistead on Cemetery Ridge after he was wounded. It was actually Henry Bingham, a member of Hancock's staff. This was done to keep the movie rolling along rather than introduce a new character in its final moments—but it was another fabrication.

- It is very doubtful that Armistead's nickname was "Lo." There is simply no credible evidence to that effect. I find myself apologizing to Civil War Roundtables when I tell this part of the story because they become so disappointed. But the novel and movie have had such a tremendous influence on battlefield visitors that "Lo" has been accepted as Armistead's nickname by acclaim and probably will remain so far into the future. I deal with it in the appendix of my book and invite readers to form their own opinions.

- Lee and Longstreet didn't meet in Lee's headquarters on the night of the second day—the gripping movie scene to that effect notwithstanding—and almost certainly didn't sit around a campfire on the night of the third day, commiserating about their defeat in Pickett's Charge.

Author Tom McMillen was one of 800 *Gettysburg* buffs to attend the 25th anniversary showing in Gettysburg. Also there was ECW's Frank Jastrzembski (above). *Courtesy Frank Jastrzembski*

And yet none of this takes away from the movie's grandeur, its edge-of-the-seat combat action, or its unprecedented effect on battlefield visitation. Shaara never said he was writing an academic history of the battle, and Maxwell never touted his film as a documentary. If viewers mistook the obvious drama for facts and footnotes, that was not the fault of the author or the director. The magnificence of *Gettysburg* lies in capturing this seminal battle in the most easily understandable of human terms. You left feeling you had seen Pickett's Charge as it happened. You were exhausted.

I had the pleasure of attending the 25th anniversary celebration of the movie in October 2018 in Gettysburg. Eight hundred giddy movie buffs crammed themselves into the town's Majestic Theater to hear Maxwell's opening oratory and mingle with the actors who played Pickett, Hancock, Hood, Richard Garnett, A. P. Hill, and E. P. Alexander (a gracious Patrick Gorman, who played Hood, even told my wife she should have "gone to the right"). The film was almost five hours because it included several scenes that never made the final Hollywood version, but few in the audience fidgeted and no one complained.

After all these years, it remains, hands down, my favorite war movie of all time (having dramatically unseated "Patton," the previous champion). If it departed from actual history at various points, so be it. An entire generation of Civil War enthusiasts, including me, were drawn into a lifelong fascination with the epoch event of the 1800s because of Maxwell's big-screen adaptation of Shaara's award-winning novel. Many of us have spent a few decades digging into the "real" stories behind some of the characters in the movie and book. And yet when *Armistead and Hancock* was published last summer, reviewer Ethan S. Rafuse of the *Civil War Times* wrote, "It is surprising that until now no one has seen fit to undertake a book-length reconsideration of the evidence to determine whether the story of Hancock and Armistead is in fact true."

Beyond that, as my friend, Matt Callery of the *Addressing Gettysburg* podcast, points out, the movie also made a profound economic impact on the little town of Gettysburg, driving visitation and commerce at hotels, restaurants, pubs, and shops in the square to previously unattainable levels since 1993.

We could use a similar artistic effort to entice the scholars and battlefield visitors of the future.

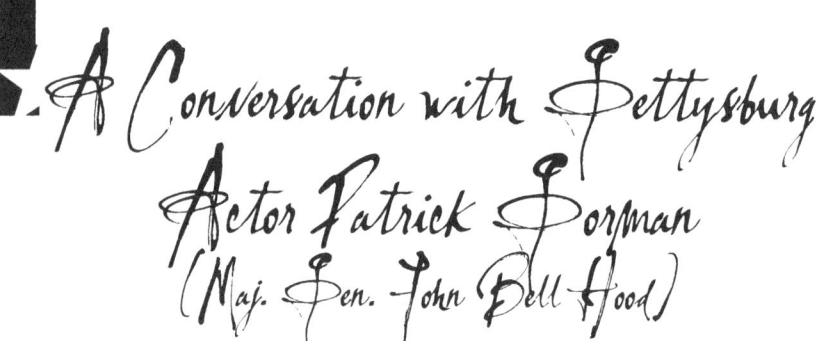

A Conversation with Gettysburg Actor Patrick Gorman (Maj. Gen. John Bell Hood)

by Frank Jastrzembski

Originally published as a Q&A at Emerging Civil War on July 2, 2018

I have been enamored with the film *Gettysburg* (1993) ever since middle school, so I jumped at the opportunity to interview actor Patrick Gorman (who memorably portrayed Maj. Gen. John Bell Hood). Gorman has been a performer in the entertainment industry for over 60 years. His impressive resume includes over 55 films, 90 television episodes, 300 commercials, and 14,000 stage performances. In 2019, he appeared in *Avengers: Endgame*. Below are my questions and Gorman's answers.

How did you end up with the role of Maj. Gen. John Bell Hood in the film *Gettysburg*?
When I read for the film, I wanted to play [Brig. Gen. Lewis A.] Armistead. That's who I was hoping to read for when I read *The Killer Angels*, but they had already cast Richard Jordan. (He was perfect.)

A Conversation with *Gettysburg* Actor Patrick Gorman 137

Patrick Gorman (above) and as John Bell Hood in *Gettysburg* (right). *Courtesy Patrick Gorman*

They wanted me to read for Hood, and I'm glad they did. I could relate to Hood more personally, even though Hood was "the blond giant"—he was like 6'2, had really broad shoulders, and had a brooding, sad look. Well, I'm 5'10, and I don't have broad shoulders, but I got cast.

Originally, when I heard Robert Duvall [first cast as Lee but had to drop out and was replaced by Martin Sheen] was going to do *The Killer Angels*, a Civil War story, I said to my wife (married then, not now), "You know, there's gotta be something for me in this film . . . Sheridan? Something!!!" I had a picture taken in the process of growing my hair back from a shaved head and had a bit of stubble, and this dark look in my eyes.

I delivered the picture to the casting office disguised as a messenger, which in fact I was at the time as my "B-Job." (My agent didn't submit me, I did that.) Nobody in the office knew me, and I got away with delivering my own submission like it came from an agent. Joy Todd, the casting person, called me in because of the picture. Later I found out that when they saw the picture, they said, "We just pray that he can act because he is the only one who even comes close to Hood." They really had a difficult time getting anyone they liked to read for that role (Hood).

And the funny thing is, I don't really look like him at all, but I had something. And incredible luck. The fact that I have a lot of Civil War fans validates that I guess, because apparently I was very successful in getting Hood's persona across.

How did you prepare for it? What kind of research did you do on the general?

Of course, I read *The Gallant Hood* and all the books I could that referenced him. (*Advance and Retreat*, of course, but all the books I could find where he was mentioned.)

Hood was, to me, a romantic, tragic character, and a man with an incredible constitution. How he survived the war with those terrible wounds and the destruction of what he believed has always fascinated me. He was a rising star up until Gettysburg, and from then on, as with the Confederacy, it was all downhill.

The criticisms leveled against him by some historians don't hold water. Most of the damning ones were made by secondhand accounts. No general, not even Lee, could have saved Atlanta or Franklin. The truth and the measure of the man, for me, has to reside in the fact that, after the war, and even after his death, the men who served under him still honored him.

I can't say I identify with him but, hopefully, I was able to penetrate something of his persona in order to embody him in the film. It is not necessary for an actor to "like" a character he plays. In fact, it's not even pertinent. You must not, in my opinion, judge your character. You have to attempt to see with his eyes and act with his resolve. You have to believe in them, and they have to breathe.

I served in the military, but as an enlisted man, so I have no real experience of the kinds of decisions he had to make. But, of course, that's what the imagination is for. That's what the research is for, and I have always had great respect for the profession of arms. For me, the military has one true function, to protect the nation, the society which they serve. The military is for defense but that also means you have to be a master of attack as well. I have always been drawn to the military, martial arts, and the history of warfare. Hood was a perfect character for me to address. Attack, that's how I think of him.

Although I had experience as a horseman (I grew up playing cowboys and Indians, riding bareback on real horses), Hood was an expert (he was going to teach cavalry tactics at West Point when the rebellion started), so I had to work on my skills. I made friends with the film wranglers and encouraged them to find me a mount that would make me look good and not be too much for me. They were a great help and acted as my staff in the film. Also, they made sure I had a Hope saddle because, apparently, that is what he rode. Yes, although a native Kentuckian, he was partial to Texas and the Texans, and I even had the honor to be made an honorary Texan by the reenactors from Texas in the film.

My mount was "Badger," and he'd done more major films than I had. We worked well together. With luck and his smooth gait, I never fell off. The fine points for my confidence in playing him came later, as I rode into the reenactor encampments in character as Hood. They welcomed me as the good general, and I learned lots of anecdotal stuff that I didn't find in books. They helped set the mood for how it might have been. I owe them a lot. The whole film did. By the time I went before the cameras, I felt comfortable as Hood.

You have great chemistry with Lt. Gen. James Longstreet (Tom Berenger) in the film. How did you two establish such a great rapport?

Tom Berenger was the heart of the production for me. He really checked on every one of his generals to find what kind of research and passion we brought. While filming, he organized a Friday Night Confederate Officers Club meeting at the Farnsworth House. He was an inspiration and a gentleman. I'd only first met him at the table read of the script on location before we began filming. I noticed that at the breaks during the reading, he was sorting out boxes of swords to give to his staff, his generals, and I thought, how thoughtful that he'd gone to props and brought them to the reading. He was more than thoughtful because he had gone out on his own dime and purchased swords for each one of us, and they were all different and personalized. Mine was a CSA cavalry saber with an actual 1862 CSA blade but with a replica hilt and sabretache. It was inscribed: "Maj. General John Hood 1st Corp. Compliments Lieut.-Gen. James Longstreet Army of Northern Virginia." A personal and generous gift which meant a lot. He cemented the Confederates together in a very important way. Besides, he was a pleasure to work with, and I just got along with him extremely well. A joy to work with.

Have you had a chance to read *The Lost Papers of Confederate General John Bell Hood* **(2015) or** *John Hood: The Rise, Fall and Resurrection of a Confederate General* **(2016) by Stephen M. Hood? If so what is your take on them?**

Yes, I read them as a gift from Stephen, and they validated what I'd always surmised from what I found, especially about the drinking and the laudanum. Those reports were all secondhand, not by anyone who was there. Petty and envious.

I see that you are listed for the role of Maj. Gen. Charles F. Smith in the *To Appomattox* **TV series project. How do you plan to prepare to play Grant's mentor and friend?**

Again, a fascinating character. Read all that I could, and this is a truly admirable man. Hah! Even look forward to leading the green troops into battle with muskets unloaded. Hopefully also, to play the younger and older version. Have done some makeup versions of both, though I am decidedly too old to play him. I believe I can pull it off. Besides, a bit of historical license here. Not many people will know what he looked like—except you and probably lots of reenactors. Thanks for your piece on him [a 2018 ECW post]. Excellent.

You mentioned that it took director Ron Maxwell almost two decades to turn *Killer Angels* **(***Gettysburg***) into a film. Do you think there will be another Civil War film like** *Gettysburg* **or** *Gods & Generals***?**

Well, if they could just get *To Appomattox* before the cameras, it would give it a good run. I've read all the episodes and they are wonderful. It should be a series, just as *Gods and Generals* should have been. But surely there are projects out there that could rival the success of *Gettysburg*. Certainly, *Glory* was a great film, and there are really so many untouched stories in our history that have yet to be addressed. We need these stories to stir up our youth to examine the Civil War. Certainly, the issues which caused it are yet to be entirely resolved. Movies can inspire and educate along with being entertaining. *Gettysburg* proved that I think.

What is your favorite Civil War book?

Grant's memoirs and anything that Shelby Foote ever wrote.

I read about your passion for Aikido and Japanese calligraphy. Can you tell me more about both of these interests?
I've been, and still am, training in Aikido (over 33 years). I have trained in other martial arts before that growing up and for most of my adult life. The principles of Aiki are profoundly valuable in life as well as martial arts. It made a difference in how I live and how I pursue my craft. All martial arts have their limitations when confronted with real fighting, but the principles remain useful, and practice makes "perfect." Awareness, focus, and being in the moment, coupled with skills long honed, is what it's all about.

Japanese calligraphy (shodo) has fascinated me since I was very young. Originally, it was the love of the Chinese characters, and then when I learned about Japanese arts and language, I found that the Chinese characters were also used in their "alphabet." I am not fluent in Japanese or in the writing of the language, but I do learn characters and practice what I know just for aesthetic reasons. At one point, where we practiced shodo as part of the Aikido training, I had some of my samples published in Japan. An honor, but as an American student training in Aikido in America. I think I have a snapshot of shodo that I was doing in my off-hours and in the Gettysburg Hotel during filming.

1. The Gettysburg Soundtrack

by Dan Welch

Originally appeared on the Emerging Civil War blog on January 17, 2020

Gettysburg was now an obsession. My first trip there had captured my imagination. At the tender age of five, my parents, with a push primarily from my father, arranged what became the first of many yearly family trips to the small Pennsylvania town. A toy musket, kepi, and my father's retelling of those historic events kept me wanting to come back year-after-year to further explore and refight the battle with those accoutrements and my imagination in hand. One trip in the early 1990s, however, was different.

As we drove around the battlefield, taking the National Park Service's self-guided auto tour, something we did multiple times from start to finish during each trip, we were confused as to why some of the areas of the park were closed. Plus, Gettysburg itself was more busy than usual. Reenactors were everywhere, which for me was great! I now had more soldiers to join my ranks to refight this battle. Through talking with other visitors and shop owners in town, my parents discovered that a movie about the battle was being filmed in parts of the park. As a matter of fact, at one particular shop in town, we were perusing keepsakes with none other than Robert E. Lee! The name Martin Sheen meant nothing to me at the time.

Following the release of the movie *Gettysburg*, on yet another family trip back to those hallowed grounds, my parents picked up the soundtrack to the movie on cassette before leaving town. They had not seen the movie yet, and they didn't plan on taking such a young kid to see a four-hour war movie, but the film's soundtrack might be something nice to listen to on the long drive back home.

The scene was set. My father driving with my mother in the passenger seat of our Chevrolet station wagon. My sister in the back seat, leaned back, with her cassette Walkman on, sleeping off yet another boring (to her at least) family vacation to Gettysburg. I was in the large cargo area at the far-back of the vehicle, drawing and coloring pictures of soldiers, monuments, and Lincoln. My British soldiers had numerous battles on streams and rocks drawn on these pieces of paper, as well. With our course set for home, the cellophane was ripped open, the cassette removed from its case, and pushed into the radio console in the front. The opening song on the album, "Main Title," cut through the relative calm and quiet of the car, save my cavalry charge across the back of the cargo area of the station wagon. I was immediately hooked.

After side one finished, my mom pushed eject, turned it over to side two, and let the album play out. It was a different time for media to say the least. When the soundtrack finished, I asked to have it played again, from the beginning. My very patient family played it over and over for me all the way home. It was nearly a six-hour drive back then.

Although it was meant to be a cassette for the whole family to listen to and enjoy, once we returned home, it practically became mine. It was stored in my room on my cassette spindle tower but was rarely found there. I listened to it all the time. I played it on my Walkman while doing everything. When we went anywhere in the station wagon, I asked for it to be played, especially when it was on the way to see a reenactment or encampment.

By the end of the decade, the tape was worn out and produced a muted, garbled sound. It was okay, however. My love of history had taken a momentary back seat to girls and garage bands. Before entering college, just two weeks before my first class as a freshman, my family took a last trip together back to Gettysburg. It had been many years since our last time there, as those awkward teen years didn't include family vacations. Feeling nostalgic, I wanted to listen to that old soundtrack, but technology had marched forward and cars didn't include cassette players any longer. Plus, that old, worn-out cassette wouldn't play anyhow.

At some point during the trip, I purchased a new copy of the soundtrack on CD. Not only was my interest in history rekindled, but so too was my love of this soundtrack. The whole ride back home at the end of this trip was once again filled with the music that had accompanied the movie all those years ago.

Over the next couple years, as I worked through my undergraduate program in music education, I continued to revisit the battlefield at Gettysburg during every break between semesters. Each time, I listened to the soundtrack on the drive there, the drive back, and during the countless hours I spent driving around the battlefield. It has remained a staple during visits to other Civil War battlefields and trips with a history focus. As a seasonal ranger with the National Park Service at Gettysburg, I also make sure to play it in the car on my way to and from the park each day on July 1, 2, and 3 each summer.

I am not the only one that has fallen in love with the soundtrack, however. The more I became involved with different circles in the larger Civil War community, the more copies of the soundtrack I found stashed in cars and wedged in car CD players. R. E. Turner, the vice chairman of Time Warner in 1998, agreed with the allure of the score, writing in the five-year-anniversary commemorative edition insert, "The score of *Gettysburg* reflects the drama, intensity and passion of the film. It is one of the most beautiful soundtracks I've ever heard."[1] Randy Edelman, the soundtrack's composer, disagreed. He contended that the score did not receive much interest in the immediate period around the film's release. "It's not as though there was an immediate response [to the music]," he wrote.[2] "Obviously, there are many people who love this kind of thing, the Civil War setting. But it wasn't like there was a tumultuous response when the movie came out, or when it first aired on cable for that matter. It was something that just seemed to happen from the viewers' emotional response to the music, that created this groundswell of ongoing affection for my score."

One of the strengths of the score, and perhaps one of the reasons why it has received as much attention as it has over the decades, were the numerous

---

1 R. E. Turner, *Music from the Original Motion Picture Soundtrack "Gettysburg"* (New York: Milan Entertainment, Inc., 1998), 4.

2 Randy Edelman, *Music from the Original Motion Picture Soundtrack "Gettysburg"* (New York: Milan Entertainment, Inc., 1998), 13.

compositional themes that Edelman had created. The composer wrote an easily identifiable theme for each prominent character or officer in the film. These themes were ever present anytime these characters were on-screen. The themes interweave so much into the rest of the compositional fabric that the overall lack of period music in the over three-hour film is hardly noticed or missed. Listeners become so enamored with the themes that Randy Edelman composed that upon successive listens, few would notice their absence. Edelman later recalled the reasoning for this lack of period pieces in his score. "I didn't have the luxury of time to research the music of the period for *Gettysburg*," he noted, so "I let the picture and the tremendous emotion of the characters dictate the music at every turn. . . . I tried to follow each officer thematically through the story, interweaving the colors of each character."[3]

Outside of Edelman's score, however, there were several scenes in which reenactors with period instruments or reproductions of period instruments performed popular airs of the day. With so much interest in the music of the film, even in the first year after the film's debut, a follow-up recording was released. Titled *More Songs from Gettysburg*, this extended release included recordings of those period pieces that had appeared in the film but were not originally included in the original soundtrack. Also on this second release was a recitation of the Gettysburg Address by actor Jeff Daniels. The actor, who had portrayed Colonel Joshua Chamberlain, recited Lincoln's words with the same stentorian voice he used during the re-created fight for Little Round Top. All the while, punctuating the background of those long-remembered words was the "Main Theme" that had been composed by Edelman for the original soundtrack.

Still, diehards of the movie and soundtrack wanted more. In 1998, on the fifth anniversary of the film, a deluxe commemorative edition of the soundtrack was released, containing two discs of the score and an insert full of interviews, fun facts, and images from the film. This edition did not incorporate the historical pieces that had been added to the follow-up release to the original score in 1994, however. Nevertheless, the re-released and expanded score has provided those avid listeners a larger musical story to explore. By the time of the commemorative edition's release, the popularity

3 Ibid.

of the score had expanded as well. Writing in the edition's insert, Turner noted, "As this compilation is being prepared . . . U.S. Olympic skating team member Todd Eldridge, [is] choreographing his long program in competition to a selection of Randy Edelman's music from the soundtrack. . . . Eldridge's choice indicates not only the enduring mark that Ron Maxwell's film made on the cultural landscape of the '90s, but more than that, how deeply the score from this film resonated within the collective consciousness of those who saw the film."[4]

Five years after the film's release and the popularity of the soundtrack, the composer still could not believe its success, writing, "The use of the music, apart from the film, is just wonderful and not a little mind-boggling: It closes the Olympics, it opens the Super Bowl, and I recently attended a performance of the score by the Boston Pops. I hope it goes on and on."[5]

As a classically trained musician and music educator, I could tell you the nuances of Edelman's soundtrack. I could walk you through a harmonic analysis of the score, point out the composer's different uses of cadences at the end of numerous musical phrases, and diagram the many themes, laying out a case for what musical form each piece in the score takes. Looking at it through this lens, however, would only strip away the magic that this soundtrack holds for me and so many others. Perhaps it is fitting to just enjoy it, let it do "what it is supposed to do, which is to set the mood," and "impart a sense of the era."[6]

---

4 Turner, *Music from*, 5.

5 Edelman, *Music from*, 13.

6 Robert Katz, *Music from the Original Motion Picture Soundtrack "Gettysburg"* (New York: Milan Entertainment, Inc., 1998), 17.

I. The 2nd South Carolina String Band
and the Pop Music of the Civil War

by Chris Mackowski

A version of this article appeared in the August 2008 issue of Civil War Historian. *The band has subsequently retired, although fans can still find their music on YouTube: @2ndSouthCarolinaStringBand.*

Joe Ewers stands on the stage and plucks one of the strings on his five-string banjo. His slouch hat sits at a rakish angle, and a pair of blue tassels, so faded that they look gray, dangle over the broad brim.

He plucks, twists a knob to get the instrument in tune, then plucks again.

To the side of the stage, two other members of the 2nd South Carolina String Band stand in front of a 34-star American flag and chat with a pair of reenactors who've come for the concert. They pause the conversation so someone can grab a snapshot—Confederates in front of Old Glory—then pick up where they left off.

The concert hall, an American Legion hall on East Middle Street in Gettysburg, fills to capacity. Women with long hoop skirts swoosh down the side aisles. On the stage, Ewers tunes his second banjo, emblazoned with a South Carolina palmetto tree, to the accompaniment of the hall's eager chatter and the click of hard-soled boots on laminate floor. "It's an ancient Chinese

Joe Ewers on the banjo (left) and Bob Beeman on the jawbone (right) at the Gettysburg concert where they recorded their live album *Lightning in a Jar*. *Chris Mackowski*

melody," Ewers's brother Fred, one of the band's two fiddle players and the on-stage maestro, will later explain to the audience. "He'll play this melody several times this evening. It's called 'Too Ning.'"

Fred has much fun with the audience at his brother's expense. "What's the difference between a banjo and a trampoline?" he asks. "You take off your shoes before you jump on a trampoline."

The 2nd South Carolina String Band, one of the oldest and best-known groups of Civil War musicians, has assembled here in a town where the Ewers brothers once both lived, to celebrate their twentieth season of reenacting. The band is commemorating the anniversary by putting on a pair of concerts that will be used as the basis for a live CD.

"We play this music a lot differently now than we played it back in the day, when we first got started," Joe Ewers explains later. "At reenactments, we'd be out burning powder during the day and then playing around the campfire, having a good time during the night. That's how it all got started."[1]

Because of that informality, the band members didn't initially take their roles as musical interpreters seriously. "We were playing modern instruments and, basically, grade-school arrangements," Ewers says. "As we matured in the hobby and matured in our music, that began to change."

Vocalist and guitarist David Goss likened it to the experience of the actual soldiers. "We were a pick-up group just like the camp bands were," explains Goss, who works as a college history professor when he's not making music. "Everyone just brought the instrument that he owned."

Over time, the crowds around the campfire grew, and by the early nineties, the band started getting invitations to play events. "That's when we

---

[1] Interviews were conducted in person on March 8 and 9, 2008.

started taking it more seriously," Goss says. "We knew the watchdogs and the thread-counters would be paying closer attention, so we started holding ourselves to the same higher standard we held ourselves to with our military, our physical impressions. We held our music to that, too."

Band members began to make the switch to period instruments and wear attire more appropriate for musicians. The advent of the internet also made it easier for the band to research their songs, so they began to play arrangements more authentic to the nineteenth century.

"We've tried to constantly improve our instruments, our instrumentation, our arrangements, our knowledge of the background stories of these songs," Goss explains. "We want to be true to our music."

* * *

Sometimes, remaining true to the music can be harder than people suspect.

"Some of that music can get pretty dangerous," Ewers says. "The minstrel music, from traveling minstrel shows, that was the pop music of the antebellum era. It had simple, catchy melodies, and some of the lyrics were funny. But the basis of a lot of that music was making fun of the differences between people, between whites and Blacks."

For that reason, Goss says, the band remains about 90 percent true to the songs in their catalog. "Some bands stay 100 percent true to those kinds of lyrics, but that really narrows the kinds of audiences you can play to," he says. "Our feeling is that if a song is overtly offensive, then what's the point? People stop listening and can't enjoy the music."

And that, says Goss, is the whole point of the music from the era. He cites Stephen Foster as an example. Foster, the author of such standards as "Camptown Ladies," "My Old Kentucky Home," and "Hard Times Come Again No More," produced pop music to make a profit, which meant he had to write music that appealed to broad audiences. "Some of the music from the time period tends to be formulaic," Goss admits. "It's like the doo-wop music of the 1950s. It's simple but entertaining."

Still, the band does get occasional complaints about content. "We're not making any political statements," Goss affirms. "We're just playing the music as it was played back then. They took their politics, their attitudes about race, and they expressed themselves through their songs. But the mentality of the songwriters does not reflect our mentality."

Goss admits, though, that he has to put himself in the place of the songwriters and the singers. "Their songs are reflective of a certain mindset. I have to ask myself, 'Why would they do what they did?' and put myself in their place," Goss says. "It's a form of acting, really."

Adopting the persona of, say, Old Dan Tucker allows the band to interpret the song in a true-to-period way. "He's a character well known to me," Goss grins. "But he is just a character."

Most audiences understand the difference between the music and the musicians. At a 2006 Bucktails reenactment in northcentral Pennsylvania, the band finished its set with "Southern Soldier," roaring out the lines "I'll march away to the firing line / And kill that Yankee soldier!" The blue-coated crowd roared back with cheers and applause, ignoring the song's sentiment and appreciating its full-bore energy and the band's musicianship. At the song's conclusion, the Bucktails jumped to their feet for a standing ovation.

But, as Ewers points out, "the wounds are still tender" for some people, even generations later. That made it tough for the band, in its early years, to sell records in some places.

"Our first two albums were a kind of Civil War Top 30 favorite parlor songs, the basic catalog that most Americans are more or less familiar with," Ewers says, noting that the mix included popular songs from the North and the South. "On the second album, we included 'Marching Thro' Georgia' and 'Lincoln and Liberty, Too,' a pair of songs with catchy melodies that dealt with subjects quite incendiary to Southrons: Sherman's March to the Sea and Abraham Lincoln. We were told by several of our vendors that they could not sell that album at many of their best venues in the South—or worse, they wouldn't even offer it."

The band compensated by compiling selected songs from those albums onto a best-of CD, *Hard Times*, one of four studio albums the band has available. The concert album recorded in Gettysburg recaptured—and reinterpreted—some of that older material. "The idea is to revisit our older material that we played back when we were farby," Ewers says, using a reenactor's term—*farb*—which refers to inauthentic hobbyists. "That early material is just great stuff, but now we play it much differently, and much better."

Aside from their CDs, the band has also contributed music to a pair of Ken Burns documentaries, they've performed in the movie *Gods and Generals*, and they still hit the road every season to play at seven or eight events. During the Sesquicentennial, with so many commemorative events and celebrations going on, the band only got busier—and things didn't let up afterwards. "The band is having a rather more successful season than last year—an 1865 series year, and as you well know, there wasn't much to 'celebrate' from that year," he chuckles, his inner Southerner showing. He rattles off a list: an encore to a gig in Danville, Virginia, in April . . . a dance in Martinsburg, West Virginia, "where Ol' Jack trashed the rail facilities and made off with the rolling stock and engines" . . . the Gettysburg anniversary ("best weather there EVER, and I lived there for 14 years!") . . . Cedar Creek for the 155th Manassas event. "All in all, a much better year than last," he says, admitting that last year had nonetheless been good.[2]

"The best part is that there are no prima donnas," Ewers says of his bandmates. "Everyone brings something to the party. We do what we do for love."

* * *

The cow jawbone never goes out of tune. Bob Beeman plays it by running a thin stick, as dainty as an orchestra conductor's baton, across the teeth like a washboard. Then the stick plinks its way back over several individual teeth, maybe three of them, maybe four, depending on the rhythm of a particular song. On other songs, Beeman may shake a tambourine, which rattles like an eastern diamondback, or he may play two sets of rib bones that he can clack together between his fingers, his wrists bobbing through the air like a boxer trying to stay loose before striking.

Like Goss and the Ewers brothers, Beeman is one of the band's original five musicians. John Frayler, the band's drummer, retired back in 2000. The band eventually recruited banjo payer Tom DiGiuseppe, fiddler Mike Paul, and fife players Greg Hernandez and Joe Whitney. Another fife player, Marty Groody, also did a stint with the band, leaving in 2000 when he moved to Florida.

2 Interview, 16 July 2016.

Joe Whitney, Mike Paul, Fred Ewers, Tom DiGiuseppe, David Goss, Joe Ewers, and Bob Beeman rest under the shade of the tent at the Manassas 150th. *2nd South Carolina String Band*

"All those instruments may sound more like the 2nd South Carolina Orchestra than just a band," Goss admits. "It's unlikely any company had a guitarist, two fiddle players, two fife players, and a couple of banjos. A guitar was very rare. Maybe a fiddle, maybe a banjo, probably a fife and a drum because they were marching so much. But when the army was in camp, especially in winter encampments, a musical group like this would've been possible."

Music was very much a part of a soldier's life, Goss explains. Some regiments performed minstrel shows. Others performed light operas. Navy men on the ships of the Charleston blockade had bands. Even in POW camps, there are accounts of soldiers putting on performances.

DiGiuseppe, the 2nd South Carolina's historical researcher, explains that music broke the tedium that plagued most soldiers. "It forged bonds between them and reminded them of home and why they're fighting," he says. "Most of those songs that they would sing—prewar songs that would remind them of home—were parlor songs. But what's ironic is that folks at home were singing the newer, patriotic songs, which makes sense if you think about it: 'I want to be with Johnny. He's in the field. I'll sing these songs that help evoke that.'"

Modern fans of Civil War music commonly but mistakenly assume that those patriotic songs, so popular in their day, made up the standard musical fare around the campfire. "You rate popularity by sheet music sales," DiGiuseppe says. "Sheet music is published for piano. Well, I haven't ever seen a piano in the field."

However, soldiers did commonly bring well-known songs from home and adapt them to their own experiences. "Listen to the mocking bird" became "Listen to the minie ball" and "Listen to the parrot shell" in a version called "The Siege of Vicksburg." Or, instead of singing "Hard times come again no more," soldiers tired of the usual army fare of hardtack sang "Hard crackers come again no more."

The best-known example might be "Dixie," DiGiuseppe says. Dan Emmett, a native of Mt. Vernon, Ohio, and living in New York City, wrote the song in the 1850s for a minstrel show. "That song is about a Black man talking about his mistress who married a gigolo," DiGiuseppe says. "It has nothing to do with the war—except it has that chorus."

Soon, Southern soldiers began creating their own pro-Confederacy verses to match that chorus. Confusing matters even further, several published versions of the song appeared that contested Emmett's authorship. Emmett, meanwhile, concerned that the Confederacy had co-opted his song, volunteered to write the fife and drum manual for the Union army.

For the concert crowd in Gettysburg, Mike Paul starts "Dixie" as an elegy with long, slow pulls of his bow across his fiddle. About a third of the concert audience rises to its feet. Men remove their hats. As the rest of the 2nd South Carolinians join in, the song picks up steam and pep, and by the time Goss sings the first chorus, the band is busting through the song with a roomful of backup vocalists singing along.

It would come as a surprise to some of the audience to learn that Company I of the 2nd South Carolina infantry originally formed in Salem, Massachusetts—a place where, as Ewers admits, "It ain't easy being Confederate." The rifle company reenacted together for twelve years before disbanding. The musicians, though, have carried on the name and traditions of the unit that originally brought them together and gave them a home, even though the band members are now "spread out from Massachusetts to Manassas," Ewers explains.

"We've had people ask us, 'You boys from South Carolina?'" Goss says. "You can see their smiles sink when we tell them no. 'Well,' they'll say, 'you gave it a try.'"

* * *

The morning after the concert, the band gathers in a second-floor photography studio off Steinwehr Avenue. Fred Ewers, who has momentarily traded his fiddle for a nineteenth-century tripod camera, has taken the band's picture for the album cover. He washes photographic chemicals over the tin plate, and a reverse image of the band ghosts into view. "Nice contrast," someone says as the image gets more distinct.

"That's why I like to use tin," Fred says. He rinses off the plate and dabs the picture with a cotton swab. The chemicals have stained his fingertips black.

On three tries now, they've held still for fifteen seconds while Fred has attempted to capture them on tin. Indeed, the third time proves to be the charm. It's a wrap.

Joe Whitney begins to take down the handmade, wall-sized Stars and Bars he'd hung as a backdrop from one of the ceiling's exposed wooden beams. Mike Paul packs his fiddle away. Bob Beeman clicks and clatters his bones before tucking them into a pocket.

DiGiuseppe and Goss have a long day's drive back to northern Massachusetts still in front of them. Meanwhile, Greg Hernandez and his wife, Denise, will head in the opposite direction, toward New Market, Virginia, and their home on the edge of the battlefield there. Since then, Joe Ewers and his wife have moved to New Hampshire.

"It's such an undertaking to get everyone together," Ewers admits, striking an almost valedictory tone. "It's gotten harder and harder as everyone's aged and our schedules have gotten more complicated. But we've had a long run, and . . . this is an evergreen product. Every year, new young people who are interested in the Civil War, who learn about it in their studies at school, will discover this music."

But it's Hernandez, who always looks like he can barely contain a smile, who stops on his way out the door to have the last word. "You have to enjoy what you do. You have to have fun with it," he says. "We do this because it's a lot of fun."

I. Driving Dixie Down

by Patrick Vecchio

My most in-depth lesson in American Civil War history began on July 28, 1973, even though I didn't realize it. That's the day I heard a band called The Band perform along with the Grateful Dead and the Allman Brothers Band at the Summer Jam in Watkins Glen, New York. I was there with 599,999 of my closest friends.

The lesson, which I still didn't realize had begun, continued a year later in Orchard Park, New York, where a football stadium full of fans gathered to hear Eric Clapton on his 461 Ocean Boulevard Tour. The Band opened, and even though I was there to see Clapton, The Band was by far the better act.

At each concert, The Band played "The Night They Drove Old Dixie Down," which, even though they were playing on bills with rock bands, is by no means a rock song. The subjects and sounds of The Band's music often evoke an earlier America, and this song about the Civil War fits right in with their songs about old-time medicine shows and whistle stops.

There's an interesting wrinkle to this piece of musical Americana. Robbie Robertson (the group's guitarist), who wrote the song, is Canadian. Even though he was born north of the 49th parallel and farther north of the Mason-Dixon Line, "The Night They Drove Old Dixie Down" is a fully realized song, so well crafted that it has been covered by Johnny Cash, Joan Baez, John Denver, and the ever-popular "host of others."

A first-time listener, though, doesn't need to know who The Band is or that the Civil War is the subject of the song. The opening trumpet figure immediately sets a mournful tone and signals there's a story to be told. This story immediately seizes the reader's attention because it's as old as literature: a man examining the aftermath of war and trying to make sense of it.

In this case, the man introduces himself:

> Virgil Caine is the name, and I served on the Danville train.
> 'Till so much cavalry came and tore up the tracks again.

At least, that's the way I always had heard the second line. That's the way Joan Baez sang it. Her version was in the Top 40 for 13 weeks and reached as high as number 3, according to *Billboard* magazine.

However, a close listen to The Band's live performance on their *The Last Waltz* album reveals a minor but significant change: "Till Stoneman's cavalry came and tore up the tracks again."

Stoneman? Never heard of him. Who was he, and why were he and his cavalry tearing up railroad tracks? With that question, my Civil War lesson was underway.

Here's what I learned: In late March 1865, Union General George Stoneman and 4,000 soldiers were dispatched into the western parts of Virginia and North Carolina—not to fight, but instead to destroy anything they could find of service to the Confederacy. The war wasn't over yet, but in weeks, it would be.

Among Stoneman's targets were the Danville-Greenboro railway line, the East Tennessee & Virginia Railroad, and the North Carolina Railroad. An important part of their mission was to cut off escape routes for Confederate General Robert E. Lee.

It would not do right by Robertson, though, to consider "The Night They Drove Old Dixie Down" simply as history in 4/4 time. After all, Bob Dylan was awarded a Nobel Prize for Literature. Robertson is no Dylan (although The Band backed and recorded with Dylan in the '60s and worked with him in later years), but Robertson is an incisive storyteller whose work deserves a look through a literary lens as well as a historical one.

Virgil Caine tells us Stoneman "tore up the tracks" of the Danville line, and history tells us the general and his men ripped up mile after mile of rails in the South. Because railroads were so crucial to the South's war effort, Robertson may be using torn-up rails as a metaphor for the Confederacy itself as the end of the war neared.

If that seems like a bit of a reach, consider these lines, which further suggest Robertson's use of metaphor:

> Back with my wife in Tennessee
> When one day she called to me,
> "Virgil, quick, come see,
> "There goes the Robert E. Lee."

At first, this reads like a reference to the Mississippi River steamboat named after the Confederate general. It was launched in 1866—the year after the war ended. If Caine's wife is calling for him to come see the steamboat, they likely lived along or near the Mississippi River in western Tennessee after the war.

However, interpreting this depends on whether the phrase "Back with my wife in Tennessee" refers to a time or a place. Does Robertson use "back" to refer to the place Caine returned to after the war, or is he using the word the way somebody telling a story might, as in "back when I was young"? Is he referring to a time *before* Caine worked on "the Danville train"—that is, before Stoneman's raid in 1865?

If so, then Caine's wife's "quick, come see"—especially the word "quick"—foreshadows the Union's Tennessee campaigns in 1862–63. During those campaigns, Union troops drove Confederate forces back along the Nashville & Chattanooga's route.

As for Virgil Caine, he's the personification of twisted, torn-up rails—or, to put it another way, he is the South. Metaphors don't sing, though, so we relate to Caine as a man, and we relate to his enduring dignity: "Now, I don't mind chopping wood, and I don't care if the money's no good." The "I don't mind" and the "I don't care" suggest undiminished self-respect, even though his side lost the war.

The phrase "the money's no good" is further evidence that Robertson leaves listeners room for varied interpretations. The likeliest reading is that Robertson is saying Caine's pay for chopping wood is next to nothing. But perhaps Robertson is referring to Confederate currency, even if Caine isn't. Robertson may be using the currency as another metaphor for the postwar South.

Regardless of how Robertson uses those words, the song's next lines are straightforward. Union troops plundered the places they conquered for supplies and spoils, and their rapaciousness made Caine bitter:

> You take what you need
> And you leave the rest
> But they should never
> Have taken the very best.

In the song's closing verse, Robertson finishes telling the story of the war as he began it: through one man's Southern perspective:

> Like my father before me
> I will work the land
> And like my brother above me
> Who took a rebel stand.
> He was just 18, proud and brave
> But a Yankee laid him in his grave.

Robertson again is veiling the meaning. Is Caine's brother "above me" as in being older, or is he "above me" in the sense that he has gone to glory? Given Caine's enduring dignity, the second viewpoint seems more plausible: His brother is not a casualty but a martyr, among the "the very best" from the previous verse.

Either way, the word "above" collides with its antonym, "below," just four lines later, and Robertson ends the closing verse with the perfect word for describing Caine's—and the South's—situation:

> I swear by the mud below my feet
> You can't raise a Caine back up when he's in defeat.

This conclusion is flush with Caine's bitterness, which is also expressed by Robertson in the irony-laced final chorus. The combination of bells ringing and people singing would seem like a joyful occasion—but not here:

> The night they drove old Dixie down
> And all the bells were ringing
> The night they drove old Dixie down
> And all the people were singing.

Who was ringing the bells? Victorious Union troops. And what were they singing? A song of mockery that sounds like taunting on a schoolyard playground: "Na, na la na, na, na."

As noted earlier, it's interesting that a Canadian musician could write such a fully realized song about the American Civil War. It's nearly as interesting to note that three of the four other members of The Band were Canadian, too: Rick Danko, Garth Hudson, and Richard Manuel.

The song's vocals, though, were handled by Levon Helm, The Band's lone American. He was born in Arkansas—a Southerner.

Steve Earle's "Ben McCulloch"

by Jon-Erik Gilot

Originally published as a blog post at Emerging Civil War on January 19, 2020

I've been a longtime Steve Earle fan, and I'm here today to share something with you . . .

Steve Earle is cooler than crap.

Here's a guy who cut his teeth in the music business under the tutelage of the great Townes Van Zandt. A guy who has consistently put out high-quality albums for more than 30 years. A guy whose talent extends beyond the realm of music.

A Texas native, Earle flexed his acting muscles in two of the finest television series this author has ever seen, *The Wire* and *Treme*. He's written a novel and an off-Broadway play. He's remained as relevant and as necessary as ever when other artists of his vintage have faded into obscurity.

And like you and me, Steve Earle fashions himself as a Civil War enthusiast. This interest has spilled over into his songwriting and soapboxing at his concerts. Earle has written a number of songs either referencing or directly relating to the Civil War. And while his jaunty ode to Buster Kilrain—"Dixieland," from his acclaimed album *The Mountain* with the Del McCoury Band—might be the first of these songs to come to mind, I'd direct readers to an earlier, edgier Earle song highlighting another son of Texas, Ben McCulloch.

The name Ben McCulloch might be foreign to some Civil War enthusiasts, especially those who shy away from Western Theater studies. A longtime soldier, legislator, and lawman, by May 1861 McCulloch had been named brigadier general in the Confederate army and soon after defeated a Federal army under Nathaniel Lyon at the battle of Wilson's Creek. McCulloch was killed at the March 1862 battle of Pea Ridge, a significant loss of a steady hand at command in the Confederacy's Western Theater.

A masterful songwriter, Earle relates the story of a common soldier serving under McCulloch, the highs and lows undoubtedly common to soldiers North and South during the early days of the war. Let's break down some of the lyrics:

> We signed up in San Antone, my brother Paul and me
> To fight with Ben McCulloch and the Texas infantry
> Well the poster said we'd get a uniform and seven bucks a week
> The best rations in the army and a rifle we could keep

Earle here demonstrates the incentives that no doubt enticed many men to enlist, especially those on the lower end of the economic spectrum, including arms, uniforms, regular pay and food. This optimism would be tempered with the realizations of what awaited them: discomfort, disease, and death.

> When I first laid eyes on the general I knew he was a fightin' man
> He was every inch a soldier, every word was his command
> Well his eyes were cold as the lead and steel forged into tools of war
> He took the lives of many and the souls of many more

> Well they marched us to Missouri and we hardly stopped for rest
> And then he made this speech and said "We're comin' to the test"
> Well we've got to take Saint Louie boys before the Yankees do
> If we control the Mississippi then the Federals are through

Both sides recognized the need for control of both St. Louis and the Mississippi River. Nathaniel Lyon secured the arsenal in St. Louis in the spring of 1861, and while the city would remain the occasional target of military action over the next four years (most notably Sterling Price's 1864 expedition), it would remain under Federal control throughout war.

> Well they told us that our enemy would all be dressed in blue
> They forgot about the winter's cold and cursed fever too
> My brother died at Wilson's Creek and Lord I seen him fall
> We fell back to the Boston Mountains in the north of Arkansas

At Wilson's Creek, the narrator sees his brother's life cut short in battle. While Sterling Price led his Missouri State Guard northward into the heart of the state, McCulloch instead took his army back into Arkansas. The narrator seethes in frustration in the chorus and final verse:

> Goddamn you Ben McCulloch
> I hate you more than any other man alive
> And when you die you'll be a foot soldier just like me
> In the Devil's infantry
>
> And on the way to Fayetteville we cursed McCulloch's name
> And mourned the dead that we'd left behind and we was carrying the lame
> I killed a boy the other night who'd never even shaved
> I don't even know what I'm fightin' for, I ain't never owned a slave
> So I snuck out of camp and then I heard the news next night
> The Yankees won the battle and McCulloch lost his life

Here we feel the confusion and disillusionment that no doubt pervaded the thoughts of men on both sides of the conflict, ultimately leading to the narrator's desertion the day before the battle of Pea Ridge, where McCulloch was killed by an Illinois soldier.

The song offers a Civil War soldier's full range of emotions in a way that history books don't always convey. Take a listen for yourself sometime. . . .

1. Steve Earle, "Dixieland," and the Irresistible Charm of Buster Kilrain

by Chris Mackowski

Originally published as a blog post at Emerging Civil War on September 1, 2011

The myths of Gettysburg rear their heads in the most unexpected places.

At a Steve Earle concert in Rochester, New York, a couple of weeks ago, the folk-rocker launched into a pair of songs related to the Irish. Before he did, though, he launched into a history lesson—and lo and behold, who should suddenly appear in the story?

A lot of people who fought in the war, particularly for the North, were recent Irish immigrants, Earle told the audience. Because those recent arrivals weren't necessarily invested in the idea of union, they had to be given other reasons to fight. So, for them, Earle said, the war was a class struggle.

"I love my job," said Earle, well known for his left-leaning politics and support of the working class. "It's amazing all the pinko bullshit I can slip into my songs."

Then, like a whack-a-mole that pops out of its burrow, Earle begins to sing his song "Dixieland" in the first-person voice of Buster Kilrain.[1]

---

1 Steve Earle, "Dixieland," *The Mountain*, Warner Records, 1999.

"I am Kilrain, and I'm a fightin' man, and I come from County Clare," the song's narrator declares.

There's no mistake that this is the same Buster Kilrain—the same *fictitious* Buster Kilrain—who appears in Michael Shaara's Pultizer Prize–winning novel *The Killer Angels*, because the song's narrator comes right out and says it: "I am Kilrain of the 20th Maine, and we fight for Chamberlain."

An odd choice, using the 20th Maine as a platform for singing about the Irish and class struggle, I thought. And an odd choice to use Buster Kilrain as the avatar of that story.

"Kilrain is English in origin, making it an insulting moniker for any true Irishman of the 1860s," points out historian Tom Desjardin in his excellent book *These Honored Dead: How the Story of Gettysburg Shaped American Memory*. "Further, it is unlikely that there would have been a 'Buster' Kilrain in the 20th Maine, for the unavoidable reason that 'Buster' did not become a popular name until Buster Keaton became a famous movie actor fifty years after the Civil War."[2]

That hardly matters, though. In art, truth trumps fact—and Earle's song sounds *true*.

As Desjardin notes, people continue to reshape the story of Gettysburg into images that satisfy their own needs. For Earle, that means reshaping Kilrain, the story of the Irish, and the battle of Gettysburg into a story of class struggle. "I damn all gentlemen, whose only worth is their father's name and the sweat of a workin' man," the song's narrator says.

It's hardly a wonder that Earle fell under Buster Kilrain's charismatic spell. To this day, years after the novel was adapted into the movie *Gettysburg*, people still show up at the battlefield looking for Kilrain's name on the 20th Maine's monument.

"It does not seem to bother people that the character is a middle-aged, overweight private who follows his commanding officer around telling him what to do while calling him 'darling,'" writes Desjardin. "Nor does it seem to register that the Kilrain to whom they refer is a Hollywood version of a character from a novel. The little Irish soldier is so endearing, they simply

---

2 Thomas Desjardin, *These Honored Dead: How the Story of Gettysburg Shaped American Memory* (Cambridge, MA: Da Capo Press, 2003), 179.

wish he were real and follow that instinct despite all the evidence to the contrary."³

Earle must've liked the character so much, in fact, that he chose to keep Kilrain alive. In the novel and film, Kilrain gets killed, but in the song, the Irishman appears to have survived—or he sings from beyond the grave. "When the smoke cleared out of Gettysburg, many a mother wept," he sings from a post-battle point of view. "For many a good boy died there, sure, and the air smelled just like death." That's an after-the-battle perspective Shaara's Kilrain didn't have.

When I first heard the song, I didn't know whether Earle knew his song's protagonist was fictitious when he chose to write the song from Kilrain's perspective.⁴ "I stole this character from a book called *The Killer Angels* by Michael Shaara," I've since heard Earle admit. "And the character that's talking to you in this song is a composite character."⁵

It's hardly important to Earle's songwriting, though. While historians frequently get rankled when artists co-opt history—because facts are usually the first casualties—from the artist's perspective, what matters is the emotional and intellectual impact of the work.

The irony here is that Earle isn't even co-opting history; he's co-opting other art to make art of his own. What matters to Earle, then—and to the majority of his fans—is whether he writes and performs an entertaining song and whether he makes the point he sets out to make:

> Well we come from the farms and the city streets
> And a hundred foreign lands.
> And we spilled our blood in the battle's heat
> Now we're all Americans.

Buster Kilrain, I suspect, would approve.

---

3 Desjardin, *These Honored Dead*, 179.

4 Since originally writing this piece, I've learned that Earle did, of course, know Kilrain was fictitious.

5 See Earle's performance at the Operation Ceasefire Concert in Washington, DC, on 24 September 2005. https://youtu.be/Y1pNQD4xD_8?t=27.

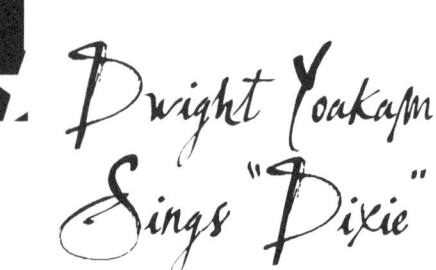

Dwight Yoakam Sings "Dixie"

by Chris Mackowski

Originally published as a blog post at Emerging Civil War on November 9, 2021

We don't know who either of the men are, but for the sake of our discussion, let's call them "Dwight" and "the old rebel." We don't really even know that the rebel is old, except that he has "old blue eyes." The bottle has aged him, and the streets have ravaged him—in fact, have ravaged him to the point of death. Dwight, there in time for the old rebel's "dying breath," tries to comfort his passing with a tearful rendition of "Dixie."

That's the premise of Dwight Yoakam's 1988 song "I Sang Dixie," the second release from his album *Buenas Noches from a Lonely Room*. The song reached #1 on Billboard's country charts, and in 2019, *Rolling Stone* placed it as #26 on its list of the "40 Saddest Country Songs of All Time."

I'm a big Dwight Yoakam fan, but to be honest, I hadn't heard that song in maybe ten years. It just hadn't shuffled up on iTunes, I guess. But the other day, it did, and "I Sang Dixie" quickly earwormed itself into my head. As I've sung it to myself—over and over, with intentional twang—and relistened to it, I've wondered how well the song has held up over the last 33 years.

In the song, Dwight (as we're calling the narrator) seems to have found the old rebel on a sidewalk somewhere in Los Angeles—"this damned old LA street," as the old rebel curses it.

This must be Yoakam, the songwriter, giving voice to something he probably pondered himself at some point. Early in his career, after giving the "urban cowboy" sound a try in Nashville in the late '70s, he moved to southern California, where his style of honky-tonk meshed well with what he later characterized as "the Bakersfield Sound" typified by Buck Owens and the Buckaroos. He gained traction, releasing his first album in 1986. It went double-platinum, but in the lean times and the good times, LA can offer different kinds of troubles.

The old rebel, as he damns the LA streets, conjures a time "way down yonder in the land of cotton" where "old times there ain't near as rotten" as they are in LA. "Don't you see what life here has done to me?" the old rebel asks.

Those turn out to be his final words. He closes his old blue eyes and falls limp against Dwight's side. "No more pain," Dwight sings. "Now he's safe back home in Dixie." Elsewhere, Dwight urges the Lord to please take the old rebel's soul "back home to Dixie," and the old rebel himself urges Dwight to "run back home to that Southern land."

In both instances, Dixie means "home" and stands for an idealized paradise. In one case, that means the South; in the other, it's heaven. From the song's perspective, they're one and the same.

Dixie—as a concept—has an additional patina of nostalgia glossing it, too, because the old rebel is dying. The grass was not greener on LA's side of the fence, he discovered the hard way, and he longs for the green, green grass of home. While it's too late for him, he urges Dwight to "listen to me, son, while you still can." Run—don't walk, don't mosey, don't take your good sweet time about it—back home.

This urgency is juxtaposed against the casual disregard people on the sidewalk show for the little human drama playing out. "People just walked on by as I cried," Dwight sings. This isn't any different than any other stretch of sidewalk on any given day where people walk by the homeless and pretend not to notice them.

But there's symbolism built into the interaction, too. After all, Dwight is singing "Dixie" as the old rebel dies—and people *still* just walk on by. They are among the uninitiated, for surely if any of them knew what they were hearing, they would understand and stop and be moved. If you're not in the "Dixie" club, then you don't get it.

The song "Dixie" evokes an old South filled with old bearded men in white suits who all went by the name "Colonel." (Dwight Yoakam, originally from Kentucky, knew the image well.) Good old boys, never meanin' no harm, tried to catch the eyes of young belles. Magnolias and moonlight abound. And if there are any Black people, they're happy, loyal servants—not a slave in sight.

In Yoakam's 1988 song, Dwight (the narrator) evokes a similar romanticized Dixie by not only singing "Dixie" but by also making comforting comparisons to home and heaven. Many people today still conjure up similar nostalgic images.

But that perception of Dixie, once widespread, has undergone a significant change in the last 33 years (and particularly in the last six). With its underpinnings of racial violence built on slavery, Dixie was hardly the idyllic haven for everyone who lived there. Members of the Dixie club today balk when that part of the picture—left out for a century and a half—gets mentioned (and I'm sure there are readers who just went, "Aw, why'd you have to go and spoil this piece by bringing up slavery and racism?").

I think this adds an extra element of lament to Yoakam's song. The very premise that originally made the song so sad is, itself, dying. Those who still think of Dixie in that romanticized way are mourning its loss; everyone else just walks on by.

That aside, I still think Dwight Yoakam's "I Sang Dixie" is a fantastic song.

1. Hurrah for Homespun!

by Sheritta Bitikofer

Originally published as a blog post at Emerging Civil War on December 14, 2021

Poetry and songs that came out of the Civil War, entertaining as they are, served as a useful vehicle for rhetoric that supported their respective sides. Songs like "The Bonnie Blue Flag," "Marching through Georgia," "Dixie," and "The Battle Cry of Freedom" are just a few of the most widely celebrated songs of the war that contained this sort of political or ideological twist. Another, lesser known, not only evokes pro-Southern/Confederate values but serves as a link to Revolutionary times just ninety-something years prior.

The song in reference is "The Homespun Dress," written by Georgian Carrie Belle Sinclair, who was the niece of steamboat inventor Robert Fulton and a volunteer nurse in Savannah's Confederate hospitals. Born in 1839, she was in her early twenties during the war. Her song, ideally played to the tune of "The Bonnie Blue Flag," describes Southern women who proudly wear homespun. Verses promote the wearing of homespun as a mark of Confederate patriotism, scorning the finery of pearls and diamonds worn by Northern ladies, admitting to the plainness of homespun but asserting that the act of wearing it makes a declaration of "what Southern girls for Southern rights will do." One verse in particular reads,

> We scorn to wear a bit of silk,
> A bit of Northern lace,

But make our homespun dresses up,
And wear them with a grace.[1]

The spirit of the song itself harkens back to a previous generation when the wearing of homespun made another similar political statement.

In the years leading up to America's separation from Britain in the eighteenth century, economic as well as political independence were in the forefront of the minds of citizens and early leaders. Up to this transitory phase into independence, America had been heavily entrenched in the British system of economy. Colonies were obligated to produce raw materials that would be shipped to Britain to be manufactured into finished goods, which would then be purchased by British subjects. Laws and restrictions on local manufacturing put the American colonies at a disadvantage, making economic independence a struggle in those early Revolutionary years. To make matters more difficult, Congress agreed that nonimportation and nonexportation efforts would

"The Southern Girl, or Homespun Dress" music sheet, published by A. E. Blackmar of New Orleans, 1865. *Library of Congress*

"obtain redress of these grievances, which threaten destruction to the lives, liberty, and property of his majesty's subjects in North America."[2] By

---

1 Arthur Palmer Hudson, "The Homespun Dress," in *Folksongs of Mississippi and Their Background* (Chapel Hill: University of North Carolina Press, 1936), 265–66 (can be accessed at https://www.civilwarpoetry.org/confederate/songs/homespun.html).

2 Worthington C. Ford, ed., *Journals of the Continental Congress, 1774–1789* (1904; repr., Washington, D.C., U.S. Government Printing Office, 1968), 75–80.

depriving Britain of the raw goods America provided, they hoped to wear down Parliament into negotiations.

On the flip side, cutting off America from foreign trade amped up the pressure on newly formed American manufacturers and mechanics—producers of finished products—to produce the goods needed for survival. This really didn't take off until after the Revolution, but until then, most manufacturing was done from the home by local families or artisans. Thus, an economic boycott of British goods was encouraged, and the homespun movement gained momentum. Language used to promote nonimportation and homespun—or general homemade goods—relied on ideas of virtue, saying that these efforts would suppress extravagance and promote frugality as colonists rejected foreign luxuries.[3] In essence, the wearing, production, and selling of homespun also declared independence from Britain as much as the Declaration did, politicizing the association with homespun. Seniors at Harvard College promised to wear homespun at graduation, despite the protests from the faculty saying that such an act would "inflame the minds of a true and loyal people" to the patriot cause for independence.[4] Accelerating the demand for domestic goods would then compel the creation of formal manufactures, and prevent the development of "a state of the most abject slavery" at the hands of the British or any other foreign entity.[5]

During the Civil War, a parallel can be seen in the secession of the South from the Union, both politically and economically, just as the American colonies separated from the mother country of Britain. These comparisons were made in contemporary times by Confederate sympathizers, declaring their own secession as a second revolution. However, historians now understand the act of secession and the initiation of a revolution to be two completely different movements. As Nathan Hall explains, "From the republic's beginnings, revolution was stated to be a universal human right,

---

[3] Lawrence A. Peskin, *Manufacturing Revolution: The Intellectual Origins of Early American Industry* (Baltimore: Johns Hopkins University Press, 2003), 37.

[4] Adam Anderson, *An Historical and Chronological Deduction of the Origins of Commerce* . . . (London, 1764; repr. New York, A. Kelley, 1967), xv.

[5] "Philo-Americanus," *New York Journal*, August 16, 1770, 2.

and secession a formal procedure of law."⁶ Due to the specialization of the agricultural industry in the South, citizens below the Mason-Dixon Line depended on the import of goods they did not have the infrastructure to produce, primarily from Northern industrial states and from abroad. As the conflict progressed, commerce with the North became just as difficult as trading with other countries like France and Britain as the blockading of seaports commenced. Likewise, cotton and other raw materials that were exported from the South would be missed by other countries that benefited from their trade and end up rotting on plantations or on port city docks. Just as during the Revolution, the lag in importing and exporting goods was predicted to aid the Southern cause, either by making it stronger in the way of building up domestic manufacturing on the basis of necessity, or by winning foreign recognition so the blockade might be challenged and exportation could resume.

Colonial kitchen with woman spinning, from *A Brief History of the United States* by Joel Dorman Steele and Esther Baker Steele, 1885. *Brief History of the United States*

Confederate leaders, like Congress during the Revolution, called for the South to become more economically independent as they also sought political independence.⁷ Just like during the Revolution, concepts of virtue and patriotism were presented to challenge any aversions to wearing or producing homespun. The *Southern Illustrated News* reported in 1862 that "not five out of five hundred ladies would be caught in the street in a homespun dress."⁸ In response, Confederate President Jefferson Davis

---

6 Doug Crenshaw and Nathan Hall, "Questions of Secession (Part One)," *Emerging Civil War* (blog), April 29, 2020, https://emergingcivilwar.com/2020/04/29/questions-of-secession-part-one/.

7 Drew Gilpin Faust, *Mothers of Invention: Women of the Slaveholding South in the American Civil War* (Chapel Hill: University of North Carolina Press, 1996), 45.

8 *Southern Illustrated News*, December 20, 1862.

called for women to set aside their vanity, stating that homespun was "becoming to them" and that they should "prove to the world that the Southern woman's principle and patriotism are not subordinate to the pride of the eye."[9] Coupled with the patriotic reasons for producing homespun, Davis hit on the idea that women viewed homespun as plain, unattractive, and least preferred against other fashionable styles of the day. This effort to appeal to women's preoccupation with fashion and appearance was nothing new. Decades earlier, Elkanah Watson understood the importance of women in the early republic textile industry and endeavored to appeal to women's presumed vanity by creating homespun "fashion shows" to be held at his agricultural fairs. These cloth shows were designed to cast women as both producers and consumers of American-made fabrics.[10]

In essence, the Confederate government instilled the economic and patriotic imperative to produce homespun goods and promoted thrifty lifestyle changes to compensate for their growing shortages. Necessity as much as patriotic fervor compelled women to bring out their spinning wheels from storage in order to spin and weave clothing for themselves, their families, and the soldiers in the field.

For the elite class of Southern women, this created a social and identity crisis, since the task of weaving and spinning were typically relegated to the enslaved or were associated with poorer women who had neither the means nor convenience of purchasing their clothes. Some soldiers, once they heard that their women were taking up the task, were outraged. Will Neblett told his wife, "I do not like the idea of your weaving. It is mortifying to me."[11] Other soldiers, as James Broomall covered so well in his book *Private Confederacies*, appreciated receiving clothing made by their loved ones, as it forged a connection with the home and family they left behind, and forged their identities as gentlemen soldiers.[12] Thomas Ruffin Jr. wrote, "[The men begged] that we shall try to get the materials, & have the clothing made at

---

9 *Milledgeville Confederate Union*, January 13, 1863.

10 Peskin, *Manufacturing Revolution*, 179.

11 Will Neblett to Lizzie Neblett, June 17, 1864, Lizzie Neblett Papers, Briscoe Center for American History, University of Texas, Austin, Texas.

12 James J. Broomall, *Private Confederacies: The Emotional Worlds of Southern Men as Citizens and Soldiers* (Chapel Hill: University of North Carolina Press, 2019), 36.

Adult silk dress made by Mary Evalina Toler, Virginia, 1861, on display in 2018 at the former Museum of the Confederacy in Richmond. *Sheritta Bitikofer*

home: & . . . they say that they can fight better in clothes made at home."[13]

The homespun movement hit numerous roadblocks. Those women who wished to take up the textile-making craft, but had never done so prior to the war, often lacked the instruction and tools necessary to do so. One unexpected shortage was in cotton cards, which were used to comb the fibers before spinning it into thread. Until the war, cotton cards had been produced outside the South, and the supply of cotton cards already within the Southern market began to dwindle as the war progressed. In the end, poor white and enslaved women who were already engaged in textile-making carried on with their production or increased their output, while women unfamiliar with the practice did not make a monumental impact in meeting the demand for textiles in the Confederacy. These women turned to purchasing more expensive goods that were run through the blockade, recycled old linens, or rehabilitated discarded garments to meet their needs.[14]

Instead of upping their homespun game, women took on knitting and sewing as their way of showing support for the soldiers in the field. Mary Gray remembered, "Many of us who had never learned to sew became

---

13 Thomas Ruffin Jr. to Thomas Ruffin, May 26, 1862, Box 30, Folder 450, Ruffin Papers, Southern Historical Collection, Wilson Library, University of North Carolina at Chapel Hill.

14 Faust, *Mothers of Invention*, 48–49.

expert handlers of the needle, and vied with each other in producing well-made garments; and I became a veritable knitting machine."[15] Others found the task more difficult but let their enthusiasm override their usefulness and sent deformed garments to the soldiers anyway.

While homespun didn't take off as it did during the Revolutionary War era—nor did it save the South from economic ruin—Southern women took pride in their ingenuity, and the concept of homespun became fixed in the iconography of the Confederate war effort.

The heavy emphasis on the nearly nonexistent homespun movement in Civil War memory can be traced back to the need to compare the Confederate cause to a greater, more recognized, and widely accepted event in American history. In their contemporary times, the people who participated in the American Revolution were seen as heroic, self-sacrificing, and virtuous. They were the epitome of patriotic success. The idea of following in their footsteps and enacting a "revolution" of their own was a strong arguing point in legitimizing secession from the Union. Homespun manufacturing was only one characteristic shared by both events, but the similarity was seized with both hands and incorporated into Confederate memory. The image of a Southern woman laboring over a spinning wheel for the cause of Southern independence transitioned beyond the wartime years, eventually wedging itself into the Lost Cause rhetoric alongside the more realistic images of women knitting socks for their soldiers and sewing patchwork dresses for their daughters.

One instance where this devotion to homespun in Confederate memory can be seen is in a South Carolina Confederate Veterans reunion in Orangeburg, which took place May 14–15, 1894. Here, Mrs. Louise Salley Hartwell—a granddaughter of Dr. Alexander S. Salley, a brigade surgeon in Brig. Gen. Joseph B. Kershaw's brigade—sang "The Homespun Dress" while wearing the subject of the ballad, a wartime homespun dress that had belonged to Mrs. Mary Ward of Spartanburg, South Carolina. The article that reported the event described that everything about the dress, from "the cotton from which it was woven and spun and the indigo, walnut and pine bark from which the dyes were made was produced on Mrs. Ward's

---

15 Mary Ann Harris Gay, *Life in Dixie during the War* (Atlanta: Constitution Job Office, 1862), 42.

 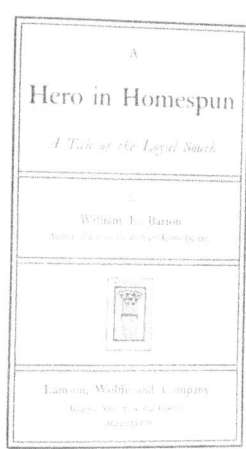

A Hero in Homespun, 1897, by William Eleazar Barton, published by Lamson, Wolffe and Company, Boston. *A Hero in Homespun*

plantation in Spartanburg County. The cloth was spun, woven and dyed at home, and this, a very pretty blue-and-tan plaid, was an 'everyday' dress."[16] The 500 veterans were moved to tears not only by her singing but by her appearance, likening her to "their old sweethearts." The article includes the lyrics to "The Homespun Dress" and an image of Miss Hartwell, evidence that the concept of homespun did not die with the war but continued in the hearts and minds of Southern veterans and civilians.

When looking at the big picture of social, political, and economic shifts in the South during the war, women's new responsibilities as caretakers of their homes and plantations, without the assistance of men, created a far more lasting impact than any level of undertaking in domestic manufacturing. Still, the comparison of national endeavors in self-sufficiency between the American Revolution and the Civil War are uncanny, in rhetoric if not in practice.

---

16 Reported by J. B. Lewis, of Anderson, SC, Adjutant General, South Carolina Division, UCV, "The Homespun Dress," *Confederate Veteran Magazine*, vol. 32, July 1924, 256.

by Meg Groeling

Originally published as a blog post at Emerging Civil War on December 13, 2011. The piece has become an annual ECW tradition, reposted each holiday season, and remains one of our all-time most popular posts.

The Christmas carol "I Heard the Bells On Christmas Day" was originally a poem. Written by Henry Wadsworth Longfellow, it was arranged and set to music by John Calkin, who took it upon himself to edit out two stanzas which refer directly to the Civil War, thereby creating yet another easily forgettable holiday musical offering and entirely gutting the meaning of the original 1863 work.

By that time, 1863, even the New England abolitionists were appalled by the amount of blood and violence their cause had created. Although the Emancipation Proclamation was signed on January 1, eight hundred thousand slaves outside the Confederacy were not covered under its authority. The War seemed no closer to ending than when it had started, despite Union victories at Gettysburg and Vicksburg. The summer of Union optimism had turned into its winter of discontent.

Henry Wadsworth Longfellow was already of bleak heart when his son was wounded during the Mine Run Campaign: Longfellow's wife had burned to death in a household accident in 1861. *Library of Congress*

Although Longfellow condemned slavery, he was not a fire-breathing abolitionist. He was, however, a close friend of Charles Sumner, who *was*. Sumner condemned "the peculiar institution" whenever and wherever he could, in harshest terms. Sumner delivered his infamous "Crime Against Kansas" speech on the floor of the Senate in May, 1856. This speech was particularly personal and inflammatory. Two days later, Preston Brooks, a Congressman from South Carolina and a cousin of one of the men insulted in the speech, approached Sumner and clubbed him over the head with his cane. Sumner was nearly killed.

Twelve years before, in 1842, Longfellow had published a thin book of poems for Sumner's group, The New England Anti-Slavery Association. Longfellow himself claimed that the poems were "so mild that even a Slaveholder might read them without losing his appetite for breakfast," but Sumner was satisfied with it, and the group reprinted it for further distribution.

Longfellow followed politics closely and, by 1860, realized that there must be some sort of resolution to the problems which beset the nation. His most famous poem, "Paul Revere's Ride," was written in time for a Christmas publication in *The Atlantic Monthly*. He hoped it would be a call for a new Revolution, although he, like so many Americans, never envisioned one so long and brutal.

Longfellow, like many in the country on both sides of the conflict, endured a significant amount of heartbreak during the war. The fall of Fort Sumter, the secession of the southern states, including Virginia, and Great Britain's declaration of neutrality were just some of the incidents that brought grief to the poet.

The most personal tragedy was the death of his wife, Fanny, in 1861. Her clothing caught fire (a frequent occurrence at the time, unfortunately) as she lit the household candles, and she was badly burned. She died the next day, sending the writer into a prolonged period of grief.

Two years later, their seventeen-year old son, Charles Appleton Longfellow, ran away and joined the Union Army. Initially, the distraught father did not know where to find his son. The young man had gone to Washington, D.C. to seek a friend, Captain W. H. McCartney, commander of the 1st Massachusetts Artillery. Not wanting to enlist the son of a family friend, McCartney wired Longfellow for permission for "Charley" to enlist. Patriotically, he gave it.

This was not the harebrained scheme of a teenager to get away from home and his father's preoccupation with the death of his mother. Charley wrote, "I have tried hard to resist the temptation of going without your leave, but I cannot any longer. I feel it to be my first duty to do what I can for my country and I would willingly lay down my life for it if it would be of any good."

The young man was soon promoted to lieutenant, and his first combat experience came at Chancellorsville. In June, Charley contracted typhoid and malaria, and was sent home to recover. He rejoined his unit on August 15, 1863.

On November 27, as part of the Mine Run Campaign in New Hope Church, Virginia, he was severely wounded by a bullet that entered his left shoulder, travelled across his back, nicked his spine, and exited the right shoulder. He was carried by ambulance to a field hospital on the Rapidan River, and then sent to a hospital in Washington. His recovery was not at all certain.

Longfellow learned of his son's injury on December 1, 1863, and left immediately, along with his younger son Ernest, to recover Charley. All during his journey to the capital, the father was not certain if he would be bringing back a wounded son, or a dead one.

In the midst of his sorrows—the War, a dead wife, a young family to raise alone, and a son who hovered near death—Longfellow thought of all the other households in the Union whose holidays were marred, some forever, by the events of the last three years. He did what writers do: he wrote. The resulting poem was the one we know as "I Heard the Bells On Christmas Day." The poem was not intended to join the pantheon of sugary sweet Christmas carols already in place.

There are two stanzas of the poem that never made it to the song we know today. They describe the effect of the War, and the sadness of the inhumanity it had caused, so antithetical to the spirit of Christmas. Below is the entire poem:

"Christmas Bells"

I heard the bells on Christmas Day
Their old, familiar carols play
And wild and sweet
The words repeat
Of peace on Earth, goodwill to men!

And thought how, as the day had come,
The belfries of all Christendom
Had rolled along
The unbroken song
Of peace on Earth, goodwill to men!

Till, ringing, singing on its way,
The world revolved from night to day,
A voice, a chime,
A chant sublime
Of peace on Earth, goodwill to men!

Then from each black, accursed mouth
The cannon thundered from the South,
And with the sound
The carols drowned
Of peace on Earth, goodwill to men!

It was as if an earthquake rent
The hearthstones of a continent,
And made forlorn
The households born
Of peace on Earth, goodwill to men!

And in despair I bowed my head;
"There is no peace on Earth, " I said:
"For Hate is strong,
And mocks the song
Of peace on Earth, goodwill to men!"

Then pealed the bells more loud and deep:
"God is not dead; nor doth He sleep!
The Wrong shall fail,
The Right prevail,
With peace on Earth, goodwill to men!

Charley survived, and by December 8, he was back in Cambridge to recover at home. He lived, but the wound was considered too severe to allow Lieutenant Longfellow to return to his unit. He was mustered out on February 15, 1864.

The Civil War in Surprising Places: The Pop Culture Delights of Emily Dickinson's Poetry

by Cecily Nelson Zander

Originally published as a blog post at Emerging Civil War on January 14, 2021

As a high school student, I always dreaded our annual Emily Dickinson poem assignment, because, to be honest, the nineteenth-century poet from Amherst, Massachusetts, never really spoke to me. One can only consider "Hope is the thing with feathers" so many times, after all. In graduate school, however, I underwent an attitude adjustment after taking a course entitled "One Hundred Years of American Poetry," which covered the 1830s to the Great Depression. I entered the class fully convinced that I would carry on with my Dickinson disdain, but then "A Bird Came Down the Walk" changed my mind. As Meg Groeling's excellent ECW series on Walt Whitman reminds us all, the Civil War had profound and unexpected effects on American literature.[1] These effects are visible in both the poetry and

---

[1] See Meg's "Weekly Walt Whitman" series, from October 2020–October 2021, at www.emergingcivilwar.com.

letters of Emily Dickinson, and are currently being delightfully investigated in the Apple TV+ series *Dickinson* (now in its second season).

Emily Dickinson
Library of Congress

The subject of the Civil War in American literature has been treated in a variety of ways. The works began with Edmund Wilson's *Patriotic Gore* (1962), a Lost Cause–tinged forebear of the "Dark Turn" in Civil War era studies. More recently, Timothy Sweet, Craig A. Warren, and Stephen B. Cushman have injected new life and ideas into Civil War literary studies.[2] There are, however, few monographs that treat Dickinson among the war poets or the war writers.[3] This is perhaps because Dickinson, like her contemporary Louisa May Alcott, wrote about the war from such a vast distance. It is hardly a coincidence that historians have paid far more attention to Southern women writers during the war—as they saw the conflict firsthand. Women like Dickinson and Alcott, meanwhile, had to treat the conflict far more abstractly. Alcott's *Little Women* can thus be viewed as both a work of Civil War literature and a perfect encapsulation of the experience of the Northern home front during the conflict. The war intrudes enough to make the plot interesting but causes no lasting damage to the March family (save for Jo's loss of her "one beauty" after a haircut undertaken to fund a train ticket to Washington for Marmee).

Emily Dickinson's writing production peaked during the Civil War (perhaps half her poems were drafted in the years 1861–65), though her poetry often shows little relation to the cataclysmic event. As was her wont, Dickinson tended to write about the Civil War via metaphor, but

---

2 Timothy Sweet, *Traces of War: Poetry, Photography, and the Crisis of the Union* (Baltimore: Johns Hopkins University Press, 1990); Craig A. Warren, *Scars to Prove It: The Civil War Soldier and American Fiction* (Kent, OH: Kent State University Press, 2009); Stephen Cushman, *Belligerent Muse: Five Northern Writers and How They Shaped Our Understanding of the Civil War* (Chapel Hill: University of North Carolina Press, 2017).

3 One notable exception is Shira Wolosky, *Emily Dickinson: A Voice of War* (New Haven, CT: Yale University Press, 1984).

she also contributed poems to a U.S. Sanitary Commission publication. They represented her small, personal contribution to the Union war effort.[4] Dickinson's brother Austin, meanwhile, paid $500 to hire a substitute to serve in his place rather than take part in the war himself.[5] During the war, Dickinson maintained a correspondence with Thomas Wentworth Higginson, the abolitionist literary critic who served as the colonel of the First South Carolina Volunteers, one of the first units of freedmen raised for Union service.

Despite the loose connections of their protagonist to the war, the producers of *Dickinson* have taken on the Civil War ably. The show begins its second season in the year 1859 ("it's almost the sixties," one character exclaims). Dickinson's first season introduced audiences to Emily and her family—older brother Austin, younger sister Lavinia, father Edward, and mother Emily (Em)—and the world of Amherst, where the arrival of the railroad is causing immense excitement and the Whig Party has selected Edward Dickinson as their candidate for Congress. Emily interacts, fancifully, with some of the leading literary lights of her era—including Louisa May Alcott and Henry David Thoreau (who isn't nearly the transcendentalist Emily thinks he is).

The show embraces the weird qualities of Dickinson's poetry—Death comes alive for Emily, and she speaks to a giant bee more than once—but it also delves deeply into the complex and rapidly changing politics and social culture of the 1850s. One standout episode from the first season is "We Lose—Because We Win," set on the day of the November hustings. Emily's father nervously awaits the result, which will tell of his successful election to Congress, worried that the Whig Party might be losing its grip on the district after a too-close-for-comfort race. Meanwhile, Lavinia and

---

4 "From the Stacks . . . Three Early Dickinson Publications," *Modern Books and Manuscripts* (blog), Houghton Library at Harvard University; https://blogs.harvard.edu/houghtonmodern/2009/06/03/earlydickinson/comment-page-1/.

5 There is an interesting history dealing with literary figures and the Civil War. Another New Englander and author, Henry James, avoided military service due to injuries sustained while serving in a volunteer fire company in 1861. His younger brothers Garth and Robertson both served. Henry James struggled with the Civil War in much of his writing and spent decades parsing his lack of participation, most famously in *Notes of a Son and Brother*. See Tess Hoffmann and Charles Hoffmann, "Henry James and the Civil War," *New England Quarterly* 64, no. 4 (December 1989): 529–52.

Emily gather with other young women from the village to cross-stitch and discuss the fact that "the Kansas-Nebraska Act was just a massive overreach on the part of the Slave Power." Lavinia explains that if she were allowed to vote, she would vote Republican. The girls also debate the possibility of secession, and Emily predicts that the nation is hurtling toward civil war, and that "one million men will die, and then a million snowflakes will fall on their graves." Meanwhile, the Dickinson's Irish maid tells Mr. Dickinson that her brothers were assaulted while trying to vote, by members of the anti-immigrant, anti-Catholic Know Nothing Party. Such small details make the series constantly delightful for anyone steeped in nineteenth-century history and literature.

In the first three episodes of Season 2, the audience meets a new character who will only tell Emily, "I'm Nobody." As it turns out, Nobody is a specter who haunts only Emily as she wrestles with whether to pursue fame and publish her poems. Nobody wears a white muslin shirt under a dark blue coat studded with brass buttons and lighter blue wool trousers. Emily believes she recognizes him from somewhere, but he refuses to tell her more. To the historian's eye, it appears that Nobody is a Union soldier with a serious warning for Emily about events to come. By season's end he is revealed to be Frazar Stearns, an Amherst college student and good friend of Emily's brother Austin who was killed at the battle of New Bern, in North Carolina, in 1862. Stearns's death likely prompted Emily to write a slate of her most explicit war poems—including "Victory Comes Late" and "To Know Just How He Suffered."

Anyone who enjoys pop culture with a historical bent will likely find something to enjoy in *Dickinson*, which satisfies not only visually and musically but also factually. And anyone who hasn't considered Emily Dickinson in a while, or who, like me, did not think they could find much to like in her poems, might think about her as a Civil War figure and a war chronicler. Though it did not touch her immediately, Emily's various responses to the war and her social circle's abiding investment in ideas about abolition, politics, and feminism, represent the degree to which the war (and its years of coming) pervaded deeply into the lives of ordinary people.

1. Uncle Remus, Brer Rabbit, and Their Continued Influence

by Ashley Webb

"Bred en bawn in a brier-patch, Brer Fox—bred en bawn in a brier-patch!" [yelled Brer Rabbit] en wid dat he skip out des ez lively ez a cricket in de embers.[1]

The ending to the folklore tale "How Mr. Rabbit Was Too Sharp for Mr. Fox," of Brer Rabbit and Brer Fox, above, is well known, regardless of where the reader has come across the tale. The entire story, which is comical in its forthright use of trickery and persuasion between the characters, has been passed down orally since before the Civil War, most likely stemming from the African continent. A teenage Joel Chandler Harris collected the stories between 1862 and 1866. Eleven years after the end of the Civil War, Harris noted the importance of these folktales, publishing and unintentionally ingraining them into Western pop culture for generations. His narrator, Uncle Remus, and the retelling of the folktales revolutionized children's literature and influenced countless authors and entertainers throughout the late nineteenth and twentieth centuries.

---

1 Joel Chandler Harris, *Uncle Remus, His Songs and His Sayings* (New York: D. Appleton and Company, 1895), 19.

Between 1862 and 1866, Joel Chandler Harris, a red-haired, shy, and illegitimate son of an Irish seamstress, ventured to Turnwold Plantation in Georgia, after dropping out of school in 1862. At Turnwold, Harris took a position working with owner Joseph Addison Turner to publish war news in *The Countryman*. During his free time, Harris visited with plantation slaves, whom he felt comfortable around after growing up as a pariah in the antebellum Georgia school system. Here he absorbed stories of Brer Fox, Brer Bear, Brer Wolf, and the trickster antics of Brer Rabbit.

It wasn't until 1876, ten years after he left Turnwold, that Harris published the first "Uncle Remus" story in the *Atlanta Constitution*. Originally, Harris's articles placed the Uncle Remus character in postwar Atlanta, having him "drop by" the *Constitution* offices to share anecdotes of life for Blacks during Reconstruction. Soon after, Harris saw an article in *Lippincott's Magazine* retelling many of the African-American folktales that he heard during his time at Turnwold. This sparked the start of a popular and influential series of folktales using the Southern African-American dialect and featuring the African folktales orally passed through generations of slaves. Two other individuals, Alcée Fortier and William Owens, both published works on the same folktales around a similar time frame, but neither received the publicity or critical acclaim that Harris received with the Turnwold renditions of Brer Rabbit.

The most well known of these tales, "The Wonderful Tar-Baby Story," followed up with "How Mr. Rabbit Was Too Sharp for Mr. Fox," both of which detail the story of Brer Fox as he creates a "contrapshun" made of tar and topped with a hat to catch Brer Rabbit. Uncle Remus describes how Brer Rabbit sees the Tar-Baby, says hello, and gets upset when the Tar-Baby never responds. Brer Rabbit proceeds to smack, hit, and kick the Tar-Baby until completely stuck. Brer Fox comes out of hiding behind the bushes, rolling on the ground laughing—excited that he finally caught Brer Rabbit. He contemplates how he's going to kill Brer Rabbit:

> 'I'm gwineter bobby-cue you dis day, sho,' sez Brer Fox, sezee. . . .
> 'I don't keer w'at you do wid me, Brer Fox,' sezee, 'so you don't fling me in dat brier-patch. Roas' me, Brer Fox' sezee, 'but don't fling me in dat brierpatch,' sezee.

"'Hit's so much trouble fer ter kindle a fier,' sez Brer Fox, sezee, 'dat I speck I'll hatter hang you,' sezee.

"'Hang me des ez high as you please, Brer Fox,' sez Brer Rabbit, sezee 'but do fer de Lord's sake don't fling me in dat brier-patch,' sezee.

"'I ain't got no string,' sez Brer Fox, sezee, 'en now I speck I'll hatter drown you,' sezee.

"'Drown me des ez deep ez you please, Brer Fox,' sez Brer Rabbit, sezee, 'but do don't fling me in dat brier-patch,' sezee.

"'Dey ain't no water nigh,' sez Brer Fox, sezee 'en now I speck I'll hatter skin you,' sezee.

"'Skin me, Brer Fox,' sez Brer Rabbit, sezee, 'snatch out my eyeballs, t'ar out my years by de roots, en cut off my legs,' sezee, 'but do please, Brer Fox, don't fling me in dat brier-patch,' sezee.

"Co'se Brer Fox wanter hurt Brer Rabbit bad ez he kin, so he cotch 'im by de behime legs en slung 'im right in de middle er de brier-patch. Dar wuz a considerbul flutter whar Brer Rabbit struck de bushes, en Brer Fox sorter hang 'roun' fer ter see w'at wuz gwineter happen. Bimeby [Brer Fox] hear somebody call 'im, en way up de hill he see Brer Rabbit settin' crosslegged on a chinkapin log koamin' de pitch outen his har wid a chip. . . . Brer Rabbit wuz bleedzed fer ter fling back some er his sass, en he holler out:

"'Bred en bawn in a brier-patch, Brer Fox—bred en bawn in a brier-patch!' [yelled Brer Rabbit] en wid dat he skip out des ez lively ez a cricket in de embers.[2]

With the *Lippincott's Magazine* article as the catalyst, Harris transitioned Uncle Remus to be the mouthpiece of Southern African Americans, keeping the same humor and veiled resistance to reconstruction, the war, and slavery as with the earlier Uncle Remus. Harris, who understood the importance of language and oral traditions, wrote his stories in dialect, preserving the nuances of African-American speaking patterns, colloquial phrases, and aspects of the African diaspora. In an introduction to his first edition of *Uncle Remus, His Songs and Sayings*, Harris wrote, "My purpose has

---

2 Ibid., 17–19.

been to preserve the legends themselves in their original simplicity, and to wed them permanently to the quaint dialect—if, indeed, it can be called a dialect—through the medium of which they have become a part of the domestic history of every Southern family; and I have endeavored to give to the whole a genuine flavor of the old plantation."³

Written in dialect, "Brother Rabbit" and "Brother Fox" became "Brer Rabbit" and "Brer Fox." *Library of Congress*

In the fictionalized autobiography *On the Plantation* (1892), Harris related his time on Turnwold Plantation, placing many of the tales in an antebellum setting. Northerners craved the unfamiliar visions of the South prior to the Civil War, and Southerners craved what they saw as humor, but what Harris saw was a way to "undermine racism . . . during the South's most viciously racist era."⁴ In writing in dialect, Harris was able to veil his opinions on the failures of Reconstruction and the treatment of African Americans. This phonetic transcription influenced other writers such as Mark Twain, Zora Neale Hurston, William Faulkner, Ralph Ellison, and Toni Morrison.

The difficulty in reading the dialect along with Harris's veiled opinions of slavery and Reconstruction under the guise of Brer Rabbit didn't affect its popularity. In 1880, Harris's first volume of tales, *Uncle Remus, His Songs and Sayings*, sold 7,000 copies within its first month.⁵ Brer Rabbit and Brer Fox became household names, and Mark Twain commented that despite his

---

3 Ibid., vii.

4 Wayne Mixon, "The Ultimate Irrelevance of Race: Joel Chandler Harris and Uncle Remus in Their Time," *Journal of Southern History* 56, no. 3 (August 1990): 461, http://www.jstor.org/stable/2210286 (accessed October 5, 2016).

5 Robert Cochran, "Black Father: The Subversive Achievement of Joel Chandler Harris," *African American Review* 38, no. 1 (Spring 2004): 21, http://www.jstor.org/stable/1512229 (accessed October 1, 2016).

shyness and lack of public persona, Harris was an "oracle of the nation's nurseries."[6] Little did Harris know that the relatable anthropomorphic characters of Brer Rabbit and Brer Fox would not only revolutionize early twentieth-century children's literature but would regale wartime children through cartoons, and provide thrills and chills to millennials via none other than Disney World.

Harris's publications and retelling of the Brer Rabbit tales sparked a frenzy, not only for more trickster tales but for more humanlike animal characters. The idea of anthropomorphism in tales wasn't original: The Brothers Grimm translated their fairy tales into English in 1823, Hans Christian Andersen published his tales in the 1830s, and Lewis Carroll published *Alice in Wonderland* in 1865. However, the foreignness, yet relatability, of Harris's characters pushed Brer Rabbit into a different realm than the folktales of Europe. Brer Rabbit, who is cunning and humorous, when placed into the setting of everyday human life, altered children's literature along with the concept of make-believe in post-antebellum childhood. As a result, Brer Rabbit directly influenced Beatrix Potter (*The Tale of Peter Rabbit*, 1902) and Rudyard Kipling (*The Jungle Book*, 1894), which then trickled down to Kenneth Graham (*The Wind in the Willows*, 1908) and A. A. Milne (*Winnie the Pooh*, 1923)—all legends in early twentieth-century children's literature.

"Brer Rabbit Steals Brer Wolf's Fish"—a sketch by Beatrix Potter that looks much like another mischievous rabbit Potter would become well known for. The Trustees of The Linder Collection and the Victoria & Albert Museum, London

---

6 Mark Twain, *Life on the Mississippi* (Boston: James R. Osgood and Company, 1883), 471, in *Documenting the American South*, http://docsouth.unc.edu/southlit/twainlife/twain.html (accessed October 7, 2016).

Since Brer Rabbit's initial debut in 1876, and after the folktales' first round of publishing in 1880, Joel Chandler Harris wrote an additional 185 stories involving Brer Rabbit, Brer Fox, and the rest of the gang. In 1893, Beatrix Potter illustrated a series of eight Brer Rabbit tales to be published in a reprint. Potter loved the idea of the prey outsmarting the predator, as well as the way Harris "turned the ordinary into extraordinary."[7] Later the same year, Potter detailed her first illustration of Peter Rabbit in a letter to a sick family friend. Peter Rabbit was not a trickster like Brer Rabbit—Peter escaped on sheer luck—but Potter's initial illustrations of Brer Rabbit set the stage for Peter and Benjamin Bunny. Additionally, Potter's "The Tale of Mr. Tod" is a modified version of Uncle Remus's tale "The Awful Fate of Mr. Wolf."

While Beatrix Potter never publicly claimed that Brer Rabbit influenced the Peter Rabbit tales, Rudyard Kipling acknowledged the impact of Brer Rabbit on his own stories. Kipling, author of *The Jungle Book*, was directly influenced by Harris's publications as a teenager in England. In December of 1895, Kipling sent a copy of *The Second Jungle Book* to Harris, declaring that his debt to Harris was long-standing. Kipling wrote,

> I wonder if you could realize how "Uncle Remus," his sayings, and the sayings of the noble beasties ran like wild fire through an English public school when I was about fifteen. We used to go to battle (with boots and bolsters and such-like) against those whom we did not love, to the tune of Ty-yi-tungalee: I eat um pea, I pick um pea, etc., and I remember the bodily bearing into a furze-bush of a young [boy] solely because his nickname had been "Rabbit" before the tales invaded the school and—well, we assumed that he ought to have been "bawn an' bred in a briar-patch," and gorse was the most efficient substitute.[8]

The humanlike characteristics of animals continued to make an impact, not only through books, but in comic books, cartoons, movies, and other

---

7 Linda Lear, *Beatrix Potter: A Life in Nature* (London: Macmillan, 2008), 131.

8 Julia Collier Harris, *The Life and Letters of Joel Chandler Harris* (New York: AMS Press, 1918), 334–35.

forms of popular entertainment in the late nineteenth and early twentieth centuries. Bugs Bunny, who made his debut in 1940, is a direct descendant of Brer Rabbit. With World War II occupying many people's minds, children needed an underdog who could serve as a distraction from the war. Much like Brer Rabbit outsmarted Brer Fox, Bugs would outwit Elmer Fudd, Wile E. Coyote, Daffy Duck, Yosemite Sam, and countless others using the same powers of persuasion. Looney Tunes episodes involving Bugs Bunny are still televised today, further solidifying the legacy of Brer Rabbit.

In 1946, the popularity of Uncle Remus changed. Walt Disney (1901–66) created *Song of the South*, a live action/animation film depicting Uncle Remus and Brer Rabbit. Disney's Uncle Remus doled out life lessons to the movie's main character, Little Johnny, which coincided with catchy songs such as "Zip-a-Dee-Doo-Dah." About creating the film, Walt Disney remarked, "There is something endlessly appealing and satisfying in Joel Chandler Harris' droll fables of animals who behave like humans. . . . I was familiar with the Uncle Remus tales since boyhood. From the time I began making animated features, I have had them definitely in my production plans. But until now, the medium was not ready to give them an adequate film equivalent in scope and fidelity."[9]

The movie brought in $3.4 million to the box office and ranked higher than *It's a Wonderful Life* in *Variety* magazine's "Top Grossers of 1947."[10] The depiction and direction of the film, while perhaps not intentional, never initially stated the date the movie was portraying, giving the impression of perpetuating the institution of slavery and, alternatively, echoing Lost Cause sentiments. This, along with the portrayal of the film's hierarchy of whites and Blacks, created controversy. Despite its high-grossing stay in the theater, the movie was poorly received by critics as well as with the African-American community. The NAACP and other civil rights groups picketed theaters throughout the country, using the film as a stepping stone to target the larger issue of racism. This controversy over *Song of the South* continues

---

9 Walt Disney, *Walt Disney Presents "Song of the South"* (New York: RKO Pictures, 1946), 13.

10 "Top Grossers of 1947," *Variety* 169, no. 5 (January 1948): 63, http://www.archive.org/stream/variety169-1948-01#page/n0/mode/2up (accessed October 20, 2016).

today. The movie received its last limited release in the 1970s and has yet to return to the public eye from the Disney vault.

Despite the poor reception of the movie, Disney's pre-release Sunday cartoon strip, *Uncle Remus & His Tales of Brer Rabbit*, continued to run until 1972. Comic books, Little Golden Books, and larger illustrated volumes capitalized on the household popularity of Disney and Brer Rabbit, retelling many of the stories without the iconic Uncle Remus. Additionally, Disney's version of Brer Rabbit continues to play a part throughout Disney theme parks. In 1989, Disney World's Magic Kingdom introduced Splash Mountain, a whirlwind water ride adventure in which park designers modified "The Wonderful Tar-Baby Story," the ending of which is detailed at the start, to encompass a more politically correct harrowing adventure with Brer Fox, Brer Bear, and Brer Rabbit. The ride details the story of *Song of the South*, without Uncle Remus, and includes songs, animatronic scenes, and a grand finale plunging riders down a steep drop into a briar patch. California's Disneyland, Japan's Disneyland Tokyo, and Florida's Magic Kingdom had variations of the Splash Mountain attraction. In 2022, Disney finally announced a reimagining of the ride based on another of its movies, *Princess and the Frog*.

Although Harris's work is now considered controversial, fueled and further facilitated by Walt Disney's *Song of the South*, Harris preserved African-American folklore, dialect, and diaspora, capturing items that would otherwise largely be forgotten. Harris not only popularized each of these after the Civil War but ingrained the stories throughout both the North and Reconstruction South. Additionally, the popularity of the tales created lasting effects on popular culture today, as seen throughout children's literature, cartoons, and even amusement parks. Not only have the African folktales and regional Georgian dialects been preserved, but the folktales remain alive 150 years later.

1. The Book I Threw
(and Then Picked Up Again)

by Sarah Kay Bierle

First published as a blog post at Emerging Civil War on August 18, 2020

The first book I ever threw across a room? *The Red Badge of Courage* by Stephen Crane. (Assigned reading in high school literature class.) That afternoon started a little journey of reality and history—I just didn't know it when I pitched the book.

Henry Fleming, the fictional young soldier in a fictional Union regiment in the battle of Chancellorsville, irritated me to no end when I first read the book as a teenager. Fleming did not fit my ideal of a Civil War soldier. He was a coward. He had no religious faith. And then spent half the book rationalizing his flight from the battle lines and his regimental comrades. The Civil War soldiers I had read about were all perfectly brave. The story was just a story, and it did not fit with how I thought battle happened for a soldier, so after I finished the class work, I promptly pitched the story from my mind. That book was just about a confused soldier who ran away and badly represented real guys in blue or gray.

Or was it? Fast-forward. I read a lot more history books and primary sources and started getting an idea that battle was a fearful, confused experience for most Civil War soldiers. They did not understand a fight with the details that researchers and arm-chair historians enjoy. A soldier did not experience battle with his regiment as nice, orderly little lines on a map. But it took me an embarrassingly long time to understand that.

The Red Badge of Courage came up in an ECW conversation one year at the symposium. I gave an inward shudder at the title, but then almost fell off my chair when Chris Mackowski started talking about how he appreciated the novel and its battle descriptions. Something must be wrong! Either we did not read the same book or I must have really missed something. Intrigued, I decided to revisit the story.

Ten years after I threw the book across the room, I opened another copy and felt like I was reading it for the first time. No, Henry Fleming will never be my favorite literary character (I feel pretty safe writing that), but the story of the common soldier and the confusion of battle came through the pages so clearly and matched words or episodes from primary sources. It was a piece of literary brilliance and it had historical backing.

Stephen Crane published *The Red Badge of Courage* in serialized form in 1894 and as a novel the following year. Born in 1871, he had no first-hand experience of the Civil War or even combat. However, he listened to stories from Civil War veterans which most critics believe influenced his war novel. By stripping away the need to wonder if the regiment was real and if the details were one hundred percent accurate, Crane lets the reader focus on "The Youth" (Henry Fleming) and his handful of comrades in a company in a very green regiment. It's not a history of the Chancellorsville Campaign or a regimental history. The novel becomes a study in the feelings and emotions of war, from questioning, fears, self-preservation, shame, and conviction toward redemption, acceptance, courage, passion, patriotism, and self-realization.

While it should be noted that many Civil War soldiers did not run away from their regiment in battle like Private Fleming, their letters and journals reflect the range of feelings and even statements like "I would run if I could." Desertion or cowardice was handled severely if the soldier was caught; execution, hard labor, drumming out of the regiment, or other creative punishments could follow, depending on the unit and the commanding officers. Sometimes fear of losing reputation among comrades or the rumors that would get back to a hometown was enough to keep a soldier in the

The Book I Threw (and Then Picked Up Again) 195

ranks. Other times, the patriotic ideas or "band of brothers" comradeship held a soldier to his post of duty.

The micro-details of history woven into the story give a color and authentic feel, again reflective of the real soldiers' lives in camp, on the march, in battle, and recovering in the aftermath of a fight. The descriptions of the "snap-shots" of the battle scenes also challenge a reader to ponder what privates saw in the battle smoke. For example:

> In another direction he saw a magnificent brigade going with the evident intention of driving the enemy from a wood. They passed in out of sight and presently there was a most awe-inspiring racket in the wood. The noise was unspeakable. Having stirred this prodigious uproar, and, apparently finding it too prodigious, the brigade, after a little time, came marching airily out again with its fine formation in nowise disturbed. There were no traces of speed in its movements. The brigade was jaunty and seemed to point a proud thumb at the yelling wood.
>
> On a slope to the left there was a long row of guns, gruff and maddened, denouncing the enemy, who, down the woods, were forming for another attack in the pitiless monotony of conflicts. The round red discharges from the guns made a crimson flare and a high, thick smoke. Occasional glimpses could be caught of groups of toiling artillerymen. In the rear of this row of guns stood a house, calm and white, amid bursting shells. A congregation of horses, tied to a long railing, were tugging frenziedly at their bridles. Men were running hither and thither.
>
> The detached battle between the four regiments lasted for some time. There chanced to no interference, and they settled their dispute by themselves. They struck savagely and powerfully at each other for a period of minutes, and the lighter-hued regiments faltered an drew back, leaving the dark-blue lines shouting. The youth could see the two flags shaking with laughter amid the smoke remnant.

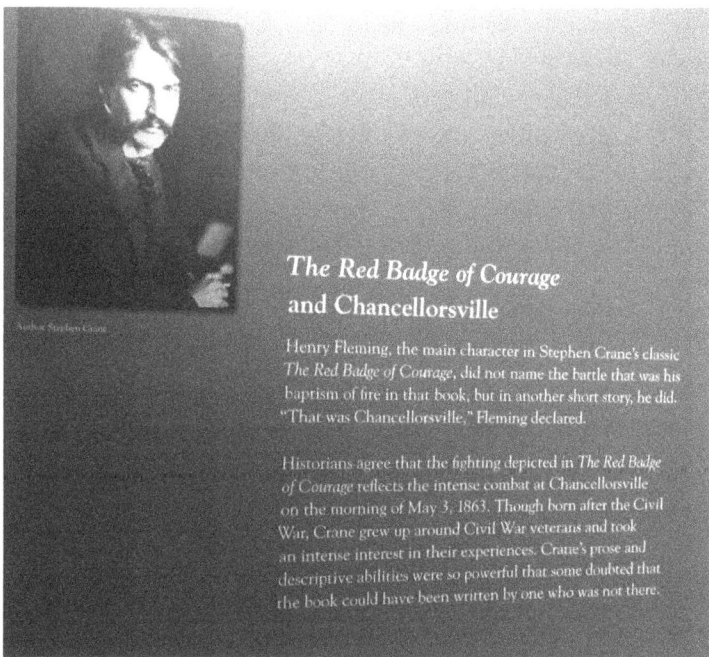

An exhibit at the Chancellorsville Battlefield visitor center details the connections between Crane's story and the May 1863 battle of Chancellorsville. The panel mentions another Crane short story, "The Veteran," in which *Red Badge*'s protagonist also appears. *Chris Mackowski*

So why did I hate this book for ten years and think of it only as the book I'd thrown across the room? Looking back, I find Henry Fleming as the example of my own "misconduct." Like "The Youth," I wanted war to be glorious and that's the way I thought it was when I was in my teens. Similar to Henry's flight and discovery of the red road with staggering wounded, a post-college study on Gettysburg field hospitals shattered that idea of glorious war for me. Later and hundreds of research pages further, the idea of an orderly battle experience for the common soldier was swept away. That next time I picked up the story to re-read it, my notions about what I thought the Civil War was had already been dismantled and I could appreciate the literary journey and concept of combat emotion and limited point of view which is ultimately mirroring the experiences of real soldiers.

I have to confess. I've spent the summer of 2020 engrossed in studying *The Red Badge of Courage*, and it's been an interesting season to approach the story for a third time. Already prepared to appreciate the story, I was able to look closer at what the author accomplished and how the tale can be a powerful teaching point and discussion starter for topics like Civil War medicine, battle for the common soldier, and the Chancellorsville campaign.

While it's been an enjoyable literary and historical experience, it's also been a positive reminder that it can be helpful to go back and re-look at the books or situations we thought we hated. Does a deeper understanding grow an appreciation? Or at minimum give a more nuanced perspective? I find myself challenged to be less quick to judge, more open to listening and learning, and then making informed theories or thought positions.

Thankfully, an ECW colleague unknowingly pushed me to re-read *The Red Badge of Courage,* allowing me to revise my opinion formed in my high-school "wisdom." Have you experienced something like this in your history journeys? Finding that notions change as time and research goes on. Was it a good feeling? Slightly regretful? Or a "break-through" moment for you?

Andersonville Offers Wonderful Writing Amidst Horrific Suffering

by Chris Mackowski

Originally published as a blog post at Emerging Civil War on April 27, 2017

Every so often as we read, we writers run into a sentence that is so spot-on perfect that we say, "Damn, I wish I'd written that." Such writer-envy is not uncommon, and at its heart, it springs from a deep appreciation for fine craft.

I recently came across just such as sentence as I was reading MacKinlay Kantor's novel *Andersonville*.[1]

Published in 1955, *Andersonville* tries to capture the uncapturable: life inside the infamous Confederate prison known as Camp Sumter. The novel won the Pulitzer Prize for fiction the following year.

One of Kantor's strengths as a writer is his characterization—not just the way he describes his characters but the way he makes them sympathetic through their personal stories. As I read one such character sketch, I came across one of those writer-envy sentences.

At the beginning of Chapter XXXI, Kantor introduces an Irish priest, Father Peter Whelan, who has been ministering to the imprisoned men.

---

1 The edition I'm reading is a tenth-printing paperback from 1964 published by Signet Books. The edition I'm citing is the 60th anniversary edition issued in 2016 by Plume.

Kantor has mentioned Whelan once before in the novel, but because Andersonville is largely a series of episodic character sketches, Whelan finally gets his due to step into center stage for a bit. His is a man who "went into death when he slept" because he worked so ceaselessly. "He must hasten," Kantor writes, "he must treat far and pray long, he must not let the flames sear the young pale souls which had been caged within rotting ribs and horny skin, but which would soon be freed." He is so rushed, he employs the short form for all his prayers and rites. "It is a sadness but— Give it, give it— Quickly— "[2]

It is within this context that I stumbled across what was, for me, a pitch-perfect sentence that made me go, "Damn, I wish I'd written that":

> Father Peter Whelan was a very old man, aging a year each day he served in Andersonville.

Can you even *imagine* the weight on this man? And Kantor captured it in one single, brilliant sentence.

Damn, I wish I'd written that sentence.

Aside from his extended scene in Chapter XXXI, Whelan plays a central role a short time later in Chapter XXXIII when the "Raiders" are executed for their crimes against their fellow prisoners. Predatory gangs of toughs that ruled through violence, the Raiders were led by six notoriously brutal "bosses." The one Kantor writes about most, Willie Collins, is such a vile human being that I felt the same burning for justice and blood that the wretched men in the stockade felt. Confederate authorities let the prisoners finally try and sentence—and execute—the ringleaders. Whelan tried desperately to minister to them on their way to the gallows.

The scene as Kantor writes it strongly evokes a Palm Sunday reading of the Passion, with a chanting crowd, prayers of intercession, and a Pontius Pilate-like Henry Wirz, commandant of the prison, trying to absolve himself of any guilt. "To you I now return these men, good as I got them," he decrees. "You say you try them yourself, you find them guilty. Nothing do I have to do with this—it is you, you prisoners."[3] The entire episode, which comes about halfway through the novel, is wonderfully crafted.

---

2 Father Whelan's quotes come from, respectively, pp. 328, 330, 331, 328. I didn't want to insert them into the text because I thought they'd disrupt the flow too much.

3 pg. 353.

Most of the chapters read like self-contained episodes unto themselves, interspersed with chapters about several recurring characters, real and fictional. Kantor's version of Wirz, for instance, has a sympathetic side to him as a man in way over his head, nagged by an unhealed war injury, still trying to do the best he can; at other times, he's as comically cross-tempered as a spastic Donald Duck who can only swear and sputter ill-humoredly. (Wirz's boss, on the other hand, Confederate Gen. John H. Winder, is truly a despicable human being made of bile and spite.)

Or take a skulky Union prisoner named "Chickamauga":

> His protruding eyes, green as peas, would glow devilishly. . . . [H]e had the sort of deformed lip which made it impossible for him to enunciate with complete clarity. . . . Chickamauga talked to anyone, everyone, jabbering on in every waking moment. . . . It was difficult to believe that he had come to exist through the natural process of conception and birth and growth; it was as if he were a changeling from a Grimm tale, delivered by a troop of elves, and wicked elves at that. It was impossible to believe that anyone had ever loved him, and yet somewhere sometimes someone must have kissed his horrid face and held him tenderly.[4]

Beyond his compelling characterization, Kantor's writing often shines when he offers description, although it always seems to catch me off guard. That might sound contradictory, but it demonstrates Kantor's ability to surprise and delight the reader—no small thing with a topic as grim as Andersonville. Take these two lines that have both just hung with me days after I first read them:

> Low in the west a bent flake of moon was receding and would soon be gone.[5]

> He had a mane of hair black as a crow's back at midnight in the dark of the moon.[6]

---

4 pp. 221-2.

5 pg. 393.

6 pg. 455.

A flake of moon. A crow's back at midnight in the dark of the moon. Damn, I wish I'd written those things. What a pleasure to read the work of a writer who can show me the world in such ways.

I'm just reveling in good writing here—and I want to urge you to revel in it, too. *Andersonville* is one of those novels we've all heard of, and many of us have probably seen the old Ted Turner production from TNT, but I wonder how many Civil War buffs have actually read it. I assure you, it is a novel worth revisiting: even after sixty years, it still holds up wonderfully well. As ugly as Andersonville was, *Andersonville* offers much that's amazing.

Of the 45,000 Union soldiers imprisoned at Andersonville during its 14-month window of operation, some 13,000 died. A monument in Andersonville National Cemetery captures the grief of the suffering. It is one of twelve monuments in the cemetery; another eleven stand in the site of the former prison. "Because so little remains of the historic prison," says a National Park Service wayside, "the monuments form a prominent part of the Andersonville landscape." *Chris Mackowski*

Thoughts on Madame Castel's Lodger

by Sean Michael Chick

Originally published as a blog post at Emerging Civil War on October 8, 2018

New Orleans has produced a fair number of notable authors, in particular George Washington Cable, John Kennedy Toole, and Anne Rice. However, it is more famous as the inspiration for writers of the first rank: Thomas "Tennessee" Williams III, William Faulkner, Mark Twain, and Truman Capote to name but a few. Its unique cultural mixture attracts people looking for something different. Many are drawn to whatever is en vogue, given whatever the era's proclivities might be.

New Orleans has often changed how it sells itself to the world. Before the 20th Century, it was gambling and commerce. Today, it is culture, whether it is food, music, architecture, or the night life. I was born in 1982, during the transition away from the city selling itself as the Creole version of the Old South and towards a depiction of the city as a Cajun outpost. Atlanta sold *Gone with the Wind* memorabilia, but we sold steamboat cruises, plantation tours, and antebellum artifacts. This is when the Garden District became a major tourist attraction.

The wellspring of this type of history was Grace King, who during the Gilded Age and Progressive Era, wrote about grand Creole families.

Whatever her faults, King remains a wealth of anecdotes and family trees. The descendants of the great founding families such as Marigny, Toutant-Beauregard, de la Ronde, Villeré, and the rest draw much of their family knowledge from King. For many, this was the "real" New Orleans.

This era was epitomized by the novels written by Virginia native Frances Parkinson Keyes. She was one of the first popular female authors of the twentieth century and counted Franklin Roosevelt among her fans. She wrote some sixty novels, memoirs, and travelogues from 1918 to 1970. Many of them were about New Orleans. In 1944, she bought a fine French Quarter home at 1113 Chartres Street that was the postwar lodging of Gen. P. G. T. Beauregard. She renovated it and made sure it would operate as a museum after her death. Today, it is the Beauregard-Keyes House.

Keyes was obsessed with Beauregard's story and, in the 1940s, started writing a novel about his life. In 1962, *Madame Castel's Lodger* was published to positive reviews. It represents one of the last literary blushes of the Lost Cause mythology.

There is hardly a plot in *Madame Castel's Lodger*. Beauregard returns from the war and rents a room from Simone Castel. They are attracted to each other but do nothing about it; Keyes was a moralist at heart, although given to romantic flourishes. Instead, Beauregard recounts his life to various people in a strict chronological order. There is a fictional subplot about Beauregard trying to find Lance Castel, a soldier in the Orleans Guard Battalion who has been missing since Shiloh. Lance is found, but it is a moment wholly lacking in drama.

The book's lack of drama can be seen in the book covers, which often contradicted the narrative. The American hardback simply showed the house. The British edition showed an incorrect house but depicted one of the best scenes in the book, when Beauregard comes to seek lodging. Paperbacks depicted scenes that never occurred: steamboats, carriage traffic jams, and even moss-covered romantic meetings with a Confederate officer who looks like Ashley Wilkes. Just try to imagine Beauregard blonde and clean shaven.

The Lost Cause elements are of the moonlight and magnolias variety. Indeed, Keyes even has Beauregard defending this, saying it was real and not a myth. Issues of race and slavery are dodged. The central Lost Cause facet is the idea of rebuilding Southern society after the war—in this case, getting a job. Gone are the politics and the tumult, replaced with a dull subplot about getting employment. Beauregard's internal debate about

To have the book covers tell the story, P. G. T. Beauregard was quite the breathy bodice-ripper during his stay as *Madame Castel's Lodger*. While is postwar career was indeed marred by scandal, they were not *that* kind of scandal. *Author's Collection*

whether to ask for a pardon, which he grappled with, is mostly missing. On the better end, Lost Cause villains Benjamin Butler and William Tecumseh Sherman are portrayed in a more complex light.

It might seem cheap to dismiss the book's limitations from our vantage point; my main issue was the lack of plot, for the book is mostly a kind of Beauregard biography. The ideas of memory and loss are explored but not in depth. Where the book is of some interest is Keyes's attention to detail. Her sense of Louisiana geography is superb, no minor thing for me. I was raised on Hollywood movies where New Orleans is just the French Quarter and the swamp, with nothing in between. Keyes loved romance and old Creole families, and those are best parts. Her attention to detail in this regard is superb, and I actually learned some family lore from the novel. Keyes was friends with Beauregard's granddaughter, Laure Beauregard Larendon, and repeated some family stories. Keyes's mistakes are more apparent in recalling Beauregard's military career, but even then, they are more minor than damning. Keyes is also good for finding graves and plantation names. She even copied some letters and grave inscriptions that are today so worn down as to be unreadable.

Unfortunately, Keyes did not get to the heart of the matter. She was perceptive in understanding Beauregard's dreams but not his limitations.

His personal blemishes are absent. He was not kind to the memory of his second wife, Caroline Deslondes. He was deeply jealous of Robert E. Lee. He could be exceedingly petty and mean, and in *Madame Castel's Lodger* he is neither. He is instead a nearly perfect Creole gentleman, undone by fate more than his own hand. Both of his wives die, Louisiana secedes, and he runs afoul of Jefferson Davis—and in each case, he has no choice in the narrative. In reality, he did. He could have been better to Caroline, stayed loyal to the U.S., and not feuded with Davis. All of this is the stuff of tragedy, of a talented man making bad or at least difficult choices. Keyes instead went in for melodrama.

Keyes's Creole Old South is almost gone as a part of New Orleans's popular memory. In her day, the emphasis was on powerful Creole families made up of grand eccentrics who could recall off-hand, their European lineages, mostly French and Spanish, with the occasional person from England, Portugal, Belgium, and Italy finding their way into the family tree. This was not the world of Anglo-Americans coming to make money, nor that of the poor Irish, Germans, and Italians who streamed into the city. Most importantly, it was a version of Creole life divorced from its African influences and blood relations. For Keyes, King, and the rest, the "real" New Orleans was a white Creole past that emphasized the colonial era. Today, New Orleans sells itself in part as a center of African-American culture. One person I know designed a shirt that says, "Everything you love about New Orleans is because of black people." We sell ourselves not as a Southern city or one on the outskirts of Cajun country, but as the "northernmost Caribbean city."

King and Keyes have their uses and their limitations. If they fundamentally erred, it was in thinking they knew the "real" New Orleans. Today's historians and artists often mock King and Keyes. I have heard many tour guides scoff at King as saccharine and privileged. Keyes is all but forgotten except for the odd reference to her only work still in circulation, *Dinner at Antoine's*. They are ignored, while others pursue a new version of the "real" New Orleans, one that will inevitably be eclipsed by another type of authenticity we sell to ourselves and the world.

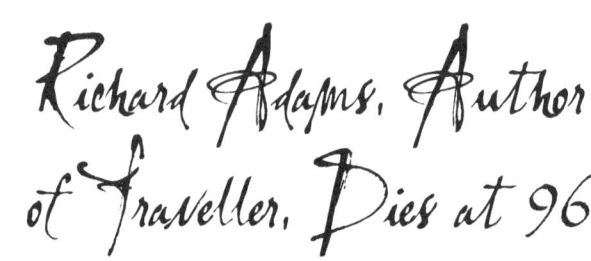

Richard Adams, Author of Traveller, Dies at 96

by Chris Mackowski

Originally published as a blog post at Emerging Civil War on December 28, 2016

While most of the pop culture world was mourning the death this week of *Star Wars'* Princess Leia and '80s pop icon George Michael, I heard the quieter news of the death of one of my favorite authors, Richard Adams. Best known for his novel *Watership Down*, Adams also authored a book known to many fans of Civil War–related literature, *Traveller* (1988), which tells the tale of Robert E. Lee's famous gray horse.

Starting in the spring of 1866, Traveller is stabled on the campus of Washington College (now Washington & Lee University), where he enjoys a quiet retirement, while "Marse Robert" serves as president of the college. In memoir-like fashion, the horse tells his life story to a pair of cats, Nippy and Baxter, owned by one of Lee's daughters, Mildred. Written in a kind of southern dialect—by an Englishman, no less—the book is sometimes tricky to read, but it's a pleasant and creative tale. *Kirkus Reviews* called it an "inventive and affecting blend of historical chronicle and animal fable that gallops right into the heart of beast, man, and war."[1]

---

1 "Traveller," *Kirkus Reviews*, May 15, 1988. https://www.kirkusreviews.com/book-reviews/a/richard-adams-12/traveller/ (accessed 30 November 2022).

Richard Adams reads from his best-known work, *Watership Down*, in 2008. Andrew Reeves-Hall

To research his novel, Adams relied heavily on sources well known to most Civil War buffs: *Recollections and Letters of General Robert E. Lee*; *General Lee, 1861–1865*, by Walter Taylor; *Memoirs of Robert E. Lee: His Military and Personal History*, by A. L. Long; and *Personal Reminiscences*, by J. William Jones. He also leaned on Douglas Southall Freeman's *R. E. Lee*—which he "most enjoyed"—and Charles Bracelen Flood's *Lee: The Last Years*.[2]

"Anecdotes of Lee and Traveller are, of course, innumerable," Adams wrote in the author's note of his book.[3]

To get inside Traveller's head, so to speak, he drew on the research of Lucy Rees's *The Horse's Mind*.

Unfortunately, *Traveller* remains the only one of Adams's major novels that's gone out of print. Paperback and ebook versions are available for his other major books, *Watership Down* (1972), *Shardik* (1974), *The Plague Dogs* (1977), and *Tales from Watership Down* (1996), with nearly a dozen other minor works also published during that time through 2010.

Like most of his fans, I came to his work through *Watership Down*, a tale about a group of wild rabbits driven from their home. The book follows their quest to establish a new home. He invented the story for his daughters, told to them just before bedtime. Eventually, they persuaded him to write the stories into book form. Six publishers rejected the manuscript before it was finally picked up—and then it became a worldwide phenomenon. Although originally a children's take, he claimed it was appropriate for kids from nine to ninety—an assessment millions of adults would agree with.

So, I first came to *Traveller* in the late '80s as a Richard Adams fan, not as a Civil War buff. I read the novel as a fan of good writing and

---

2 Richard Adams, "Notes and Acknowledgments," *Traveller* (Alfred A. Knopf, 1988).

3 Ibid.

interesting stories, not as someone interested in history or Civil War-related literature. I've carted that paperback with me through college and three subsequent graduate degrees, two children, eight relocations, and into a second marriage. The book is, as you might imagine, a little worn on the cover with small flecks and nicks, and a pair of water stains blossom across the closed page edges.

To be honest, it's been so long since I've read the book that I can't even tell you how accurate or inaccurate its historical elements are. One look at his list of sources reminds me what a Confederate-centric book it is—but then again, it's told from the adoring and loyal perspective of Lee's horse, so it wasn't really supposed to be nonpartisan to begin with.

Traveller died in 1871 and is buried just outside Robert E. Lee's crypt on the campus of Washington and Lee University in Lexington, Virginia. *Chris Mackowski*

What I do remember about the book is a larger lesson that Adams himself embodied, too. He was not afraid, as a writer, to take a risk with his work. He committed himself to a tale and stayed as *absolutely true* to it as he could, which in turn gave it life, depth, context, and resonance. *Traveller* rings true, not because the history is true or its historical interpretation is true, but because Traveller's perspective and voice are absolutely, 100 percent true to what they should be. That's the only way to make a story like that—or a story about nomadic rabbits—at all believable enough to read, let alone sustain over the length of a novel.

Richard Adams died at 10 p.m. on Christmas Eve at the age of 96.

A Beautiful, Despairing Journey with a Coal-Black Horse

by Chris Mackowski

Originally published as a blog post at Emerging Civil War on July 27, 2012

There's a kind of myth-making happening in Robert Olmstead's novel *Coal Black Horse*. Set in the middle of the Civil War—itself a fertile era of American mythology—Olmstead's story follows a fourteen-year-old boy sent from Virginia to find his father in the Confederate army and bring him home. "You must find him before July," the boy's mother tells him as she sends him on his quest.

And thus the myth-making begins.

Coal Black Horse feels every bit like the story of a Greek hero sent on an impossible quest, who learns along the way the deep reservoirs of perseverance and strength he possesses but never knew he had. It feels like an epic story passed down, through oral tradition, from generation to generation.

And if that's all the novel was content to be, it would still be an interesting diversion. But what Olmstead crafts, instead, is a story that undergoes a metamorphosis along with is main character. As Robey Childs journeys from the wilds of rural western Virginia—and the wilds of his own youth—toward the harsh reality of war, the novel undergoes a subtle but powerful transformation of its own.

Robey comes from a world peopled by the kind of offbeat, slightly surrealistic characters you'd expect from a child's imagination. There's a hunchbacked blacksmith, an "upside-down boy" who walks on his hands, a man whose skin teems with lice. Robey's mother is clairvoyant.

Even Robey possesses a touch of the fantastic. "On one night alone he grew an entire inch and when morning came he felt stretched and his body ached and he cried out when he sat up," Olmstead writes. The result is a little like Mark Twain meets Homer.

This slight sense of surrealism—the way the world looks to an imaginative innocent—fades away the closer Robey gets to the armies. People lose their charm, they get grittier, they get bleaker. As Robey loses his innocence, so does the rest of the world.

Olmstead does not get gratuitous with his descriptions of battlefield violence, but he doesn't shirk from the horrific experience of it, either. The war is grim. The world is grim. The book gets grim—but even at its most grim, the book never loses its poetic beauty. It's as if Olmstead has infused his novel with truly beautiful writing as a way to refute the terrible things he has to write about.

For instance, one evening on the battlefield, Robey notices, "[a] heavy dew had fallen and the wetted field that stretched out before them beneath the moon was so like a wide path of white jewels on blue velvet." Olmstead is a writer who appreciates the beauty of the world, and he takes time to supply readers with plenty of sensory descriptions.

The war is not incidental to the story, but *Coal Black Horse* isn't really a war story. Robey's journey doesn't end at the battlefield. He must take his newfound knowledge—which might well be a curse—and learn to live with it. If the world is so grim, is there any place for beauty, for imagination, for innocence?

At the center of the story is the coal black horse the novel gets its name from. Olmstead sought to create an iconic figure from the horse—a task he succeeds at, perhaps too well. As any horse-lover knows, every horse has a distinct personality; in his effort to create an icon, Olmstead paints the horse in rough, stereotypical colors that fail to capture the horse as an individual. Maybe that's the point. After all, in myth, icons matter more than individuals.

But Olmstead is smarter than that. He sends readers from one kind of myth to another and then, in the end, to someplace altogether different. It's a journey both dark and beautiful, bleak and redemptive, haunting and resonant. *Coal Black Horse* is a myth of its own making—and you'll feel its power on every page.

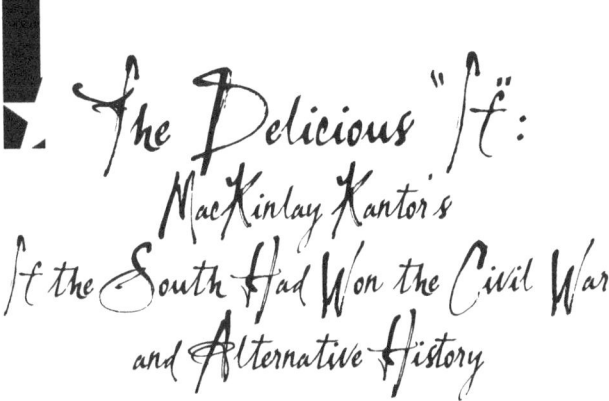

1. The Delicious "If": MacKinlay Kantor's If the South Had Won the Civil War and Alternative History

by Stephen Davis

Originally published as web-exclusive content for Emerging Civil War on February 6, 2020

For every Southern boy fourteen years old, not once but whenever he wants it, there is the instant when it's still not yet two o'clock on that July afternoon in 1863; the brigades are in position behind the rail fence, the guns are laid out and ready in the woods . . . and it's all in the balance, it hasn't happened yet. . . . This time. Maybe this time with all this much to lose and all this much to gain: Pennsylvania, Maryland, the world, the golden dome of Washington itself to crown with desperate and unbelievable victory.[1]

William Faulkner's rumination on Gettysburg in *Intruder in the Dust* is one of the most famous literary forays into imaginative history. Not the kind

---

1 William Faulkner, *Intruder in the Dust* (New York: Random House, 1948), 194-95.

of history imagined by, say, Stephen Crane pondering how Henry Fleming faced battle at Chancellorsville. Rather, it's the history about to be not just rewritten, but *recast altogether* in one's imagination. Faulkner, in short, spoke for every white Southern boy of his generation who thought about the Civil War and dreamed about how the South might have won it.

... not just of his generation, but even of mine. When I was a Southern boy fourteen years old, I was already reading about the Civil War. But when I wanted to imagine how the war might have ended differently—with a Confederate victory, as improbable as it seemed—I had a ready touchstone. In its issue of November 22, 1960, *LOOK* Magazine published as its feature article something it called "History in Reverse": MacKinlay Kantor's imaginative essay, "If the South Had Won the Civil War."

It was one of the coolest things I had ever seen in my (young) life. "Two little switches in the events of the summer of 1863 could have turned the tide for the Confederacy," the editors tweaked in their opening, as they introduced "an amazing version of history as it did not happen," written by Kantor, the "distinguished author of *Andersonville*."

I didn't even have to start reading it; just flipping the pages was exciting, drinking in Robert Fawcett's vivid, full-page pictures of Confederates overrunning Gettysburg's Cemetery Hill, Major John Mosby capturing Abraham Lincoln, and Confederate leaders celebrating with a festive ball in the White House.

The article wasn't very long, though it was spread over thirty pages. In between were *Look*'s usual lot of ads, as for Campbell Soup ("M'm! M'm! Good!").[2]

Kantor's "history in reverse" was a hit. The next spring, in April 1961—centennial year for the start of the war—a paperback edition appeared with a few new flourishes to the *Look* text. When magazine mention is made of the meeting in which a captive Lincoln pleads with Confederate President Davis for an end to bloodshed, Kantor mentions "Lamon, in his memoirs" as source. In the paperback, we get a footnote: *Recollections of a Cavalier* by Lamon (Philadelphia, 1887)–which, of course, is made-up. Added to the paperback as well are ink sketches by Isa Barnett, illustrating scenes not

---

2 MacKinlay Kantor, "If the South Had Won the Civil War," *Look*, vol. 24, no. 24 (Nov. 22, 1960), 29-42, 45, 49-50, 52, 54, 58, 60, 62.

pictured by Fawcett in the magazine. Notable is that showing Gen. Ulysses S. Grant's equestrian accident, mid-May 1863. The tumble from his horse took Grant's life and threw his army, trapped in the middle of Mississippi, into such crisis that it was forced to surrender on June 30, 1863.[3]

Kantor's "two little switches in the events of the summer of 1863" prove to be momentous indeed. After Grant's fatal accident, Maj. Gen. John McClernand takes over, and falters. McClernand dashes his troops against Gen. Joseph E. Johnston's Confederate army fortified at Jackson. Rebel cavalry cut up Federal foraging columns and the Yankees start to starve in the middle of Mississippi. Major General William T. Sherman takes over from McClernand and leads the army toward Vicksburg. There he has no better luck. Futile assaults against the river fortress held by Lt. Gen. John C. Pemberton waste away Sherman's remaining strength; the red-haired Northern commander is drilled in the head by a Rebel bullet. "The Army of the Tennessee," Kantor writes of the luckless Union force, "was trapped against the Mississippi shore" by the combined armies of Pemberton and Johnston, who had been hammering it from the rear. On June 30, 1863, it surrenders, just days after Gen. Nathaniel Banks's Union forces have been routed downriver at Port Hudson, Louisiana.[4]

Events turn just as favorably for the Rebels a thousand miles away at Gettysburg, Pennsylvania. After his infantry have routed the enemy I and XI Corps on July 1, Lee is uncharacteristically resolute in calling for assaults on Cemetery and Culp's Hills south of the town. Gen. Richard Ewell promptly sends forth his divisions, and the Confederates soon have the Yankees flying for the rear "in a panic not unlike that endured at Chancellorsville."

The rest of the battle of Gettysburg is legendary in the annals of Confederate history. Lee orders commanding heights, called the Round Tops, occupied before the enemy get there. "Jeb" Stuart attacks the Federal cavalry early on July 2 and disperses them. The Union commander, Gen. George Meade, is unable to organize his troops approaching Gettysburg into a cohesive defense, and Lee masterfully defeats them in detail. "By sunset

---

3 Paperback edition (New York: Bantam Books, 1961), 11.

4 *Look*, 31-32.

on July 3rd," Kantor explains, "the Army of the Potomac had dissolved into hopeless tatters—bleeding human garbage, a pitiful mockery of an army."

With Lee bearing down on Washington and no defense forces on hand, Lincoln sadly witnesses government authority in the capital dissolve. For the sake of the president's safety against marauding mobs, loyal aides arrange his surrender to Confederates, who safeguard Lincoln's escape to Richmond.

There remains enough of a U. S. government to allow its representatives to meet with Southern counterparts for a peace conference in September. The final agreement recognizes the secession of the Confederate States. The Southern envoys write into the treaty language familiar to them from an earlier American Revolution, "that these [States] are and or right ought to be, free and independent."[5]

This sort of stuff is too exciting for historians to make up, so it's left for novelists to do it. Turning their imaginations to Gettysburg are other fictionists less renowned than MacKinlay Kantor. Several years before the Centennial, in *Bring the Jubilee* (1952), Ward Moore had Lee winning the battle by posting artillery on Little Round Top late on July 1. Determined Confederate attacks against a pummeled Union line sweep it away; "the disorganized Federals were given the final killing blow in their vitals" by Gen. George Pickett's charge on the 3rd.[6]

Mark Nesbitt gets straight to the point in *If the South Won Gettysburg* (1980). After sweeping the Union I and XI Corps through town on July 1, Lee the next day is prepared to attack the enemy line formed along Cemetery Ridge down to Little Round Top. But Lt. Gen. James Longstreet, his trusted old war horse, argues that instead of attacking, the army should swing around and take a defensive position along Rock Creek, interposing between Meade's army and Washington. Lee agrees and so orders. Sure enough, Meade has no choice but to assault the entrenched Rebel lines July 3-4, and is bloodily repulsed.

Meanwhile Stuart's cavalry swoops down on Washington and shells the city. Congress flees, the White House is on fire, and Lincoln slips away to

---

5 Look, 37, 49.

6 Ward Moore, *Bring the Jubilee* (New York: Farrar, Straus and Young, 1952), 187.

safety. Meade, unable to break or outflank Lee's strong position and with his army wrecked from attacking, calls his senior officers together. "His Corps Commanders (those that were not killed or wounded)," Nesbitt narrates, "voted unanimously to send a request for terms of surrender under a flag of truce." Meade reluctantly agrees to see General Lee, although he tells an aide "he would rather die a thousand deaths than do that." Within two weeks of Meade's surrender, the two sides sign a peace agreement. Confederate independence is recognized, Federal troops will withdraw from Southern territory, and Confederates will end their occupation of Washington, allowing the United States government to re-establish itself in its historic capital.[7]

Civil War buffs will recognize that the key to Lee's victory in this scenario is his decision to take Pete Longstreet's advice not to attack Meade's army, but to maneuver south of Gettysburg and force the Yankees to attack. That much we know from history.[8] Nesbitt's Document of Peace, signed at Fredericksburg, naturally involves the novelist's flight of imagination —a venture as lofty as the very front cover photograph of his paperback. Beneath the title, *If the South Won Gettysburg,* a moon-suited astronaut stands on the lunar surface beside the Confederate battle flag planted in the dust.

After Longstreet, after Nesbitt, there's not much novelty for William R. Forstchen to explore in his *Gettysburg: A Novel of the Civil War* (2003). Here, too, Lee takes Longstreet's advice, marches to a defensive position south of Gettysburg and forces Meade to attack. The Confederates win the battle and destroy the Army of the Potomac. So what's new in this novel? Actually, quite a bit, at least in its clever details. "My fault, all my fault," laments the defeated army commander after the battle. But here it is not Robert E. Lee grieving (his famous words in history), but George G. Meade, just before he was shot and killed trying to escape. And when the Union infantry form for their final, fateful attack, vowing, "Maybe, just maybe, we'll do it this time," they sound a lot like Faulkner's fourteen-year-old Southern boy in *Intruder in the Dust.*[9]

---

[7] Mark Nesbitt, *If the South Won Gettysburg* (Gettysburg: Reliance Publishing Co., 1980), 146.

[8] See, for example, Glenn Tucker, *Lee and Longstreet at Gettysburg* (Indianapolis: Bobbs-Merrill Co., 1968), 50-51.

[9] William R. Forstchen with Newt Gingrich, *Gettysburg: A Novel of the Civil War* (New York: St. Martin's Press, 2003), 390, 450.

I saw Newt Gingrich, Gettysburg's presumed co-author, at a book signing in 2003. I managed to ask the Speaker if he and Bill Forstchen had caught any flak for their earlier novel, *1945,* in which they had Germany win the Second World War.[10]

"Why would we?" Gingrich answered. "It's a novel."

Which brings us back to MacKinlay Kantor's *If the South Had Won the Civil War.* Sure, it's just a novel. But for me, as a youngster growing up dreaming about Rebels and Yankees, it was the power of just such a novel which helped birth my war-passion and which has sustained it all of these ensuing years.

---

10 Newt Gingrich and William R. Forstchen, *1945* (Riverdale NY: Baen Books, 1995).

Holiday Village Reenactments and Reflections

by Neil P. Chatelain

Originally published as a blog post at Emerging Civil War on December 20, 2021

  The rattle of musketry cracked with volley after volley as officers struggled to bark commands to keep their battle lines organized amid the din. Two regiments of Federal troops were arrayed in a line of battle, facing off against a single Confederate regiment across the field on this cold, snowy, December afternoon. Spotting uniforms and insignia, it was clear this was a hodgepodge affair, with elements of the 72nd Pennsylvania Fire Zouaves mixed with the 1st Michigan. On the other end of the field, and with a slight numerical edge, was the 26th North Carolina, sending a steady stream of fire at the U.S. line. Things were getting desperate, as off in the distance Confederate reinforcements, the Louisiana Tiger Zouaves, were fast approaching to turn the tide. At the last moment however, U.S. support also arrived on the field to retrieve the moment. And these Federal troops were lead elements of the 19th Indiana, part of the famed Iron Brigade. They could be just what it might take to seize the initiative and drive the Confederates off the field once and for all.
  As the soldiers closed for the final charge, on the edge of the field, a crowd roared and cheered with delight. These are not soldiers, but spectators

A view of the Holiday Village Reenactment from the spectators' stands! *Neil Chatelain*

enjoying the scene. It is the annual village Civil War reenactment, and much of the town has crowded the central park to witness the festivities. Adults pack onto benches overlooking the battlefield, as children caught up in the spirit build their own ice-block fortifications for a snowball fight to rival the reenactment itself. Food trucks and stands offering snacks add to the festivities.

This reenactment is a merger of several elements of my own childhood and showcasing this is a great way to get into the holiday spirit while simultaneously reflecting on those who have influenced my appreciation of the conflict overall. To start with, the holiday village is a major tradition of my maternal grandmother, who began collecting and showcasing her own village of porcelain houses and townspeople in the 1980s. It quickly grew beyond what most people think of when they ponder a holiday village on a mantle or bookshelf. Hers spread to taking up an entire room of the house, approximately 100 square feet, and contained separate residential, government, shopping, and leisure districts of the town.

My older brother would set up this village each year the weekend after Thanksgiving, and by the time I entered middle school, and he was off to college, the task fell to me. It took an entire day to set everything up, with each building brought to life with individual light bulbs. It was my favorite part of the holidays. The entire setup remained until King's Day, the official end of the holiday season and start of the Mardi Gras season in New Orleans.

Holiday Village Reenactments and Reflections 219

The 2021 Holiday Village Reenactment, encircled by an excursion train. *Neil Chatelain*

When my grandmother passed, her holiday village was split between family members. I received my share, which amounted to about one-eighth of her original collection, when I got married. Since then, I have continued setting up my own holiday village annually, adding more modern pieces each year (including a massive dog costume parade that my wife adores and a lighthouse acquired in Estonia). My own holiday village now contains 35 buildings (half being originals from my grandmother), a residential district, shopping district, downtown area, an airport, train station, cemetery, and park! It is spread across the whole house at this point.

The Civil War soldiers taking part in the village reenactment are a mixture of metal and plastic painted miniatures. The Iron Brigade soldiers, members of the 72nd Pennsylvania, the Louisiana Tigers, and half of the 26th North Carolina were made by Britain's miniatures. The 1st Michigan figures, with their distinctive red Maltese crosses, and half of the 26th North Carolina are plastic figures I found at a battlefield park gift shop.

These also have a childhood connection. I began collecting metal Civil War figurines in middle school and, growing up in New Orleans, I always begged my mom to take me to the one store in the French Quarter that I knew had them. This initial collection likely sparked because of my memories of setting up my grandmother's village, and as a child I wanted something akin to that for myself, tailored of course to my passion for studying the Civil War. About once a year, I would have the chance to add a new set to my collection. This amassing continued until I graduated high school, when Hurricane Katrina flooded my childhood home. We gathered and cleaned figures found in the muck that was once my bedroom, eventually replacing pieces that were lost forever. If you look closely, you can still see paint damage and marks on some of the figures from the flood damage.

A final childhood memory links these two together, and that is Civil War reenactments. I had the great privilege as a high schooler of spending parts of my summer each year traveling from Louisiana to most of the major battlefield parks in Mississippi, Tennessee, Georgia, Kentucky, North Carolina, Virginia, Maryland, and Pennsylvania. There were always reenactors present at these battlefields, and even if they were not re-creating a skirmish, seeing them in camp stepping into character was great. My dad also took me several times to the annual reenactment at Camp Moore, Louisiana, which helped link reenacting to visiting sites even more.

Thus, as the holiday season commences each year, I take some time to merge these three childhood memories into something that showcases my love of family traditions and my passion for studying the Civil War era. Hopefully seeing this can bring you a good laugh or help you reflect on what made you so interested in the most defining challenge of the United States while you also celebrate the holiday season.

Civil War Wargaming

by Scott L. Mingus Sr.

Joyous shouts of Huzzah! Huzzah! ring out from one side of the table. Across the way, disappointed moans and mutterings simultaneously fill the air. In between the two groups of opposing wargamers, miniature Union and Confederate armies do battle on a carefully laid out tabletop, replete with scale-model houses, tiny woodlots, crafted hills, fields, and roads. Stone walls, streams, and fences provide terrain obstacles for the "generals" to move their wee warriors to glory or shame on the sham battlefield. Rules sheets, dice, measuring tapes, rulers, and liquid refreshments typically complete the scene as teams of wargamers oppose each other, discuss possible joint strategy, or loudly debate the merits of Richard S. Ewell as an effective corps commander at Gettysburg or whether Stonewall really would have made a difference.

The players can take the hypothetical role of a brigade commander, regimental leader, squad leader, or common soldier, depending on the type of game they're playing and the specific set of rules they're using. They must decide which units to move and where, when to fire and at what target, how to position and protect supporting artillery, where to move leader figures to maximize their effect on troop morale and combat enhancement, and how best to achieve the ultimate objective of seizing and controlling key terrain features while routing or demoralizing opposing forces. Dice rolls (or computer-based random number generation) give game results based upon mathematical probabilities. This is heavily influenced by the type of weaponry, distance to the target, training level of the units being modeled, morale levels, previous casualties, terrain effects, the presence or absence of hard or soft cover or a friendly charismatic leader, attacking and defending unit formations, whether the attacker or defender moved during this game turn, visibility and "fog of war," and a myriad of other factors, depending upon the complexity of the rules set being used for the game.

The "game master" who organizes and oversees the wargame may elect to refight a historical battle, using the same approximate troop positions as the actual battle with similar objectives (in essence, playing out the actual tactical situation using the players' decisions independent of the actual movements and combat). Another popular option is to present a derivative "what if" scenario with alternative troop setups, reinforcements, or other significant changes to the historical narrative. For example, the game scenario may have General Ewell attack Cemetery Hill on the night of the first day at Gettysburg, or have Meade counterattack on July 4, or have Sickles defend his original Cemetery Ridge line. In other cases, the game master will arrange a hypothetical battle on nonhistorical battlefields to offer fresh tactical challenges. The game master is also usually responsible for keeping the game moving, interpreting rules, judging any disputes or conflicts that may arise, and providing an enjoyable social experience for the players.

Gaming buffs enjoy their hobby for a wide range of reasons. Some like the tactical challenge of trying their hand at seeing if they can break through Confederate lines at Atlanta or some other situation. Others like testing the "what ifs," enhancing or refuting, at least in miniature, whether Sickles should have moved forward to the Peach Orchard–Emmitsburg Road line at Gettysburg. Many gamers find their primary enjoyment in researching battles, units, flags, etc., and re-creating battlefields in miniature with model railroad quality. Some are much more into the social aspects of the game experience and care less about the appearance of the terrain or the situation than they do about having a good time with their friends while discussing the War Between the States or the merits of George Pickett as a commander.

The American Civil War is one of the four most popular conflicts/periods to wargame, either on the tabletop with scale model miniatures and model railroad terrain or with more traditional board games, or on the computer screen with one of any number of popular software titles. Many wargamers, particularly those born in the 1950s and 1960s, can trace their love for the hobby back to their childhoods, when a combination of external factors helped spark a lifelong interest in toy soldiers and refighting long ago battles of the bitter War Between the States. The Civil War Centennial, from 1961 to 1965, sparked a myriad of TV programs, all sorts of toys and playsets, movies, parades, reenactments, books, and other remembrances. The availability of mass-produced plastic soldiers, led by Louis Marx & Company's 54mm blue and gray warriors and, later, boxes of 20mm Airfix™ figures, gave boys (and some girls) a supply of fighting forces to command and lead on to imagined glory. For others, a road trip to Gettysburg, Shiloh, Antietam, or Vicksburg, or some other monument-studded battlefield, added to the overall wonderment and helped stoke an interest in children and teenagers to learn more and more about their history and heritage. As one wargamer has put it, "That family road trip to Gettysburg and a box of toy soldiers under the Christmas tree, and we were hooked for a lifetime." Indeed.

Miniature Wargaming

Miniature wargaming can trace its origins as a strategy game back to chess, which greatly abstracted war through its long lines of common pawns, strong fortifications, workmanlike knights, and powerful senior leaders. The goal of each is straightforward: destroy enough of the enemy's strength to allow you to maneuver into a favorable position and then execute the final winning attack. In the fifth century, noted Chinese military strategist Sun Tzu formally defined "The Art of War" in his classic text of the same name. Elements of his thoughts find their way into the often complex and detailed rules sets that modern wargamers use to define the methods by which their miniature armies are composed, their fighting abilities, their movement rates, morale, and combat resolution. In Great Britain, famed author H. G. Wells published a popular book titled *Little Wars* that enthralled an entire generation of boys, teens, and even men, who battled it out on the floor or table with miniature lead soldiers. Similar books followed suit in the 1920s and 1930s, introducing other rules for sham battles, both on land and sea.

By the 1950s, military strategy enthusiasts such as Californian Jack Scruby were casting their own lines of highly detailed tin/lead alloy gaming figures and developing criteria for playing wargames, a takeoff on the old lead toy soldiers that Wells and his compatriots had earlier deployed on their floors and kitchen tables. In 1956, Scruby organized one of the first formal conventions to bring together wargamers from throughout the

Miniature wargaming layouts can be as simple as a few trees and roads to more elaborate, diorama-quality layouts. This shows one of the author's award-winning 15mm games in progress. *Scott Mingus*

region for a weekend of simultaneous gaming on neighboring tables. He, and later others, began publishing magazines and newsletters to support the growing hobby. British hobbyist Donald F. Featherstone in 1962 published *War Games through the Ages*, which became a leading book on the emerging hobby, replete with color photographs of an array of miniature armies.

To date, more than 100 different rules sets for Civil War miniature gaming are in existence. Most strictly deal with land battles (infantry, artillery, and/or cavalry), while others, such as *Smoke on the Water*, *Hammerin' Iron*, and *River Wars*, cover coastal, oceanic, or riverine naval actions. The vast amount of historical data available on the war, including armament, training methods, battle summaries, orders of battle, etc., provides fertile ground for new ideas as to how best to re-create battles in miniature. Two popular rules sets, *Fire & Fury* and *Johnny Reb*, were major contributors to the growing popularity of gaming Civil War battles in the 1990s and 2000s. They continue to retain throngs of loyal followers more than 30 years after they first came into print. They have inspired hundreds of battle scenarios and related articles by adherents.

The basics of most miniature wargame rules for the Civil War are similar: each figure represents a set number of actual combatants, from a one-to-one ratio for skirmish wargaming up to 100 or even 1,000 for larger engagements. Figures, model houses, ground scale, terrain features, etc. are all proportionally scaled similar to the various gauges of model railroading, with a 25mm scale being the most popular worldwide. Other leading scales include 10, 15, and 54 millimeters (the latter being the standard height of most traditional plastic toy soldiers), usually measured from the base of the foot to the eyeline. A number of other scales are also available to the gamer.

Specific rules apply for troop formations, morale levels, armament, combat losses, cover, charismatic leaders, taking casualties, etc. Players typically will refight historical battles to test their judgments of tactical situations, or they can create hypothetical fights without historic precedence. Game turns usually have a set sequence (often movement, fire combat, charges, and morale checks) of actions, which usually alternate between the opposing sides, although a few games rely on simultaneous movement. Figures (one to four) are typically grouped on a base and moved as a unit, or a portion of a unit. The so-called individual "stand" of figures may represent a regiment, a battalion, a company, or some other military unit. For example, a group of stands may represent a brigade of infantry (or cavalry, depending upon the figures selected). The brigade becomes the smallest operational unit on the tabletop, and the rules reflect brigade movement, combat, morale, etc. Many gamers take existing rules sets and add their own "house rules" for added playability.

One of the first widely popular brigade-level Civil War rules sets was *On to Richmond*, written by gamemaster Paul Koch and first published in *The Courier*, a leading gaming magazine, in 1982. Marylander Richard Hasenauer, inspired by Koch's rules, over a five-year time frame developed his own best-selling *Fire & Fury*, which remains arguably the most widely played Civil War rules set in the world. He borrowed a few ideas from some of the old classic books from an earlier generation, including Donald Featherstone's *War Games through the Ages* and Joseph Morschauser's 1962 work *How to Play War Games in Miniature*, and blended them with some of his own creative game mechanics to produce a fine rules set that has stood the test of time.

Almost as popular as brigade-level wargaming is the regimental level. In these sets of rules, the smallest operational unit is a regiment. While, of course, grouped within a brigade organizationally, the morale, casualties, firepower, etc. are all based upon individual regiments, not the brigade as a whole. For example, in the late John Hill's classic *Johnny Reb* system, the ground scale is 1 inch = 50 yards, and each figure represents 30 men within a regiment. Typically, a regiment would be comprised of four stands of figures, with the number of figures varying from one to four per stand depending upon the size of the historical regiment being modeled. Leaders, as with brigade and some skirmish games, can be a benefit if attached to or in close proximity to the unit.

In addition to the venerable *Johnny Reb* (now in its third iteration), other popular tactical regimental rules sets include Dale Brown's *Guns of Gettysburg* and Larry Reber's *Gettysburg Miniature Soldiers*. A newer rules set, *Longstreet*, controls battle action by a deck of action cards that offer command choices and situations to the commander. The various cards add a high level of randomness to the traditional wargame. One of the newer rules sets, *Glory, Hallelujah!*, is a 2016 Civil War variant/expansion for Warlord Games's very popular *Black Powder* series of rules.

Skirmish-level gaming, where the smallest unit is an individual figure, also enjoys a large and faithful following. Ivor Janci's *Brother against Brother* was one of the early rules sets that gained national exposure. In this system, figures (usually 25mm or 54mm) are mounted individually. Groups of figures represent a company or other small unit. Casualties, movement, etc. are done for the individual figure; combat and morale results can influence the behavior of the rest of the company. The ground scale is, of course, much larger to represent terrain in scale with individual figures.

Wargaming clubs are popular in many areas, with the leading umbrella organization being the Historical Miniatures Gaming Society, Inc. (HMGS). The largest chapter, its East group, sponsored some of the largest public wargaming conventions in the country, including its flagship convention, Historicon. That annual four-day event, in recent years held in July at a convention center in Fredericksburg, Virginia, draws thousands of wargamers and modelers each summer. The convention features hundreds of wargames that, for an admission fee, HMGS members, guests, and other gamers can sign up for in advance. Popular games often "sell out" quickly and gamers typically submit alternatives when they preregister. HMGS East also hosts a spring convention and a fall one, both usually in Lancaster, Pennsylvania.

Other HMGS chapters across the country also have their own major regional conventions, such as Little Wars in Chicago, Nashcon in Tennessee, Recon and Hurricon in Florida, Advance the Colors in Ohio, and many others. Miniature wargaming conventions primarily aimed at nonhistorical or fantasy gaming, such as the very well-attended Origins convention in Columbus, Ohio, also have a strong historical presence most years.

While much more popular in the United States and Canada, there are pockets of avid American Civil War gamers across the world, most notably in the UK, Western Europe, and Australia. Gaming conventions; figure, terrain, and accessories dealers; brick-and-mortar stores; internet websites; etc. all have parallels overseas to their North American counterparts.

While no one knows exactly how many miniature wargamers play Civil War games, they number in the thousands based upon annual attendance at conventions, the number of scenario books and rules sets sold, web and social media presence on such leading gaming sites as The Miniatures Page and the Wargame Vault, and gaming store and internet sales of supplies such as wargaming figures, period-specific terrain, buildings, etc. Wargamers are a mixed lot, ranging from college-educated professionals to skilled workers and students. Many gamers, particularly those in their 40s, 50s, and 60s, began gaming through small groups at their colleges and universities. Most also play historical board games; some also play computer simulations of wargames.

Historical Board Games

The historical board game market for Civil War enthusiasts can be traced to some popular strategy games of the 1950s, including early game designer Charles S. Roberts's mass-market *Tactics*, which was published in 1954 and updated as *Tactics II* later in the decade. It was one of the first popular wargames to use cardboard counters to represent troops, which the players moved on thick cardstock game boards that represented maps of actual or hypothetical battles. Baltimore-based Avalon Hill was one of the first companies to produce nationally distributed wargames, including the classic *Gettysburg* (which has been revised and reprinted numerous times over the years) and many other titles. From 1964 until 1998, Avalon Hill also published a bimonthly gaming magazine titled *The General*, which included tactical tips for its line of published games, rules variants, updates, historical articles, answers to reader-submitted questions on rules, and other related materials for gamers.

During the early 1960s, renewed interest in the Civil War during its Centennial helped spark a proliferation of plastic toy soldiers for children, as well as several board games that played on the theme of toy soldiers. Popular board games with a military theme, such as Milton Bradley's *Battle Cry*™, *Dogfight*™, *Broadside*™, and *Hit the Beach*™, featured small colorful plastic playing pieces of soldiers, artillery, airplanes, ships, and other martial themes. These games, while entertaining and useful introductions to history themes, were poor simulations of actual battles, strategy, or tactical situations. A heavily revised, mass-marketed version of *Battle Cry* emerged in the 1990s, with much more of a historical flavor but still at a highly abstract level.

The heyday of true historical simulation board games was the 1970s and 1980s, when Avalon Hill, Jim Dunnigan's Simulations Publications, Inc. (SPI), Game Designers Workshop (GDW), West End Games, Yaquinto, and many other companies produced a dizzying array of new titles. One of the largest and most complex was SPI's *Terrible Swift Sword*. Designed by Richard Berg in the early 1970s, *TSS* refought Gettysburg on three large maps at a regimental scale, using more than 2,000 counters for the grand three-day game. Smaller scenarios allowed the gamer to refight the Peach Orchard, Devil's Den, Little Round Top, Pickett's Charge, or John Buford's defense of McPherson's Ridge. SPI later published several spin-offs using Berg's basic *TSS* system to allow gamers to refight other major battles.

On the other extreme, SPI published a monthly magazine, *Strategy & Tactics*, that contained a smaller folio game—a stand-alone, introductory game—each month. These were generally intended for solo gaming or one-on-one gaming, with a smaller footprint and time commitment. Several Civil War titles appeared over the years that *S&T* published. SPI at times bundled individual folio games as a set for commercial sale to gamers who did not subscribe to the magazine.

Other variants of historical wargames include Columbia Games's *Bobby Lee*, which used 96 specially labeled wooden blocks as the game pieces on a colorful map of Northern Virginia. The game mechanics rely heavily on the fog of war concept, in which the opposing players do not know the strength or composition of the enemy, unlike many traditional board games where counters marked with firepower and type of unit are evident (faceup) to all players. Columbia also markets card-and-dice games in their *Dixie* series for Bull Run, Shiloh, and Gettysburg. Each colorfully illustrated card represents a single regiment or artillery battery, as well as terrain features, random events, reinforcements, leaders, etc.

Computer Games

By the mid-1990s, traditional historical board games were quickly being supplanted by the new genre of computer-based games, which allowed nearly instant play versus the often hours-long setup time required for cardboard counter-based games. Some of the more popular early software titles were TalonSoft's *Battleground* and its subsequently improved *Battleground 2* series, which grandly translated turn-based miniature wargaming into a realistic digital version on the computer screen. Their specific Civil War titles included *Gettysburg, Shiloh, Antietam,* and *Bull Run*. Online participative gaming soon became popular, and several variants of the original TalonSoft series came into being. Another early popular game was *Sid Meier's Gettysburg!* (1997) and *Sid Meier's Antietam!* (1999), two software-based games that introduced the novel concept of real-time simultaneous movement and combat versus the more traditional turn-based system of TalonSoft.

As computing became more powerful, the resulting Civil War games, in turn, became much more detailed and realistic with new releases, including *History Channel's Civil War: A Nation Divided* in 2006 and *Ageod's American Civil War* the following year, among other titles of varying popularity and playability. The year 2010 saw the release of *Scourge of War: Gettysburg*, a companion game to designer Norm Timpko's 3D *Scourge of War: Waterloo* for Napoleonic gaming. Other battles have since been released or are in the works, including Chancellorsville, Pipe Creek, Brandy Station, and Antietam. Individual "shooter" games also exist, where the player controls a single soldier from a first-person perspective.

Gaming has provided another method of increasing the awareness of Civil War history. From its colorful, visually stunning tabletop battlefields to the deep tactical thinking that often stems from board games and on to easy-to-play PC games, Civil War games have influenced tens of thousands of people.

One Man's Personal Journey

On a personal level, I first started wargaming in earnest in the early 1970s while a student at Miami University in southwestern Ohio. That hobby emanated from a childhood love of refighting Civil War battles using my collection of 54mm blue and gray plastic toy soldiers. I would look at maps in various books and in *Civil War Times Illustrated* (my parents bought me a yearly subscription starting when I was 10 years old) and re-create the key elements of the battlefields. My early college actual gaming experiences at Miami included miniature wargaming Napoleonics and later Civil War battles, and spending countless hours in our dorm with my roommate and other friends playing Avalon Hill and SPI board games, including my personal favorite, *Terrible Swift Sword*.

After graduating and starting my long career as a scientist in the global paper and printing industry, I continued playing wargames (miniatures and board games) with my friends and, later, with my children and their friends. I became enamored with the *Johnny Reb* miniatures systems and wrote a number of scenario books, as well as for a decade publishing a quarterly newsletter, *Charge!*, with original Civil War battle scenarios and other gaming articles. The games, the many hours of carefully painting tiny 15mm figures and crafting sculpted terrain boards using model railroad supplies, the deep research and subsequent discussion into aspects of battles, terrain studies at battlefields with my sons, all helped them develop a deep love for history. That, in turn, translated into master's degrees in history for both sons, who are now college professors. Today, wargaming offers me a future venue for fellowship with my six grandchildren as they grow and hopefully become interested in history.

1. Gaming the Civil War

by Sean Michael Chick

". . . from which banners still fly in the minds of some . . ."
— *The American Civil War and Wargaming, 1958–2017*

The niche hobby of wargaming is mostly found in America, and as such the American Civil War has been a popular topic. Only World War II has more titles, with World War I and the Napoleonic Wars offering some competition. For Americans, the reasons are self evident. The war was the nation's bloodiest, and it defined the country. Issues of government, economics, race, and rights are all tied up in the war. Each generation attempts to create a unified vision of the war's eternal truths.

Modern wargames were invented by the Prussians during the Napoleonic Wars to train officers, but they did not become recreational until the late nineteenth century. Fred T. Jane created rules for simulating naval warfare in 1898, and H. G. Wells crafted rules to simulate battles between toy soldiers, most famously in *Little Wars* (1913). Post–World War II America experienced an explosion in disposable income and hobbies.

In 1954, Charles S. Roberts founded Avalon Hill. Roberts made board games into a serious affair and not simply something for children to pass away the time. The first game to come out with a strictly historical topic was, fittingly enough, *Gettysburg* (1958). The subject remains the most simulated battle in the wargame market, with only Waterloo offering comparable competition.

In the world of gaming, *Gettysburg* was a watershed. The success of the title, coming right around the Civil War Centennial, launched an entire genre of gaming that has existed to this day. *Gettysburg* itself was reissued and remade no less than three times. The game was an indirect progenitor of the role-playing game *Dungeons & Dragons* (1974), itself a product of Gary Gygax and Dave Arneson's love of wargaming. Although wargaming remained a niche, it attracted several famous fans and players, including Drew Carey, Tom Clancy, Walter Cronkite, Peter Cushing, Peter Jackson, Philip Roth, Curt Schilling, Whit Stillman, Kurt Vonnegut, Robin Williams, and Edward Woodward.

Wargames sold big in the 1960s and 1970s, but by the 1980s, sales fell dramatically. The causes were various, including the rise of computer games, the increasingly complexity of wargames, and the death of big-time publisher Simulations Publications, Inc. (SPI). Gamers had more options as *Dungeons & Dragons* and its clones became popular. By the 1990s, it appeared wargames might disappear altogether. The industry survived into the 2000s with innovative game mechanics, more sound business practices, and a broadening of gaming subjects. Such obscure conflicts as King Philip's War, the Angolan Civil War, and the War of the Grand Alliance saw major stand-alone releases. The hobby has not thrived, but it has survived.

Throughout the decades, the American Civil War has been one of the hobby's biggest sellers. This is in spite of the fact that it is a difficult war to make into an enjoyable game. Yet being the nation's biggest war, it is natural it would attract attention despite its limitations. One wargame, *The American Civil War* (1974), even captured this fascination with purple prose plastered on its front cover: "Our nation's bloodiest and saddest war . . . from which banners still fly in the minds of some and hatreds still stain the lives of many."

The success of Civil War games was partly because of America's fascination with all things military in the postwar world. During the Centennial, the military aspects were played up with an occasion to celebrate shared valor and a united America that had recently destroyed the twin evils of Nazi Germany and Imperial Japan. For a people once so divided to have achieved so much was a reason for pride. Lost in the mix was the question of civil rights and racism, both legal and social.

Contemporary historians such as David Blight have held that the fascination with the war's military aspects was itself a way to dodge the thornier issues of race. After all, valor on the battlefield is easier to acknowledge than sharp differences on race. The love of the military aspects is, from this vantage point, a function of white reconciliation. However, it should be kept in mind that America was involved in a major war and utilized drafted soldiers in nearly every decade from 1917 to 1973. Warfare was experienced on a scale and savagery that surpassed the American Civil War. Furthermore, the wargamers of the 1950s–80s lived in the shadow of the Cold War and the possibility of death by nuclear annihilation or in the jungles of Vietnam. The fascination with war was no mere fad meant solely to ignore the vital questions of race but was itself a fascination with an existential threat to life and nation. Games on the Cold War going hot were also big sellers in the 1980s and even today are popular topics.

Arguably one reason wargames declined in popularity was that the threat of nuclear war faded. The draft had been revoked and the Vietnam War damped martial ardor. World War II was less of an immediate experience as the veterans died off. A preoccupation with military subjects wore off, and despite a few boosts, such as the popularity of *Saving Private Ryan* (1998), it continues to this day. The military misadventures of George W. Bush have made war less interesting and arresting; antiwar sentiment is common in both political parties. War films, which were common before the Iraq War, are now fairly rare. Part of it is that the scale of such productions makes them risky and that they have a limited international appeal. War films can do well. *Lone Survivor* (2013) and *American Sniper* (2014) attest to people's appetite for such stories, but it is hardly the heyday of *Full Metal Jacket* (1987) and *Platoon* (1986). There are exceptions to this trend, such as video games, but generally, Americans in 2017 are less addicted to war as art and entertainment.

The other effect of society being more divorced from military matters is a decline in sympathy for the Confederacy. No matter how detestable the cause, Americans found value, and even tragedy, in the experience of Southern soldiers. The end of the draft separated the society from the military. Americans have not fought a war on the scale and scope of Vietnam since 1972. As such, sympathy for the Confederacy, at least for going through the hell of losing a war, has faded. Military subjects on the Civil War, including wargames, had more relevance in the mid-twentieth century. In our age, questions of race supersede those of warfare.

* * *

William Faulkner, in *Intruder in the Dust* (1948), famously wrote that Southern youth could recall the moment before Pickett's Charge and think, "Maybe this time with all this much to lose than all this much to gain: Pennsylvania, Maryland, the world, the golden dome of Washington itself to crown with desperate and unbelievable victory the desperate gamble, the cast made two years ago." How many a Southern boy has played a game about Gettysburg with the intent of rewriting history at least in their own head? There are around seventy-five games with the name of that obscure Pennsylvania town in their very title.

Faulkner's Southern boy today would have a dizzying array of titles and subjects, but in general, Civil War games fall into three categories. There are tactical games, which feature a specific battle. Then there are operational games, which feature a campaign. Lastly, there are the strategic games that try to simulate the whole war. Each has its challenges. David Fox and Richard Berg, in their review of *The War for the Union* (1992), hit upon this with a few pithy lines: "The American Civil War is an extremely difficult topic on which to design a 'game.' A simulation? Easy. A game? A major challenge. . . . [T]here are an awful lot of people who know an awful lot about the ACW, and an awful lot of those often awful people are often quite secure, shall we say, in their knowledge. And may the Ghost of Braxton Bragg reside in your briefs if you don't get it exactly the way *they* securely envision it to have happened."

Tactical games are the most common, with Gettysburg, Shiloh, Chickamauga, and both Bull Run battles being particularly popular. Battles offer delineated sides and a narrative flow. At Shiloh, the Union is surprised and then reinforced. At Gettysburg, both armies feed troops into an ever-expanding cauldron of death. Battles also have dramatic moments, from large-scale assaults to Louisiana troops throwing rocks to stave off an attack. The attraction to dramatic battles is mirrored in the literature, where even comparatively minor scrapes such as Ball's Bluff and Belmont have full-scale monographs.

The trouble is, Civil War battles were grinding affairs in which dramatic results were rare. Although one side nearly always won, the results were usually not decisive. The classic explanation was that rifled muskets made linear formations obsolete. Current scholarship by Earl J. Hess, Brent Nosworthy, and others has dispelled this idea. The battles were not decisive due to poor assault tactics and a lack of massed pursuit cavalry. Tactical wargames have reinforced the point. It is easy for infantry to escape since cavalry units are rarely fearsome fighting formations. Attacking is often difficult, which can make for grinding affairs that leave players a bit downcast. Civil War generals were leading mass armies made up of amateurs. They had inadequate staffs. The result was a shocking number of tactical mistakes on both sides. The average tactical game plays up difficulties with controlling men. It can make for dramatic moments, but it does tend to favor the defender.

It is striking to compare Civil War tactical games to the other most popular topic in musket combat: the wars of Napoleon Bonaparte. Napoleonic games are known for armies activating with comparative ease, particularly the French. Combat resolution is often attacker friendly. Cavalry is plentiful and effective. The result is a very different experience. Dramatic and decisive results are never assured but are more common. From personal experience, people seem to have more fun fighting Austerlitz instead of Stones River.

The indecisive nature of battle, and its effect on game design, has not gone unnoticed. Fox and Berg wrote that the Civil War was one "of maneuver—not combat. Yes, there were several, huge set-piece battles of major historical import, but, with certain exceptions and with the clear vision of hindsight, these big battles did not have the lasting impact that being maneuvered out of position usually did. Just ask Albert Sidney Johnston." Both men are right, to a degree. The strategic turning movement was often more decisive than battle. Robert E. Lee beat Ulysses S. Grant and George Meade at the Wilderness, but the Union army could maneuver its way out of a defeat. Some campaigns, such as Tullahoma and Atlanta, were won less by fighting and more by marching and logistics.

The lessons about maneuver are often showcased in operational games, which usually give players more options and allow for more random but historical results. In these games, the units maneuver on a large map, often covering a whole state. The armies maneuver and look to win by marching as much as battle. There is a certain thrill to fighting a huge battle in a place where none occurred. Who knew the campaign would be decided in Bell Buckle, Tennessee?

Since many campaigns were fought with only a few battles or even just one, your average operational game tries to make every battle rigorous.

Indeed, Clash of Arms's Civil War Campaign Series features a multistep approach to battle that creates a game inside of a game. Other series, such as Great Campaigns of the Civil War and the Blue & Gray Campaign Series, feature involved battle rules meant to increase tension and force decisions, although neither is as involved as the Civil War Campaign Series.

Operational games are some of the best-reviewed Civil War games. They usually capture the dynamics of the war and are enjoyable. Yet they are not massive sellers. The battles have a drama all their own, and these games sell very well. The word "campaign" seems to keep away all but the most devoted.

There is a holy grail that often draws in the best designers and the most attention. Nearly all wargamers want a game covering the whole war, start to near finish. Yet this holy grail is more elusive than the one sought by King Arthur and Indiana Jones. Davis and Berg are particularly right when they wrote that the Civil War "was an *inexorable* war. Oh yes, there are places where it could have gone differently, and there are opportunities for 'changing' history," but "the Union Player is aware where—and why—they will occur. And he is rarely as ineffective as the Union leadership was for the first two years." With respect to it being "an *inexorable* war," your average strategic game is a rebuke to current scholarship. It also can make for tedious hours spent pushing cardboard around.

Strategic Civil War games are often inadvertently props for the Lost Cause. That view of the war upheld that Union victory was a matter of resources, first and foremost. In your average strategic Civil War game, the Union can absorb losses and have more strategic options. The idea of the "inexorable war" pans out as the South is slowly worn down in most strategic games. Your average Confederate player is more under siege than in control. The Confederate player often must hold out and wait for George McClellan to become president, the usual condition of Confederate victory. As the Rebels, you are lucky to hold Richmond by 1863, as your opponent is less likely to make the same errors as Henry Halleck.

Current scholarship, itself often drenched in admiration for the Union war effort, has refuted the "inexorable" claim. The argument goes that the Union had the tougher task, trying to conquer a stubborn people who had the advantage of defense, all the while trying to maintain a coherent war effort. The strategic Civil War games refute that claim and offer a compelling and practical case against the current orthodoxy. The Union has more resources, so they typically decide when and where the fighting will occur.

Arguably, the lack of political factors in many early strategic Civil War games, such as *The American Civil War* and *War Between the States* (1977), is the main reason the Lost Cause interpretation is upheld. Early Union setbacks were a consequence of politics. The open war between McClellan and his radical critics was a major reason Richmond did not fall in the summer of 1862. Later games include politics, such as *For the People* (1998) and *Lincoln's War* (2013). Yet even these two titles swim in shallow waters, since politics is less important than the actual fighting. They still concentrate on grand army wide maneuvers. Both concede that certain generals had more influence and thus were in command longer than they should have been. Yet both games generally fall for the trap of making politically connected generals incompetent.

According to Michael F. Holt, the war only happened because the political parties collapsed. The Civil War was a political war, fought in the midst of a political vacuum. Grant owed his first command to his patron Elihu Benjamin Washburne, an Illinois Republican who had Lincoln's ear. William Tecumseh Sherman's brother was a senator, and his adopted family, the Ewings, were among the most powerful political factions of the day. P. G. T. Beauregard ran for mayor of New Orleans less than three years before he fired on Fort Sumter; he was posted to Charleston in 1861 because he impressed Secretary of War Leroy Pope Walker. None of those three men are classically considered "political" generals, but they owed their position in part to politics. The very ability to get into West Point was as much about political connections as ability. With few exceptions, every general was a political animal, and they all knew that whoever got the most glory would become president. It had worked for George Washington, Andrew Jackson, and Zachary Taylor. It ended up working for Grant.

Due to the rotating door of commanders, the politics of the war, and the wargamer's obsession with particular personalities, leadership rules are often complicated in strategic games. It is so involved that some games discard such rules, which means bad generals are often left in the rear. A joke among players of *The Civil War* (1983) is that Ambrose Burnside, Don Carlos Buell, and Benjamin Butler are often left in Evansville, Indiana, to play poker, while Grant and company win the war. Yet most games have complicated rules for leader promotion, transfer, and removal. In *The Price of Freedom* (2008), the rules for making Grant commander of the armies is nearly a game within a game.

The difficulty of making a great Civil War game might be overstated. The hobby has its share of classics, including *The Civil War, For the People, Lincoln's War, The U.S. Civil War* (2015), *Guns of Gettysburg* (2013), and *Battle above the Clouds* (2010). Yet the number of titles has decreased. The 150th anniversary did not create enough buzz. Worthington Games released two anniversary games, one on First Bull Run and the other on Gettysburg. Neither was a big success. The games still sell but less than they did in Roberts's day. Some of that is because the war is not an easy one to simulate in an enjoyable fashion. Many Civil War games promise big returns but only mildly deliver. The other cause, though, is far deeper and dangerous to the hobby's future.

Sadly, the future of wargames, and Civil War games in particular, is in jeopardy. There are many reasons. The wargaming clientele is mostly aged. The complications of the games, always a barrier, will likely be insurmountable in a digital age of instant entertainment. The games take work and time.

On a broader level, we no longer live in the shadow of two world wars nor of imminent nuclear obliteration. War is rarely as romanticized as it was in the grand paintings of Édouard Detaille. Our ancestors were not blissfully unaware of war's horror. To quote Lord Byron, they often knew war was "a brain-spattering, windpipe-slitting art." Yet they saw war as inevitable, necessary, and sometimes transformative. Our notions are even less romantic, and we have generally acknowledged that Sherman was right. In Columbus, Ohio, he famously proclaimed, "There is many a boy here today who looks on war as all glory, but, boys, it is all hell." In 1861, Harvard students flocked to the 20th Massachusetts and made up its officers. Today, the graduates of Ivy League schools eschew military service altogether.

The raw horror of war is considered repulsive, and it can seem distasteful to make such bloody moments into games. Wargame designer and historian Philip A. G. Sabin wrote, "War games deliberately downplay the dark side of war. Casualties or destroyed units are usually removed cleanly from the board, with no simulation of the grisly aftermath in terms of the dead and wounded." Wargames are from a commander's point of view. They have more in common with *The Personal Memoirs of Ulysses S. Grant* (1885) than with *Co. Aytch, or A Side Show of the Big Show* (1882). Wargames are good for teaching command lessons but not so much for explaining what happens to the men you just hit with poison gas in *Paths of Glory* (1999). I have seen players launch tactical nukes in Germany in 1985 without so much as breaking a sweat.

Gamers often have an interest in military affairs not unlike any person's odd obsessions, some of which are turned into dissertations. Yet the subject matter is charged, particularly when a person is asked to put themselves in the role of some of history's most vicious conquerors. With World War II still a popular topic, players often find themselves battling to expand the Third Reich or the Greater East Asia Co-Prosperity Sphere.

Much of the outcry over games is specific to time and place. There is no controversy in America over playing as Genghis Khan; his horrors were inflicted centuries before America existed. By comparison, *King Philip's War* (2010), which simulates one of the most brutal Indian wars, drew protests and even mainstream attention. A 2010 article in *Salon* highlighted the game's issues. Many Native Americans saw the game as trivializing their experience. *Free at Last* (2006), which simulated the civil rights battles of the 1950s and 1960s, was never formally published because one side had to play the segregationists. The book *The Myth of the Eastern Front: The Nazi-Soviet War in American Popular Culture* (2007) devoted a whole chapter to wargames as a fetishization of Nazi Germany and demonization of the Soviet Union. The point has some relevance. In the 1970s and 1980s, wargames often depicted Germans on the game cover with Soviets rarely appearing. The 1981 cover for *Axis & Allies* featured not a single Soviet. The trend was so pronounced it was lampooned in the crude, but biting, game *4th Reich* (1985), where in a postapocalyptic world, "Puremen" slay "Mutants" from the east in a war for Europe.

Civil War games allow one to refight the war without considering its issues, which itself will draw the ire of partisans for the emancipationist vision of the war. An obsession with the military aspects can be judged as a sign of willful ignorance or blindness to the war's larger meaning. Tactical and operational games are best at dodging the bigger issues; the focus is so narrow. Larger wargames are not, and to an outsider can seem perverse. The Confederacy is increasingly viewed as an evil cause. How happy should you be winning Southern independence and ensuring the indefinite survival of slavery? Cole Wehrle, in his review of *The U.S. Civil War,* wrote, "More than one person approached me while I was playing the game publicly to ask if I sympathized with the south. Looking up from my counter-pushing, I found it hard to formulate a response. Of course I didn't sympathize with the Confederacy, but, then again, here I was cheering on my brave boys in butternut as I dotted the landscape with little counters bearing the Army of Northern Virginia's Battle Flag."

The idea that one can enjoy playing a game where Jefferson Davis might win is increasingly seen in poor taste or even as an act of racism. The new judgmental view is not universal. The contemporary poet Maya Lowy, in writing about contemporary condemnation of the Fascist poet Ezra Pound, stated "Readers *are* capable of enjoying somebody's work without being brainwashed by it, and it is demeaning to assume otherwise." Playing Jefferson Davis in a game does not make you Davis, any more than reading Pound does not make you want to buy a Benito Mussolini poster. But it can look that way to others, and appearances are enough to dissuade players and readers.

Our conception of the war is shifting. It is increasingly seen as a conflict about slavery, which means its other great issues become obscure and even alien. The films of the 2010s that dealt with the war and/or slavery, such as *Lincoln* (2012), *Django Unchained* (2012), *Twelve Years a Slave* (2013), and *The Hateful 8* (2015), leave no doubt that white Southerners were the "bad guys" of the era, although all except *Django Unchained* have their share of nuances. Yet all four are miles apart from the sympathetic portrayal of the South in *Gone with the Wind* (1939) and *Gettysburg* (1993).

Blue & Gray magazine had the tagline "for those who still hear the guns." In 2017, after thirty-four years in print, the magazine ended publication. Fewer people hear those guns. The American Civil War's prominence in the wargaming hobby is no longer as central or as assured. The war is no longer seen as a tragic fratricidal war redeemed by honor, valor, and emancipation. It is difficult to make the Civil War a fun gaming experience. Much of that is the fighting itself. The battles were grinding and indecisive. The war has an inexorable quality. More to the point, the war is no longer seen as a brother's war between states.

1. Ready, Aim, Click!: A Look at the Civil War Through Video Games

by Tyler McGraw

It was amazing to see all the battlefields I have lived on or visited right there in front of me, on a computer screen. Compared to the steady flow of *Civil War Combat* VHS tapes that my father had ordered for me, this was incredible. This was my chance to control a character in a Civil War battle—a game titled *The Civil War: A Nation Divided*.[1] Despite some wildly inaccurate features like an anachronistic Gatling gun on Little Round Top, the game absolutely made its mark on young and impressionable Civil War buffs just like me.

This was my first foray into the world of Civil War video games. In fact, it was also the first time I had heard the opening song from the movie *Glory*, as it is the main theme song of *A Nation Divided*. The game is first-person based and features twelve maps for the campaign. Among them are notable battles such as Gettysburg, Chancellorsville, Fredericksburg, and many more. Another interesting aspect of *A Nation Divided* is its wide variety of

---

1 Cauldron HQ, *The Civil War: A Nation Divided*, Activision Value, PC/Playstation 2/Xbox 360, 2007.

Civil War weaponry. The ability to use carbines, rifled muskets, and various artillery pieces made for a unique experience in gaming. I began to frequently visit the battlefields in my area because of this game, looking to compare the landscape and learn about the history.

Long before *A Nation Divided*, there was the famous *Sid Meier's Gettysburg!*[2] While I have not played *Gettysburg!*, the game made an impact on many. Named after the programmer who developed the game, *Sid Meier's Gettysburg!* is a real-time wargame and focuses more on the overall strategy of battle rather than the first-person experience. Rob Zacny, author of "Why 'Sid Meier's Gettysburg' Stopped Making Sense," writes that "Sid Meier's Gettysburg is about a shared, popular understanding of Gettysburg as not just a pivotal battle of the Civil War but one whose course and outcome was so contingent on famous accident and infamous miscalculation as to invite unlimited speculation. The scenarios themselves are unveiled with briefings that are more memetic than informative: poor Harry Heth's march for shoes, Buford's long wait for Reynolds, Longstreet's plea for a flanking maneuver, Sickles' advance into the wheat field, the Union's stand among the rocks of Devil's Den and Little Round Top, Lee's desperate conviction and Pickett's doomed charge at Cemetery Ridge."[3]

Sid Meier's Gettysburg! set a precedent for Civil War strategy games to come. Following *Gettysburg!* came *Sid Meier's Antietam!*, released in 1999.[4] Just like its predecessor, this game also focused on the overall strategy of a battle.

Another real-time strategy game worth mentioning is *Scourge of War: Gettysburg.*[5] I'm happy I have friends who are experienced in this game, as it was a bit overwhelming at first. The number of steps one must take in order to initiate combat is exhaustive. For example, playing as a corps

2 Firaxis Games, *Sid Meier's Gettysburg!*, Electronic Arts, PC, 1997.

3 Rob Zacny, "Why 'Sid Meier's Gettysburg Stopped Making Sense,'" *Vice News* (blog), accessed April 28, 2022, https://www.vice.com/en/article/5dgvqk/waypoint-101-sid-meiers-gettysburg-essay-civil-war-nostalgia?fbclid=IwAR3vcbTJrbPFpZaBnjVnDKjy0UNXNK_t33CcfuSeqlRSh2BZpXxHuTOornE.

4 Firaxis Games, Break Away Games, *Sid Meier's Antietam!*, Firaxis Games, PC, 1999.

5 NorbSoftDev, *Scourge of War: Gettysburg*, PC,. 2012.

commander means that you must send orders by using a courier to move your forces. I found out the hard way that you must be incredibly specific about what you expect your troops to do. The time it takes to do battle is also a feature that I was not terribly thrilled with. Some matches would run well into the night and still not even be close to over (the downside of "real time"!). Fortunately, you can save the battle at whatever point of the engagement you stop playing. All in all, the most enjoyable aspect of *Scourge of War* is the camaraderie. Playing with my friends was fun, and it helped that they know their history, too, because we would talk about whatever battle we were simulating and use our knowledge to try to best re-create the events of whichever scenario we played.

A more recent Civil War game is *Battle Cry of Freedom*.[6] The game is unique, as you can choose to play in either first or third person. I have not had the opportunity to play this one in depth as of this writing; however, I did play briefly upon its release in March of 2022. *Battle Cry of Freedom* has a very positive outlier rating, ranking at 82 percent, which falls on the high end for a Civil War video game. It is also unique in that it features character customization and a buildable and destroyable environment. It is a massive multiplayer experience, and battles can get extremely intense. My gripe with this game, however, is that the battlefields featured in the game are purely fictional, though community mapmakers are working on making real locations.

While not entirely focused on the Civil War, *Red Dead Redemption 2* is a favorite of mine.[7] There is no shortage of effects the Civil War had in many towns you visit throughout the campaign. In fact, there is even a battlefield to explore in one of the later missions. *RDR2* features something that is new in the gaming community: the appearance of the effects of Jim Crow and post–Civil War white supremacy in the game. This comes in the form of violent encounters between Civil War veterans and the KKK. This feature has made many players uncomfortable, but it can be used as an effective lesson about what the post–Civil War era was like. The storyline

---

6 Flying Squirrel Entertainment, *Battle Cry of Freedom*, Flying Squirrel Entertainment, PC, 2022.

7 Rockstar Studios, *Red Dead Redemption 2*, Rockstar Games, PlayStation 4/Xbox One/PC/Stadia, 2018.

is phenomenal and keeps getting better, and there are even a few uniforms a character can wear that look smartly like a Union officer.[8]

The most interactive—and my personal favorite—is *War of Rights*.[9] The title is controversial, as it seemingly focuses on the Lost Cause ideology of "states' rights," ignoring the aspect of slavery in the Civil War. However, the game focuses on the combat and battle experience of individual soldiers, both North and South. While there is some narration to the game, it does stay true to actions that took place on the battlefield.

I found out about the game during my tenure as an intern with the National Park Service, and it led me to purchase a gaming computer. While I was staffing the Wilderness Exhibit Shelter, three visitors approached for a tour I was giving. They were extremely interested in the battle of the Wilderness and asked a multitude of questions. After the tour, they informed me that they were members of Campfire Games and that they were currently developing a Civil War game. I was, of course, immediately captivated by this. I was given a business card and began my search for a gaming PC so that I could play it.

War of Rights absolutely delivered! It is a first-person shooter game, focusing on realism. There is no AI (Artificial Intelligence), so it is all player based. This means that the game has no computer-controlled characters and that all players are humans. One unique thing about the game is that you can play as a regiment, meaning that you can form a unit with friends and play together. This has given me the opportunity to make many friends who are also interested in the Civil War and form a community. I have had the opportunity to command two regiments. I led the 30th Virginia Infantry and later migrated to the 1st United States Sharpshooters.

You also have the choice to play as an officer, musician, color-bearer, private, and various other ranks, giving the player a sense of the different roles a soldier played. Each battle does have a time limit, as well as a ticket system, which dictates the number of times a soldier can fall in battle. Once

---

8 Jonathan Jones, "Red Dead Redemption 2," *Journal of American History* 108, no. 3 (December 2021): 676–79.

9 Campfire Games, *War of Rights*, Campfire Games, PC, Alpha, 2018.

tickets have been exhausted, your regiment has lost, and the next battle begins loading.

Artillery is another feature that makes this such a superb game. The artillery is extremely difficult at first because you must know how to elevate a cannon tube, sight in the gun, and estimate range. Just like the regiments, you can join a battery and support the infantry in a battle.

War of Rights is set during the Maryland Campaign of 1862. Featuring historically accurate maps, you fight in places like Harpers Ferry, South Mountain, and various locations on the Antietam battlefield. I was blown away by the realistic maps and the beauty of the graphics. The folks at Campfire Games paid attention to detail and helped make this such a unique experience.

As with any game, though, there are a few things I found troubling. One of the features that tends to be both good and bad is the in-game proximity chat. It is useful in the sense that a commanding officer can give verbal orders, and that makes cohesion as a fighting unit much simpler than written orders. The downside to that is some of the players say crude and awful things. Fortunately, you do have the option to mute and, as of 2021, you can report players for gross misconduct.

Civil War video games can be more than just a source of entertainment. For me, they led me to create a podcast and show, *The Unfiltered Historian*. When I finally bought *War of Rights*, I started streaming my gameplay with a focus on interpreting the Antietam battlefield. I received affiliate status on Twitch and continued streaming regularly. Twitch is a video streaming platform similar to YouTube, except there is a larger focus on live videos. My stream on Twitch would consist of me playing a historical game and providing personalized commentary. From there I was able to establish my brand and began shifting gears in order to make it a podcast, while still featuring historical gameplay from time to time.

Without games like *A Nation Divided* and *War of Rights*, I'm not certain I'd be as involved in the Civil War community as I am today. Even though some of the inaccuracies are almost comical, games have the potential to spark interest in many, just like they did for me.

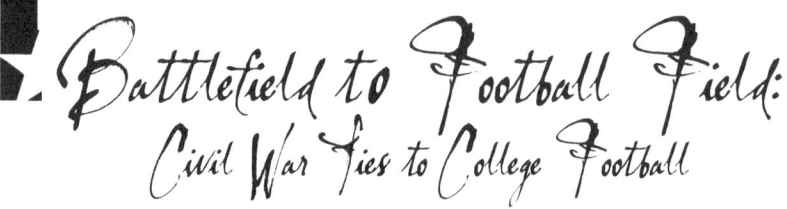

Battlefield to Football Field: Civil War Ties to College Football

by Christopher L. Kolakowski

Adapted from a post originally published at Emerging Civil War on October 11, 2014

Each fall week there are several hundred college football games contested in the United States. Every region and state hosts contests matching teams from the top-tier levels to small colleges. The pageantry and spectacle of gameday often extends beyond the four quarters of actual football. It is a large and important national industry.

"By the late 20th Century," wrote Stephen Brunt, "spectator sport had become a more significant cultural force than at any time in human history since the fall of the Roman Empire. . . . In a culture in which face-to-face connections were made less necessary by technology, in which organized religion or mass political movements were less likely to bring people together in the same place, at the same time, caring deeply about the same thing, spectator sport filled a void. To be a fan meant becoming part of a larger whole."[1]

In some states, rooting for the local university is a way to show state pride (Missouri, Kentucky, Nebraska, and Oregon are examples) or regional

---

1 Stephen Brunt, *Gretzky's Tears* (Chicago: Triumph, 2009), 167–68.

pride (Louisville, Cincinnati, Pitt, UCLA, Miami, Stanford, and Auburn, among others). In many cases, the local university is often a key part and reflection of the state or community's identity. This community expression means that at many of these games, particularly those in the eastern United States, symbols and echoes can be found that trace back to the Civil War—yet another ripple of that conflict that's still visible in America today.

Major colleges that draw their symbols in some way from the Civil War include:

Gettysburg College. Known as Pennsylvania College during the war, it was and is a prominent landmark on Gettysburg Battlefield. The nickname since 1924 has been the Bullets, inspired by its location on the Civil War's largest battlefield.

Howard University. The school is named for its founder, Maj. Gen. Oliver O. Howard, U.S. Army, who served prominently in the Civil War's Eastern and Western Theaters from 1861 to 1865.

Indiana University. The school's nickname is the Hoosiers, sharing a nickname with Indiana troops in the Civil War.

The Louisiana State University. The school's mascot is a tiger, in honor of the famed Louisiana Tigers of the Army of Northern Virginia.

The Pennsylvania State University. The team plays in Beaver Stadium, named for Colonel James A. Beaver, who served in the Army of the Potomac from 1862 to 1864. Beaver lost a leg at the battle of Reams Station and later served as governor of the Commonwealth of Pennsylvania.

The Ohio State University. The school's nickname is the Buckeyes, sharing a name with Ohio troops in the Civil War.

State University of New York at Albany. The school's alma mater calls the area and state the "mother of armies." As the New York State Normal School, students and faculty contributed a company to the Army of the Potomac's 44th New York Infantry.

West Virginia University. The school's nickname is the Mountaineers, a partial reference to some of the state's Federal volunteers and militia during the Civil War.

University of Iowa. The school's mascot is the Hawkeyes, sharing a nickname with the state and the state's troops in the Civil War.

University of Kansas. The school's mascot is the Jayhawks, from the Jayhawker bands of free-staters that battled pro-slavery elements in the "Bleeding Kansas" period of the 1850s and through the Civil War.

University of Michigan. The school's mascot is the Wolverines, sharing a nickname with Michigan troops in the Civil War. The most prominent use of the Wolverine nickname in the war was applied to George A. Custer's all-Michigan cavalry brigade, which fought in the Army of the Potomac from 1863 to 1865.

University of Mississippi (Ole Miss). The school's mascot is the Rebels, alluding to the state's Confederate service. The campus also supplied the company-sized University Grays of the 2nd Mississippi Infantry, which served from 1861 to 1865 in the Army of Northern Virginia and its predecessor formations.

The University of Nevada, Las Vegas. The school's mascot is the Rebels, which along with the scarlet and grey colors hearken back to the Confederacy. The original mascot in the 1950s was a bear named Beauregard (after Confederate General P. G. T. Beauregard) dressed in a Confederate uniform; in the late twentieth century, it was changed to a generic bearded officer and renamed Hey Reb. The men's basketball team is the Runnin' Rebels and the baseball team is the Hustlin' Rebels.

The University of Notre Dame. The school traces its Fighting Irish nickname partly to the Army of the Potomac's Irish Brigade, which fought in the Eastern Theater from 1861 to 1865. For most of its service, the brigade contained the 28th Massachusetts; the 63rd, 69th, and 88th New York; and the 116th Pennsylvania. Notre Dame's third president was Father William Corby, who famously performed a mass absolution of the brigade's members prior to their going into action at the battle of Gettysburg on July 2, 1863; a statue of Corby with his hand raised during that act, which copies a monument at Gettysburg, is prominent on campus.

Historian Dan Davis, a diehard fan of the Fighting Irish, stands inside Notre Dame stadium. "The love of our college football teams is woven into our very being," Davis said. "We feel the hurt of their defeats but remember that we are involved in the ever-important game of life, where we often look to their victories for inspiration." *Kathy Davis*

University of Wisconsin. The school's mascot is the Badgers, sharing a nickname with Wisconsin troops from the Civil War. The Badgers play in Madison at Camp Randall Stadium, located on the site of the state's Civil War–era training and mustering ground; the playing field itself is on the exact site of the former Camp Randall parade field. A memorial arch to Wisconsin's Civil War veterans today straddles one of the stadium's entrances. The fight song and cheer of "On Wisconsin" comes from Lieutenant Arthur MacArthur's exhortation to the 24th Wisconsin at the battle of Chattanooga in 1863.

Virginia Polytechnic and State University (Virginia Tech). Every home game features the visible and active presence of the school's Corps of Cadets. They drill at Lane Hall on campus, which is named for Brigadier General James H. Lane, a former Confederate general and Army of Northern Virginia veteran, who served as first Commandant of the Cadets.

Washington & Lee University. The school is named for George Washington and Robert E. Lee, the latter of whom served as college president after the war and is buried with his family on campus. At the time of Lee's presidency, the school was known as Washington College; Lee's name was added after his death. W&L's mascot is the Generals.

In addition to these individual schools, the Blue-Gray Classic was a college all-star game played in the Confederacy's first capital of Montgomery, Alabama, from 1939 to 2001 and once again in 2003.

There are other colleges and universities that have Civil War ties that are not in their symbols, such as West Point, the Naval Academy, the Virginia Military Institute, the Citadel, Harvard, Mississippi State, William & Mary, Emory & Henry, the University of North Carolina, the University of the South, Transylvania University, and many others. These schools sent alumni to war, were battlefields or hospitals themselves, or were founded by Civil War figures.[2]

It is not surprising that the Civil War is so prominent among American colleges, as the war marked the United States in irrevocable ways. As Major General J. F. C. Fuller, a British Army officer and veteran of the First World War who became one of the foremost historians of the early twentieth century, noted in 1932, "The Wars of the Roses in England and the Civil War in America were both intestinal conflicts arising out of similar ideas. In the first, the clash was between feudalism and the new economic order; in

---

2 The preceding section was drawn from a variety of widely available sources, but most notably the websites of each institution. See also James Lee Conrad, *The Young Lions: Confederate Cadets at War* (Mechanicsburg, PA: Stackpole, 1997).

the second, between an agricultural society and a new industrial one. Both [wars] led to similar ends; the first to the founding of the English nation, and the second to the founding of the American."[3]

The American Civil War was the largest world conflict between 1815 and 1914, pitting millions of men from the Union and Confederacy against each other. By war's end in 1865, over 1 million men (of a total population in the prewar United States of 30 million, 5.6 million of military age) were dead or wounded because of the war. Scarcely a town or family North or South remained untouched by the war and its effects—a generational maiming comparable to Britain or France after the First World War.[4]

In addition to the scars inflicted on people, the war's physical destruction was immense. The war occurred on an unprecedented scale up to that point in American history. Cities like Richmond, Virginia, and Atlanta, Georgia, suffered significant destruction comparable to Europe in 1945; in other places around the former Confederacy, trenches, cemeteries, and blasted landscapes marked battle sites and the passage of armies. Communities across the former Confederacy suffered depredations as armies moved and fought across the landscape, while Northern towns and counties in Missouri, Kentucky, Maryland, and Pennsylvania suffered similarly. The transformations wrought by emancipation and postwar Reconstruction also roiled the national economy for years after the restoration of peace. Many localities were never the same because of the Civil War, making the conflict a critical milestone in American history.[5]

The Civil War's battlefield activities were not the only occurrences during the war years to define the United States; two pieces of key legislation in 1862 also did much to shape America after 1865. These were the Homestead Act and the Morrill Act, which together guided and encouraged national development.

---

[3] J. F. C. Fuller, *Grant and Lee: A Study in Personality and Generalship* (Bloomington: University of Indiana Press, 1957), 17.

[4] Statistics taken from John H. Eicher and David J. Eicher, *Civil War High Commands* (Stanford, CA: Stanford University Press, 2001), 3–73. See also Fuller, *Grant and Lee*.

[5] Many sources discuss the Civil War's impact on the United States; this one is primarily drawn from James McPherson, *Ordeal by Fire: The Civil War and Reconstruction* (New York: Knopf, 1982), 486–89. See also Fuller, *Grant and Lee*, 17-42.

The Homestead Act, passed May 20, 1862, granted 160 acres in the West to anyone wishing to apply. Applicants had to improve the land and live there for five years. They also could not have taken up arms against the United States government. This act, amended and expanded after the war, drew many people from the eastern United States and many new immigrants westward into the territories.[6]

A few weeks later, Congress passed the Morrill Land Grant Act, and on July 2, 1862, President Abraham Lincoln signed it into law. The act gave each U.S. state an amount of acreage to use in the creation of a university, either by sale to raise funds, direct usage, or a combination of both. New states hereafter admitted to the Union would also receive these land grants. The act required the resulting colleges, "without excluding other scientific and classical studies and including military tactic [sic], to teach such branches of learning as are related to agriculture and the mechanic arts, in such manner as the legislatures of the States may respectively prescribe, in order to promote the liberal and practical education of the industrial classes in the several pursuits and professions in life." These requirements provided an appropriate and lasting educational foundation for the developing states and the country as a whole.[7]

The Morrill Act combined with western expansion to produce a boom in college foundings after the Civil War. Land grants ensured that each state would have at least one university, and for many new states, the land-grant college was an essential element of their development as full-fledged members of the Union. Many of these schools became deep-rooted regional organizations that expressed each state's identity and reflected the values and heritage of their respective areas. Originally limited to only loyal states, Morrill Act benefits were later extended to former Confederate states and to historically Black colleges.[8]

Of those colleges listed above, Louisiana State, Mississippi State, Ohio State, Penn State, Virginia Tech, West Virginia University, and Wisconsin all became the land-grant colleges for their respective states.

---

6 McPherson, *Ordeal by Fire*, 374–75.

7 Ibid. The Morrill Land Grant Act text is in Chapter 7 of the United States Code.

8 Ibid.

The South will rise again—every autumn Saturday on the football field. *Chris Mackowski*

In the same time frame as these laws took hold after the war, a new sport, football, was entering the national landscape. Football itself started in the northeastern United States in 1869 and grew in popularity in that region throughout the next decade. Walter Camp codified the first rules for American football in 1885, and soon the game spread to other colleges around the country. As the nineteenth century ended, schools across the United States started intercollegiate athletic programs and incorporated football. Many of these schools at this time wrote fight songs and chose symbols as fundamental expressions of their institutional and regional/state identity. Given the relatively recent conflict that defined so many places, naturally the Civil War appeared in these symbols. They have endured to this day and can readily be seen on any fall weekend.[9]

These ties between the Civil War and college football continue to connect and express the war's defining legacy on these schools and their home regions. The next time the Tigers take the field in Baton Rouge, Penn State hosts a football game, crowds pass the Camp Randall Arch to attend a University of Wisconsin game and sing "On Wisconsin," Fighting Irish football players pass the Father Corby statue, people root for the Buckeyes or Wolverines, or fans mark dozens of other gameday rituals that hearken in some way to the Civil War, know that these symbols recognize and recall legacies far beyond the schools and stadiums where they are displayed.

---

9 A brief description of college football's history is in David Whitford, *A Payroll to Meet* (Lincoln: University of Nebraska Press, 1989).

1. Re-Creating War in Peaceful Fields: Catharsis Through Reenacting

by Derek D. Maxfield

As a history professor at a small upstate New York college, I found myself in the crosshairs of a problem during the Civil War Sesquicentennial: the general disregard for living history, especially Civil War reenactors, by my academic peers on the one hand, and my own great desire to make the most of the anniversary as a teaching moment beyond the bounds of my own classrooms on the other.

When I was an undergraduate history major at the State University of New York–Cortland, I had the good fortune to secure a summer-long internship at Sainte Marie Among the Iroquois, a small museum in Liverpool, New York, along the shore of Onondaga Lake. The museum was dedicated to the story of the Haudenosaunee people, and outside stood the re-created mission (the actual site of the mission was nearby), which Catholic missionaries built and occupied for a short time in 1657. There I received a first-rate education in first-person interpretation—a method that features the interpreter portraying a particular historical personality in character—while I developed an impression of a seventeenth-century Jesuit priest.

My introduction to Civil War reenacting also dates from my time at Ste. Marie. The facility hosted a "Festival of Centuries," in which reenactors, musicians, impressionists, artists, and more participated. There were military reenactors from the French and Indian War, the American Revolution, the War of 1812, the Civil War, etc. I enjoyed strolling through time, but I was particularly drawn to the Civil War encampment.

The encampment was exclusively Union. The reenactors were serious, anxious to talk to the public, and excellent storytellers. During my visit, they stuck mostly to talking about life in camp, uniforms, and the guns they carried. Their enthusiasm was contagious.

The encampment left a good impression on me that contrasted with attitudes I had heard expressed by academics. A good example of such attitudes can be found in a 2011 article written for Salon.com by Glenn W. LaFantasie, Richard Frockt Family Professor of Civil War History at Western Kentucky University, on the eve of the Sesquicentennial. Entitled "The Foolishness of Civil War Reenactors," LaFantasie argued that "the commemoration of the sesquicentennial deserves to be more funereal than mirthful, more disconsolate then cheery." Instead of re-creating staged, pretend battles, in which "pudgy Civil War reenactors pretend to relive history," LaFantasie suggested that those interested in the war should read a book.[1]

For a purist like LaFantasie, the experience as a Civil War soldier cannot be recovered. There is much merit in that point of view—after all, reenactors only shoot blanks, not real bullets; no one dies; and therefore no bodies fester in the sun during and after battle. And of course, the "pudgy" reenactor eats better than a nineteenth-century soldier—especially the poor Confederate scarecrow, who was generally half-starved. Undoubtedly, LaFantasie is also correct that very few African Americans participate in—or even just visit—a reenactment. "For good reason," LaFantasie wrote, African Americans "are a little sensitive about slavery and anything that seems to suggest—as reenactments most assuredly do—that the Civil War was all about battles, that each side fought with equal courage and grand moral purpose, and that the war had nothing to do with slavery or emancipation."[2]

While LaFantasie made some good points, he also came off as elitist and condescending. The only way to understand the Civil War, he seemed to suggest, is to read books. In some respects, LaFantasie misses the

---

[1] Glenn W. LaFantasie, "The Foolishness of Civil War Reenactors," *Salon*, May 2011, accessed April 4, 2016, http://salon.com/2011/05/08/civil_war_sesquicentennial/.

[2] Ibid.

whole point. What he calls "playacting" is a tactile and sensory attempt to understand something books cannot provide.³ While some reenactors want to play weekend soldier to escape their dreary lives, many—most that I have dealt with—are seeking to understand what the common soldier went through. They know much of that experience is unrecoverable, but they want to get a hint of it. Moreover, they want to share their passion for the Civil War and "see themselves . . . as teachers, the self-anointed and self-effacing stewards of our nation's past."⁴

Dana Shoaf, editor of *Civil War Times* and a reenactor himself, sees the value in reenacting for both the living historian and the general public. To him, academics like LaFantasie seem a bit hypocritical. They want people to learn about the Civil War, but it seems like they "would almost feel happier if it wasn't as popular or something."⁵

The trick with reenacting, Shoaf believes, is to keep it from becoming a "dog and pony show." In recent years, production companies have taken over annual reenactments, especially at places like Gettysburg, where they can feel certain of a profit. They set up rows of bleachers to maximize visibility for the visitor but compromise the atmosphere. "It's a fine line," Shoaf says, "when it goes from historical interpretation to spectacle."⁶

War reenacting is not a recent phenomenon, according to Robert Lee Hadden, author of *Reliving the Civil War: A Reenactor's Handbook*. There were, in fact, "sham battles" and grand reviews during the Civil War. Staged re-creations were popular features of veterans' reunions and anniversary commemorations. The most famous, perhaps, was the Great Reunion of 1913, the commemoration of the 50th anniversary of the battle of Gettysburg, when more than 50,000 veterans attended.⁷

---

3   Ibid.

4   Jesse Marx, "The Rise and Fall of Civil War Reenactors," *The Week*, April 2014, accessed June 9, 2016, http://the week.com/articles/448515/rise-fall-civil-war-reenactors.

5   Chris Mackowski, "The Future of Civil War History: An Interview with Dana Shoaf (part three), *Emerging Civil War* (blog), August 2016, accessed October 14, 2016, https://emergingcivilwar.com/2016/08/12/the-future-of-civil-war-history-an-interview-with-dana-shoaf-part-three/.

6   Ibid.

7   Robert Lee Hadden, *Reliving the Civil War: A Reenactor's Handbook* (Mechanicsburg, PA: Stackpole Books, 1999), 4.

The first Civil War reenacting in the modern sense probably began during the Centennial observances, when "Manassas was again visited by the U.S. Army," Hadden wrote, "which dressed up soldiers in blue and gray costumes and let them go at each other with Garand carbines and printed cardboard cartridge boxes." Historical accuracy, as Hadden observed, was then "only a vague concept."[8]

Concern for historical accuracy in reenacting developed during the national Bicentennial commemorations of 1776 and much boosted the hobby. Once the glow faded from those events, the number of Civil War reenactors climbed, probably peaking with the 125th anniversary, when "*Time* magazine estimated that there were more than fifty thousand reenactors of all sorts in America."[9] In 2000, CNN estimated that the number of Civil War reenactors alone totaled 50,000. And while it might have been reasonable to expect that the Sesquicentennial would bolster the ranks of Civil War reenactors, that does not seem to have been the case. In April 2014, writing for *The Week*, Jesse Marx observed that "the Great Recession has taken its toll on what was already an expensive [hobby]." In fact, the numbers of Civil War reenactors "have dropped significantly in the last 15 years and may never return."[10]

The fallout from the Unite the Right Rally in Charlottesville, Virginia, in August 2017 and the murder of George Floyd in 2020 led to a renewed call for Confederate flags and monuments to be removed from public spaces. Civil War encampments, for a time, were canceled or postponed. Those that were held featured Union reenactors exclusively. Embittered by the hostile environment, many Confederate reenactors in New York left the hobby.

* * *

My glimpse into Civil War reenacting in Liverpool, though enlightening, in no way prepared me for hosting a Civil War encampment. And yet, on the eve of the 150th anniversary of the Civil War, I found myself preparing to do just that. Now a professor of history at Genesee Community College

---

8 Ibid.

9 Ibid, 6.

10 Marx, "Rise and Fall."

Passing it forward: Orton Begner (right) mentored Tom Bowers (left), who mentored author Derek Maxfield. *Derek Maxfield*

(GCC) in Batavia, New York, I felt that the college ought to find a way to commemorate the Civil War. The first step was creating a monthly lecture series, open to the public and covering a broad variety of topics. In time, the lecture series would become wildly popular.

Then I began to consider hosting a living history event. Before I could, though, I needed to do some research and find out just what was involved. Fortunately, my search for an advisor—someone to guide me—was short and successful: Tom Bowers, who had been in reenacting for over 25 years. Finding Bowers was like winning the lottery on the first try.

Tom began his reenacting career shortly after graduating from St. Bonaventure University, where he had been profoundly influenced by a history professor. Not long after, he attended his first reenactment and was spellbound. As he watched the reenactors march and drill, he thought to himself, "Wow! This is kinda cool."[11] Soon Tom was learning the ins-and-outs of reenacting, especially first-person interpretation, which involves finding a particular person who fought during the war and "becoming" that person. Through research, a reenactor develops a character and an impression and greets people as if they were that person. Third-person interpretation, on the other hand, features a person dressed as a historical figure but not in character. They speak in the present. As I knew from my experience at

11 Interview with Tom Bowers, interviewed by author, Medina, NY, April 2015.

Ste. Marie, first-person interpretation required dedication, practice, and a measure of skill.

Tom would go on to participate in the 125th anniversary commemorations of the war and later form his own unit, the 34th North Carolina Infantry. More than anything else, he enjoyed working with schoolkids, Boy Scouts, and the Trailblazers. Tom wanted the kids to put themselves in the shoes of the Civil War soldier.

During our commemoration encampments, Tom would oversee the reenactors. Because Tom was well known and respected by the members of that community, I left it to him to recruit them, help create a schedule of events that would maximize their potential—including battle scenarios—and in general act as a liaison between them and the college.

As planning developed, the weather proved to be the biggest variable of all. From the beginning, I knew the GCC encampments had to be at the end of April for two reasons. First, these events were designed, in part, to give my students a hands-on opportunity to be involved. This meant the encampment would have to be during the fall or spring semesters and near the end of the semester as a kind of culminating experience. This reality made the timing simpler: the event would have to be either in April or May on the one hand, or November or December on the other. Of course, November and December in western New York meant snow and cold. April and May were not immune from such conditions, as later events would demonstrate, but the chances for decent weather were better.

The second reason for a late-April date had to do with the reenacting calendar. We were trying to introduce a new Civil War event on the eve of the commemoration years, which already promised to be busy. Our only real hope to secure reenactors was to schedule the event right at the beginning of the reenacting season. This would work to our advantage because of the long winter of upstate New York. Like much of the population, by the time spring began to make its appearance, people were stir-crazy. Reenactors would be itching to get outdoors, anxious for the season to begin.

We held the first GCC encampment at our Lima campus center, near Honeoye Falls. The center, just outside the village of Lima, had a large field next door. As if I was not nervous enough, the weekend before the event, a snowstorm dumped eight inches of snow. Tom assured me that reenactors prided themselves on being able to hack it in any weather. I was not so

For people who can't make it to battlefields, living history events can "scratch the itch." Such events provide essential opportunities to interact with Civil War history for people who might not otherwise ever have the chance. *Derek Maxfield*

sure about the public, though. In any case, much to my surprise, everything melted by the time our event started. While I feared all the melt-off would create acres of mud, it was not bad at all.

As it turned out, the weather was sunny through the whole weekend—if a bit cool during the day, with highs in the low 50s. For soldiers dressed in wool uniforms, this was not so bad. Unfortunately, the nights were frigid, with lows in the teens. I was chagrined that Tom could say that, in more than 25 years of reenacting, our event was the coldest. I worried that the reputation might prevent reenactors from joining us for future events, but I soon learned that they took perverse pleasure in living through such events so they could tell the tale over campfires throughout their future years as a testament to their hardiness (and perhaps foolhardiness). Thus, the event in Lima passed into reenacting history.

* * *

Every reenactor I have had the good fortune to get to know had a ready supply of stories, just as, I expect, Civil War veterans did who had the good fortune of coming home. Tom Bowers recounted for me one of the most memorable weather-related stories, which involved the commemoration of the 125th anniversary of the Civil War at First Manassas in Virginia. In this case, the heat and humidity were the problem. The worst of the weekend was Sunday, when the temperature reached 110 degrees Fahrenheit by the time the battle began. Roasting in their woolen uniforms, men dropped like flies. Conditions were so bad, according to Tom, that the reenactors set aside their period scruples enough to abandon their tents and sleep on the floor of an air-conditioned Arby's one night.

While the whims of Mother Nature can be maddening to the public-event organizer, the phenomenon serves as a healthy reminder that Civil War soldiers had as little control over the weather as we do today, but considerably fewer ways of alleviating the discomforts associated with heat and cold, rain and snow. As I strolled the camps at the Lima encampment, I was surprised to see heaters in some of the tents, sleeping bags, and other modern contrivances. Is this cheating or making reasonable accommodations? Given that temperatures were in the teens overnight that weekend, I was not critical, though I hoped that the heaters would be stashed out of sight when visitors came through the camps during the day. Still, I pondered how far one should take historical accuracy as a reenactor.

As a professional historian, I am often of two minds when it comes to historical accuracy. My inclination, naturally, is to insist on as much of it as possible. On the other hand, anything that tends to inspire an appreciation for history I count as positive. As usual, Tom Bowers gave this issue perspective. Reenactors, he pointed out, act from a mixture of motivations. Almost all of them engage in the hobby to share their appreciation for the Civil War with the public. From the very beginning of our discussions about hosting an encampment, Tom made it clear that in order to host successful events, I would need to deliver an audience. In many ways, reenactors are performers, who spend a lot of money on their wardrobe and accoutrements. They want to be seen. They want to be heard. They want to be appreciated.

Some reenactors are attracted by a spiritual element connecting the modern world to the world of the nineteenth century. In this way, someone might seek to identify with an ancestor who fought during the Civil War by escaping the modern world and re-creating life 150 years ago. In this case, compromises in historical accuracy become barriers to a personal goal. There is a strong desire to get it right in order to bridge the gap in time. Beyond a certain point, though, much of the public would not know if something they view is authentic. If necessary, particularly if it makes reenacting a bit more comfortable, compromises in historical accuracy can be made without the public becoming the wiser.

However, there are some who self-identify as "hardcore" reenactors who insist upon historical accuracy under almost all conditions and tend to scoff at those who make compromises. Like many, I suspect, my introduction to this kind of reenacting originated with the best-selling book *Confederates in the Attic* by Tony Horwitz. Forever after the authentic Civil War experience that would trigger a "period rush," hardcores went to great lengths to turn back the clock. Typical of such groups, Horwitz spotlighted a Confederate group known as "The Southern Guard." Looking the part was not enough for the Guardsmen; they needed to really feel the part. So in addition to wearing real homespun clothing, they would soak brass buttons in urine to re-create the look they wanted. Inside those filthy garments, the men would prepare for the reenacting season, even dropping weight to achieve a gaunt, sinewy look typical of the underfed Confederate infantryman.

The acknowledged master of hardcore was Robert Lee Hodge, best known for his "bloat" look: dropping to the ground, contorting into a dead-man pose, Hodge would swell his abdomen to mimic the grotesque appearance of a rotting corpse. His approach to reenacting was all-the-way, take-no-prisoners stuff. He advocated "total immersion in soldierly misery," as Horwitz explained, "camping in the mud, marching barefoot on blisters, staying up all night on picket duty." He would not even object to being overrun with ticks and lice. In fact, Hodge said, "If that happened, I'd feel like we'd elevated things to a new level."[12]

One of the notable changes in reenacting over the past half century is the rise of production companies that orchestrate major reenactments, operated more to make money than pay tribute. The profit motive meant that the big national events were expensive—both for spectators and for reenactors (who pay for the privilege of participating)—but they apparently do give a better impression of what battle was really like.

"I can remember the 125th Gettysburg," recalled Orton Begner, a reenactor who, once upon a time, mentored Tom Bowers when Tom first got involved in the hobby.

---

12 Tony Horwitz, *Confederates in the Attic* (New York: Pantheon Books, 1998), 16.

> We were marching up to do Pickett's Charge; our battalion was one of the first ones in the line of Union troops filing up towards the event site. I was a First Sergent at the time, so I was marching at the head of the company. The Captain was right next to me. We're going up this hill and all of a sudden he elbows me and says, "Orton, turn around and look over your shoulder." I looked over my shoulder and as far as you can see it's a line of blue; flags flying, drums beating. . . . I said, "This is it. This is what it was like." When we got up there, for the number of men we had on the line, it was a one-to-one reenactment. The waves of Confederates that they talk about . . . it was there! The noise, the smoke, you know . . . it was just unbelievable. It really was.[13]

Spanning 50 years, Begner has witnessed the origins of the big national reenactments down through the commemorations of today. Given that perspective, I asked him what the biggest changes have been. His response surprised me. "I think a lot of people today that are in this hobby really don't know a lot about the Civil War," he declared with perceptible disappointment. "It's something to do with your friends. You put on these uniforms, and you go out for the weekend . . . and they do these things, but do they really know much about the Civil War? I don't think so. A lot of these guys don't, because I've talked to them."

"Reenactors 25 years ago knew more?" I asked.

"Yes," he answered without hesitation—quite the irony when you consider that some have called our time the "Information Age."[14]

Begner's perception, perhaps colored by nostalgia, may reflect the reenactors he met in upstate New York—a small sampling—but overall, those in the hobby today are well informed, drawing on modern scholarship and primary sources. Indeed, online forums dedicated to the hobby feature impressive debates over firearms, uniforms, historic accuracy—and even climate change since the war.

* * *

---

13 Interview with Orton Begner, interviewed by author, Medina, NY, 2015.
14 Ibid.

Another aspect of living history that lends a kind of celebrity touch are the individual impressionists. For the Civil War era, the most popular are President Abraham Lincoln, Union General Ulysses S. Grant, and Confederate Generals Robert E. Lee and Thomas Jonathan "Stonewall" Jackson. It was my good fortune to meet and work with two of these impressionists, who became valuable parts of our encampments: Thomas Schobert, who becomes Lee, and Dave Kreutz, who portrays Lincoln.

As I knew from experience, doing an impression of a particular person means endless hours of preparation as you try to really understand not only the facts of the person's life but also their character, voice, and manner. Like a reenactor, impressionists are performers. If you're going for a first-person impression, you want to convince the visitor that you *are* the person you're portraying. This can lead to challenges because there's a class of skeptical visitors who take pride in tripping up the impressionist by drawing them out of character or catching them in a factual error.

When Tom Schobert decided to portray Robert E. Lee, he was overwhelmed by the sense of responsibility that came with the role and spent a year in preparation before ever donning the gray jacket with stars on the collar. A retired army lieutenant colonel, Schobert began reenacting near the end of the 125th anniversary commemorations, participating in events at Sailor's Creek and Appomattox Court House in Virginia. But with the exception of his participation in the filming of the movie *Gettysburg* as an extra, Schobert's 25 years of reenacting was exclusively in a blue uniform.

From the start, Schobert wanted to portray a specific Union soldier. For a time, he took on the identity of an ancestor in the 53rd Pennsylvania Volunteer Infantry, but soon turned to a medical impression. Schobert chose to portray Farand Wylie, born in Bath, New York, who began his army medical career as an assistant surgeon for the 86th New York Volunteer Infantry—called the "Steuben Rangers"—before joining the 155th New York Volunteer Infantry as a surgeon. After the war, Wylie returned to Bath, where he became the surgeon for the Bath Soldier's Home.

Schobert enjoyed creating his impression of Wylie. He combed the records and even went looking for the surgeon's grave at the National Cemetery at the Bath VA Medical Center. A bit intimidated by the number of graves, he had no idea where to even begin, but as Schobert drove through the ranks of the deceased, a ray of light poked through the clouds and illuminated Wylie's grave. The remarkable experience led Schobert to petition for a

Tom Schobert (left) as Robert E. Lee stands with his "Old Warhorse," Ken Miller as Pete Longstreet. A native of Canada, Miller is a longtime Confederate impressionist and student of the American Civil War. *Derek Maxfield*

bronze marker for the grave, marking the doctor's Civil War career.

The inspiration for Schobert's Lee impression struck in 2009 while he was participating in a Civil War event at Hull House in Lancaster, New York. A look in the mirror caused him to reflect that his white beard and hair might lend itself to an impression of Robert E. Lee. When he later mentioned this epiphany to some Confederate friends, they responded enthusiastically. From that moment, Schobert set aside his Union blue and prepared to do an impression of the most significant Confederate soldier of all.

Lee, as portrayed by Schobert, made his first appearance at a memorial ceremony at Forest Lawn Cemetery in Buffalo, New York. While all the reenactors present embraced Schobert's impression, he knew he'd nailed it when the commander of the U.S. Signal Corps—who was at the cemetery that day for a different ceremony—approached him. This U.S. Army general admired Schobert's portrayal of Lee and asked to have his picture taken with him.

Schobert went on to portray Lee hundreds of times over the course of the Civil War's Sesquicentennial, but his most notable success came in 2012, when he developed a program called "Four Days after Appomattox." Just as the title suggests, the one-person program featured Lee reflecting on the surrender and the war in general. Although this scene never occurred in quite this fashion, it is based on Lee's writings and those of his staff. Schobert's Lee is thoughtful and deliberative, thinking out loud, at times quiet as a whisper and at turns a bit angry. Each time I've seen it, I've gotten the feeling that Schobert was so immersed in his character that he lost sight of the audience completely. You could believe that Schobert was Lee in much the same way that a person could believe that Daniel Day Lewis was Lincoln.

One of the interesting things about reenacting in western and central New York is the predominance of Confederate units. At most encampments and living history events, Confederate reenactors outnumber Union reenactors by margins of two-to-one or more—ironic when you consider that no state produced more Union soldiers during the war than New York. Often, when staging mock battles, organizers ask Confederate reenactors to don blue to make the sides look more even. When I asked Tom Bowers, who led the 34th North Carolina unit, he pointed out that it was much cheaper to be a Confederate reenactor because they had no real standard uniform for the rank-and-file Rebel. All you really need is a few rags clinging to your bones, maybe an old hat, and a gun. Shoes are optional, whereas a Union reenactor would have to invest in a proper uniform, shoes, accoutrements, and the gun.

After spending the Sesquicentennial with Civil War reenactors on both sides, I suspected that there was another issue at work that contributed to the lopsided Confederate ranks: the Lost Cause. The Lost Cause is the name of a school of thought about the Civil War that emerged in the late nineteenth century, led by men like former Confederate generals Jubal Early and John B. Gordon and organizations like the United Daughters of the Confederacy. Among the prominent tenets of the Lost Cause are that slavery was not a primary cause of the Civil War, both sides fought bravely for the causes they believed in, Robert E. Lee was one of the greatest men to ever live, and the South lost because they were overwhelmed by greatly superior manpower and resources.

Does the average Civil War reenactor know what the Lost Cause is? Although I cannot say for sure, my informal survey of reenactors I worked with suggests that, though many cannot identify it by name, the tenets of the Lost Cause are part of their motivation. There is also the romance of the Confederate outlook that has been perpetuated by films like *Gone with the Wind* and, to a lesser extent, the book *The Killer Angels*, which was the inspiration behind the movie *Gettysburg*.

I asked Tom Schobert if anyone ever accused him of perpetuating the Lost Cause through his portrayal of Lee. "Never directly," he replied. From time to time, he might encounter a scowling guy in a blue kepi, but no one has ever confronted him. On occasion, Union reenactors would engage in what Schobert termed "good-natured ribbing." In fact, Union and

Confederate reenactors alike generally treated Schobert with respect and even reverence—evidence that suggests the Lost Cause is alive and well in New York.[15]

That's not to say he hasn't had his share of baffling encounters. Once, when he was addressing a group of fifth graders, Schobert—dressed as Lee—asked the children, "Do you know who I am?" As he waited for an answer, he noticed a mother whisper into her son's ear. The boy raised his hand and said, "You are General Grant!"[16]

Dave Kreutz has never been troubled by being misidentified. Everyone knows who he's portraying, clad in black with a stovepipe hat and sporting the distinctive beard. Everyone knows Lincoln. In fact, long before he began to appear purposefully as the sixteenth president, people would point out to Kreutz the resemblance, and he was known to take advantage of this on the occasional Halloween. But from the beginning, Kreutz had a different means to his goal of being a credible Lincoln.

Both Kreutz and Schobert decided to do their impressions because of their resemblance to Lincoln and Lee, respectively. But Schobert was interested in a first-person impression that would be good enough to get people to suspend disbelief and believe he was Lee. In this, Schobert did well. His impression was largely developed for reenactments and encampments. Kreutz, however, never wanted to develop a first-person impression of Lincoln. His impression was based almost entirely on his appearance and developed for children and symbolic appearances. One of his most requested appearances, for example, is to read the Gettysburg Address.

A General Motors employee for "39.9 years," Kreutz developed his impression after he won a look-alike contest on Lincoln's birthday in 1996. When his peers pressed him to take off work and enter the contest, his boss declined his time-off request. With his buddies covering for him, Kreutz went anyway, but after winning the contest, Kreutz's picture made the front page of the *Buffalo News*, effectively blowing his cover. While his boss was unamused, the budding Lincoln did not lose his job.[17]

---

15 Interview with Thomas Schobert, interviewed by author, Batavia, NY, March 2016.

16 Ibid.

17 Interview with Dave Kreutz, interviewed by author, Batavia, NY, March 2016.

Kreutz credits his experiences with the Association of Lincoln Presenters (ALP) as a major influence, particularly the yearly gatherings of dozens of would-be Lincolns from all over the country. Founded in 1990 by Dan Bassuk, the mission of the organization is to bring "Abraham and Mary Lincoln to life. Through presentations that educate, entertain, and inspire, members honor the words and works of the Lincolns."[18] The conventions of ALP have been inspiring for Kreutz because he found common cause with many other impressionists and picked up valuable tips.

However, Kreutz also discovered a phenomenon not to his liking. Some of the Lincoln impressionists were so concerned with dignity that they would not joke around or tell stories as part of their impressions. Kreutz finds this baffling because Lincoln was a well-known storyteller and loved a good joke. He was even known to enjoy raunchy and racy jokes. In Kreutz's opinion, any impression of Lincoln without that side of him is not historically accurate.

* * *

Like other academics, I still retain skepticism about living history and reenacting. Many people are not suited to bring off a good impression. A historically inaccurate impression is a matter of concern because the average John Q. Public probably does not know the impression is inaccurate, and thus ignorance gets perpetuated.

However, I cannot deny the power of living history done well. Of course, you cannot recover the world as it was, but combined with the right books and teachers, reenacting and living history—done right—can engage people's senses to help them envision how other people lived. There is power in smelling the gunpowder, hearing the rumble of artillery, holding an Enfield rifle, and tasting hardtack and bad coffee.

After organizing successful Civil War living history events during the commemoration years, I have come to understand the vast potential of living history. A great burden of responsibility goes with hosting such events—especially for an educational institution. Unlike a production company that

---

18 "Mission," Association of Lincoln Presenters, accessed August 9, 2016, http://www.lincoln-presenters.org/index.html.

Inspired by the unique power of living history as a teaching tool, the author (left) presents first-person programs as Ulysses S. Grant. Here, he is accompanied by Jess Maxfield as George Alfred Townsend (right) in *Grant on the Eve of Victory*, one of several shows he has created for roundtables and historical societies. *Derek Maxfield*

sponsors an encampment to produce profit, our events—which were all free admission—emphasized interpreting the life of a Civil War soldier and promoting a better understanding of the war. Each of our events featured reenactors screened and invited by Tom Bowers; scholarly lectures; artifact exhibits with docents to explain the historic context of the objects; author appearances and book signings; and handpicked impressionists who were more interested in teaching than collecting an honorarium.

Perhaps the most poignant lessons for me came, ironically, from my students. I require all students who take my classes to complete an applied learning experience. While I give students the freedom to choose how they complete this requirement, many chose to help manage the encampments. Students were involved in all aspects of these events, from planning and public relations to set up and traffic control to participation as reenactors and event cleanup. Along the way, students had many opportunities to talk to the reenactors, impressionists, and authors.

Formal and informal debriefing exercises with my students were instrumental in improving events year to year and helping me to better understand how they perceived the reenactors. Among the things that visitors enjoy at reenactments are the sights and smells of camp life. My students pointed out that giving visitors a taste—literally—of camp life enhanced the experience of immersion. The next year, we added a family that prepared donuts over the fire and handed the donuts out to visitors. The result was delicious and educational.

One small group of young ladies struggled to see how life in the nineteenth century was relevant to them. Throughout the day, these ladies plodded through their tasks showing little enthusiasm for the military aspects of the event. That evening, a period band played the songs of the century, with a caller who taught the dance steps of the day to the unfamiliar. The ladies gathered around the entrance of the tent, watching. Twenty minutes later, they had taken seats inside the tent, watching more closely. When next I visited, about 45 minutes later, each of the young ladies was dancing and grinning ear to ear. The experience transformed their understanding of the nineteenth century. From that moment, their enthusiasm knew no bounds. One has since changed her major and is now pursuing a teaching career in social studies.

There is no doubt that battle scenarios are a big draw for the public, but one cynical student, whom I'll call Don, was unmoved by the smoke and gunfire. He said it all looked a lot like acting and wondered how the reenactors really knew what it was like. I explained that most did research. He remained skeptical. At the end of the mock battle, a bugler played "Taps," signaling the end of the scenario. Men, who a moment ago laid facedown and still on the field, suddenly rose, unharmed, and joined their comrades. Don found this "resurrection" scene, a common ritual during reenactments, especially troubling and distasteful. But soon his attention turned to the medical tent nearby, where dozens of spectators had gathered.

Doc Annabel, who portrayed a Confederate surgeon with the 21st Georgia Infantry, was a star attraction at every event he attended. After each battle scenario, he would demonstrate the surgical techniques of the day and explain post-battle triage. As fake blood spurted all over his apron, he would demonstrate how to amputate a leg. This was always a compelling scene—

and it captured Don's imagination. After the crowd drifted away, Don took the opportunity to talk to Doc.

There is more than meets the eye with Doc Annabel. By day, he really is a physician, who practices in Hornell, New York. He backs up his impression of a Civil War surgeon with 40 years of practicing modern medicine. With his little black bag in tow, he is the very image of the old country doctor. His charisma and sharp wit combine with his natural presentation style to create a spellbinding show. He even has devoted fans who follow him event to event.

When next I saw Don, he was very animated and clearly impressed by Doc Annabel—as nearly everyone is. The credibility that Doc brought to his impression had given Don a new appreciation for living history. Don remained skeptical about the average reenactor's ability to recover an authentic experience, but Doc gave him reason to reassess his previous disregard for all living history.

Watching my students' reactions when they are introduced to living history has been, for me, a highlight of the encampments. It is like a new world has opened to them. As an educator, how could I ask for more? Imperfect as living history can be, it still accomplishes much if it gets people interested in history. Discovery through living history is infinitely better than an encounter with the History Channel or, worse, Disney. Once the spark of interest is ignited, folks can go on to dig into the books and find out more.

Strike the (encampment) tent! *Derek Maxfield*

The Civil War Art Boom (and Bust)

by Richard Heisler

The glare of disapproval from the newsstand cashier felt uncomfortable. There I was, yet again, browsing and not buying anything. As a struggling college art student, I was probably not alone in using the place as a de facto library. With what little money I earned from a very part-time job in the few hours a week I wasn't in the studio or classroom, I could buy a magazine or attempt to keep myself fed with the cheapest items on the Taco Bell menu or some packages of ramen. Food won out when it came to my financial expenditure, but I still had to get my periodical fix.

What always drew me to the newsstand, in addition to the latest issue of *Art in America* or *ArtForum*, was the current issue of *America's Civil War* or *Civil War Times* magazine. It was not typical art-student material, I'll grant you, but it was an important ritual for me. As an aspiring historical painter, I was eager to see what prints were newly released by my favorite artists. This Civil War art captivated and inspired me. It satisfied my deep, life-long interests in both history and art. Pursuing a career in this type of work was a slam dunk. What else would I do? It was obvious—that is, until a leading artist in the field counseled me against the idea.

A letter arrived one afternoon in the mail in a crème-colored envelope with the unmistakable logo of my favorite artist's studio. I couldn't open

The author photographed at the 30th anniversary reenactment of his discovery of Don Troiani's *Barksdale's Charge* print. *Heisler Institute of Civil War Art*

it fast enough. Inside was a reply to a letter I'd written some time earlier asking for feedback on my student work and advice on getting started on a career as a Civil War artist. To my surprise, I was essentially told, *Good work young man, but don't pursue Civil War art as a career. Pick other subject matter.*

It was confusing at first. Why wouldn't I want to do it? Civil War artwork was mainstream. The market was scorching hot. I loved to paint the Civil War, and collectors were eager to buy it. How could it possibly be the wrong choice?

Interest in the Civil War had surged on the groundswell created by the Ken Burns PBS series, the award-winning film *Glory*, and the cult-classic *Gettysburg*. Civil War roundtables thrived, reenactment participation numbers were at all-time highs, and the collector's market for original items was soaring. On a pop culture level, it was truly the golden age of the Civil War "buff."

Hobby collecting of all sorts had broad public appeal at the time. Nostalgia was a high-octane fuel for the supercharged engine of the popular collectibles market. Whether it was decorative art featuring vintage Coca Cola advertising, vintage baseball, antique John Deere tractors, or swooning portraits of Stonewall Jackson, there was an eager audience ready to part with their money to adorn their homes with it.

For people interested in the war, limited-edition art prints and collectibles—ranging from coins to knives, book series to sculptures—were everywhere, and collectors couldn't get enough. Retailers were ready to sell you a Civil War print in the perfect blonde oak picture frame to complement a gaudy Broyhill couch fabric. A saintly yet pensive portrait of Robert E Lee lent an air of dignity to a room, hanging on the wall above the silver Time-Life books on the TV cabinet beside the VCR. A framed print also paired beautifully with the Franklin Mint Civil War chess set handsomely displayed on the end table.

There was something for everyone. An enormous range of styles provided ample variety to suit the tastes of all. Don Troiani's masterful compositions and commitment to historical accuracy dazzled those who sought an accurate look into the conflict. Appealing to others was the austere, yet dynamic work of Keith Rocco, imbued with the familiar stylings of N. C. Wyeth. John Paul Strain impressed with his technical skill. Countless artists threw their hats in the ring to get in on the Civil War art gold rush.

Leading the charge in the Civil War art market was artist/illustrator Mort Kunstler. His cotton-candy, Lost Cause romanticism and saccharin-sweet pink tonality was an aesthetic that thrived in the era of Thomas Kincaide. The omnipresent Kincade, with his kitschy, bucolic cottages drowning in flowers and sentimentality, brought "art" to the masses through affordable print reproductions. His artwork and marketing genius created an empire. It is estimated that 1 in 20 American homes had a Thomas Kinkaide print on the wall. Kunstler was the Civil War world's equivalent and likely achieved a ratio much higher than 1 in 20 in homes of 1990s Civil War buffs. He portrayed all your favorite Civil War heroes, with the same unblemished nostalgia as people's childhood sports legends. They were celebrities. There kneels Stonewall Jackson in prayer, as stoic as the Lou Gerhig you recalled from your youth, but with a healthy dash of *Gone with the Wind* styling and a polished varnish of religiosity. It was devoured by an eager audience of Civil War aficionados and those who bought gifts for them.

Where there was success, imitation soon followed. This was not just in Civil War-themed art, but in all forms of nostalgia collectibles. Soon, it all became too big for its own good. Print production outpaced demand. Civil War art "galleries," glorified frame shops, dotted the streets of Gettysburg and Fredericksburg and perhaps even your local mall. The feeding frenzy of Civil War buff consumers became an orgy of overproduction and the saturated market was bursting at the seams. It could not last. It did not last.

Much like the now nearly valueless glut of 1990s baseball cards, it was too much of a good thing. The pendulum of production and marketing had swung so far past what met consumer demand that it became the agent of its own undoing. The customers who bought these limited-edition prints, sculptures, and collectible chess sets simply had all they wanted. Missing also was a rising second generation to be cultivated to keep the market buzzing. Printing and production techniques evolved. Values shriveled under the weight of an oversaturated market. Tastes changed.

Perhaps sealing the fate of this once-ubiquitous frenzy of Civil War art and collectibles was the tragedy of 9/11. For the moment, the candle of American nostalgia and romance was snuffed out by a new global reality. The country was suddenly grappling with fear, anger, and uncertainty that a generation of Americans had not experienced. Images of Old Stonewall's picture-perfect candlelight Christmas soiree just didn't resonate with people the way it had for the past decade. The once-boiling hot market of Civil War art and collectibles cooled to just a simmer.

In the end, I was right to follow the advice of that artist I looked up to then—and whom I still admire to this day. Not staking my future on the longevity of the Civil War art market was a wise choice. I've made my art career elsewhere with no regrets. There is great art on the subject still being made. That will continue as long as people study the conflict. But the haughty days of the 1990s Civil War art and collectibles market are unlikely to ever be seen again.

The Stream of American History

by Chris Mackowski

Originally published at Emerging Civil War on May 28, 2015, as part of a series "Civil War Trip 2015"

I've spent a lot of time at ECW talking about the relationship between history and art, usually in the form of novels or movies, but in Corinth, Mississippi, sits one of the most provocative interminglings of the two.

The National Park Service's Civil War Interpretive Center, which opened in 2004, offers information about the siege of Corinth in the spring of 1862 and the battle of Corinth in the fall of that same year. There's also information about the town's contraband camp. As a satellite of Shiloh National Military Park, the center also offers information about that battle. It's a beautiful, polished visitation experience, and well worth the stop.

In a courtyard behind the building, the NPS offers a wonderfully contemplative experience: *The Stream of American History, 1770–1870*. Part fountain, part sculpture, it offers a visual representation of the birth and growth of the United States, increasing sectionalism, and Civil War.

"Beyond its inviting, initial emotional appeal, and with a complexity at first glance easily overlooked," a Park Service brochure says, "this watercourse records the flow of events central to understanding the American nation's turbulent first century."[1]

---

1 http://npshistory.com/brochures/shil/corinth-water-feature.pdf.

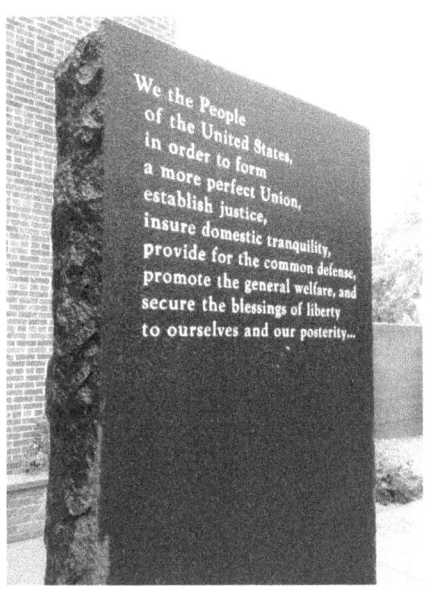

The stream of American history bubbles up around the Declaration of Independence and flows onward from the Preamble of the Constitution. *Chris Mackowski*

As I describe the monument, I'll move from left to right down the western side of the watercourse. That's important, because the flow of water and time are tied together in the memorial, so knowing which way both are flowing is important in understanding how this all fits together.

At the north end of the courtyard, a black granite monolith rises from a nearly still pool of water. On the side facing away from the rest of the memorial: Thomas Jefferson's evocative words from the Declaration of Independence: "We hold these Truths to be self-evident . . . all Men are created equal."

"Left unsaid," says the Park Service brochure, "is the contradictory reality existing when Jefferson penned this inspiring theory of government." Many critics of slavery in the republic's earliest year pointed out the hypocrisy of fighting for liberty even as some Americans denied their slaves that same right.

The flip side of the monolith features the preamble of the Constitution. Note that as we go from left to right, time moves with us—so, the Declaration came first, then the Constitution.

Thirteen notches, representing the thirteen colonies, allow water to pass from the pool into a narrow spillway. Beyond that point, which

The stream widens; the flow quickens. And the war came. *Chris Mackowski*

represents 1790, every three and half inches the water travels represents a year of time.

Along the way, small fountainheads—each representing a new state—add water to the flow. New northern states are on the far side of the stream from where I stand; southern states on the near side. The spillway widens to accommodate the additional flow and also visually represent the nation's growth in geography and population.

At 1820, the spillway flows over a lip that represents the Missouri Compromise. A little farther down, the stream flows over the Compromise of 1850. Scattered between are other small square blocks that represent smaller obstacles—creating more ripples—in the flow. They almost look like tile squares, and they're located in positions that correspond to each state (although that's impossible to know without the Park Service's handy-dandy guide).

When the water reaches 1860, the scale of the memorial changes. Dark gray blocks, each the size of a coffee table, jut into the stream. Each has a year of the war stamped on its top in white numerals.

Between them, dividing the stream, stretches a huge row of fifty-two "battle blocks" of pink granite. Each block bears the name of a battle or

"Battle blocks" show the tumult of war. *Chris Mackowski*

campaign, with campaign names inscribed in ALL CAPS. The size of each varies depending on the size of the battle. Battles fought in the Eastern Theater appear on the east side of the waterway; Western battles, where I stand, appear on the west side. "Battles commonly known by different names in the north and south have both been inscribed," the brochure says, "with each visible only from opposite sides of the stream." Is it "Manassas" or "Bull Run"? "Murfreesboro" or "Stones River"? Depends on which side you stand on.

"The watercourse is now fast moving, energetic, and irregular shaped," the brochure says.

The tumble of stones doesn't divide the watercourse straight down its center. Instead, the row of stones curve toward the Southern side of the spillway to suggest early Confederate success. I don't get this part, I admit, because Confederates in the west didn't fare so well, even early in the war.

After 1862, though, the stones bow back toward the center, and the flow of water straightens.

After Appomattox, the two sides of the stream come together again, and then the water flows through a bridge that highlights the Thirteenth, Fourteenth, and Fifteenth Amendments.

Beyond, a still pool allows for reflection. Beneath the surface, an inscription reads, "The Civil War was fought over issues of liberty. The cost was high and many issues remain to be resolved."

While the statement is true, it's a dodge of the slavery issue—but a reflection of the early 2000s, when the Park Service made an effort to avoid controversy. It wasn't until heading into the Sesquicentennial that the NPS finally decided to fully embrace slavery as the central cause of the war, and some places still deal with it more gingerly than others. This is the most ginger handling of it I've yet seen.

Another block invites further reflection: "The United States as we know it today began not with the Revolution of 1776 but rather in the new nation that emerged from the Civil War." That reminds me of the old point that, prior to the Civil War, people said "The United States *are* . . ." but today we say "The United States *is*. . . ." We're now singular instead of plural. I've heard different theories on the origins of that, but that's a rabbit hole not built into this water monument.

Overall, there is a lot happening in this plaza. Much of it is subtle—perhaps too subtle for most people to even notice. For me, though, that kind of depth and richness makes the memorial something worth visiting over and over. There is always something new to discover and appreciate and think about. It can continue to be provocative and contemplative, which is a hallmark of good art.

But even for those who don't pick up on the memorial's many levels, it is still cool and interesting to look at. That, too, makes it good art.

Does this particular art help us better understand history? I'm not sure, but it certainly gives us a new way to think about it. And that, I think, makes it great.

How does art help us better understand history? How can it help us reflect? *Chris Mackowski*

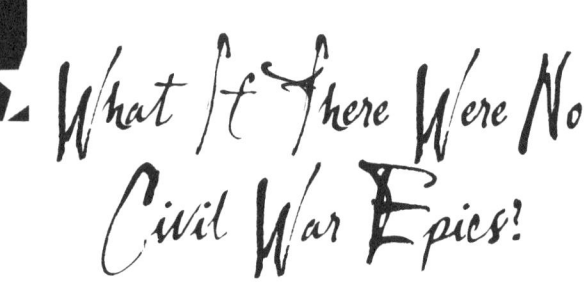

What If There Were No Civil War Epics?

by Sarah Kay Bierle

Adapted from a blog post originally published at Emerging Civil War on August 23, 2022

What if the great Civil War epics of film and television history had not been created?
The debate could be long about what should qualify for the list, but here are the ones I'll suggest for the sake of this "What If" scenario.

1. *Gone with the Wind*
2. *Glory*
3. Ken Burns's *The Civil War*
4. *Gettysburg*
5. *Lincoln*

Gone with the Wind's cinematic drama burst on the big screen in 1939, roughly based on the 1936 best-selling novel. In both the on-screen and off-screen "celebrations" of the Civil War, this film brought to life the story of a "lost civilization." The more I've been looking at late 19th- and early 20th-century Confederate memory, the more I'm convinced that *Gone with the Wind* capstoned a lot of the popular views of that movement, a grand celebration of the ideals connected to the Lost Cause. In this way, *Gone with the Wind* (the movie) had several effects. First, it helped cement a particular memory of the Civil War into mainstream and even global thinking. Second, the movie's long-range popularity helped keep the American Civil War visible in popular culture, ultimately paving paths for greater interest thirty-ish years later for the centennial anniversary. Without *Gone with the Wind*, would Lost Cause ideals have been as entrenched? Would there still have been a strong popular interest around the centennial?

Glory hit movie screens in 1989 and helped shine a spotlight on Black history and the sacrifices of African-American soldiers. It started introducing audiences to "other" stories of the Civil War and perspectives far different than those of fifty-year-old *Gone With The Wind*. *Glory* brought some of the shifting interests of academic Civil War studies to the public in an effective and dramatic film. What if *Glory* wasn't made? Would it have been even more difficult to teach and highlight African-American accounts from the Civil War?

Ken Burns's *The Civil War* is frequently pointed to as the starting interest point for many enthusiasts and historians of the current era. First aired in 1990, the long documentary series came at a crucial moment in the battlefield preservation movement, the height of Civil War reenacting, a strong point for Civil War roundtables, and the academic search for lesser-known accounts and different perspectives on the 1860s. While still highlighting major battles and campaigns, the series tried to add more voices to the Civil War saga, including politicians, civilians, and African Americans. What if the documentary had not been made? Would we have seen the renewed interest in the Civil War of the 1990s? Would we have preserved as many battlefields? Would documentary-making have changed as it did?

Gettysburg was released in 1993. Don't underestimate its power on pop culture! Many people I've talked to at roundtables, on battlefields, and in other public-history settings credit this movie with starting their interest in the Civil War. I had a teenager emphatically tell me *Gettysburg* is "the best war movie ever made." (I have questions.) Gettysburg battlefield tourism jumped, sales of anything and everything related to Joshua Lawrence Chamberlain skyrocketed, Longstreet's memory got reexamined, and sales of *The Killer Angels*, the novel on which the movie was based, finally reached the huge readership it deserved. *Gettysburg* has influenced the "emerging" generation of history enthusiasts, captured the imagination, and started many on their battlefield quests or sent them into libraries to find books and learn more about what really happened in July 1863. What if the movie hadn't been made? Would the long-range effects on interest in Civil War history plummeted more quickly?

In 2012, *Lincoln* came to theaters during the Civil War's 150th anniversary. It could be argued that it doesn't belong in this list, but I think it's possible we may look back and see the movie's importance as a reflection of changing views of the Civil War. The movie is not battlefield centric. Instead, it focuses on politics and, to some extent, 1860s society. When I saw *Lincoln* in the theaters, I thought it reflected the themes in many newly released book titles: a trend into the political and social movements and away from the long-standing military traditions connected with the Civil War. It brought abolition and Union to the big screen in a new way and in a way that reflected academic trends. It allowed some of those more academic discussions to come into the pop culture, even for just a short time. What if we hadn't had that opportunity? What if we didn't have the movie to point to for examples?

So…what if these movies and TV series hadn't been made? How would this have further impacted popular views of the Civil War? Would there have been less interest in learning about what happened? Would there have been less enthusiasm for saving battlefields?

Would you even be reading this book if it hadn't been for one of these films?

Contributors' Notes

Emerging Civil War is the collaborative effort of more than thirty historians committed to sharing the story of the Civil War in an accessible way. Founded in 2011 by Chris Mackowski, Jake Struhelka, and Kristopher D. White, Emerging Civil War features public and academic historians of diverse backgrounds and interests, while also providing a platform for emerging voices in the field. Initiatives include the award-winning Emerging Civil War Series of books published by Savas Beatie, LLC; the "Engaging the Civil War" Series published by Southern Illinois University Press; an annual symposium; a speakers bureau; and a daily blog: www.emergingcivilwar.com.

Emerging Civil War is recognized by the I.R.S. as a 501(c)3 not-for-profit corporation.

* * *

Garry Adelman is the award-winning author, co-author, or editor of 20 books and 50 Civil War articles. He is the vice president of the Center for Civil War Photography and has been a Licensed Battlefield Guide at Gettysburg for 27 years. He has lectured at hundreds of American Revolution and Civil War sites across the country and has appeared as a speaker on numerous televised documentaries. He works full time as chief historian at the American Battlefield Trust.

Edward Alexander is a freelance cartographer at Make Me a Map, LLC. He is a regular contributor for Emerging Civil War and the author of *Dawn of Victory: Breakthrough at Petersburg* in the Emerging Civil War Series. Edward has previously worked at Pamplin Historical Park and Richmond National Battlefield Park. He has written for the Emerging Civil War blog since March 2013.

Sarah Kay Bierle, author, speaker, and researcher focusing on the American Civil War, graduated from Thomas Edison State University with a BA in History, volunteers as the managing editor at Emerging Civil War, and works in the education department of the American Battlefield Trust.

Sheritta Bitikofer is a lifelong student of history. She's currently in pursuit of her undergraduate degree in American History with American Public University. Since 2016, she's published over a dozen historical fiction novels and novellas that cover many eras of history from Tudor England to the American Prohibition. She also works part-time with the University of West Florida's Historic Trust in their archives and collections department.

Neil P. Chatelain teaches history at Lone Star College-North Harris and Carl Wunsche Sr. High School in Spring, Texas. The former US Navy Surface Warfare Officer graduated from the University of New Orleans, the University of Houston, and the University of Louisiana-Monroe. Neil authored *Defending the Arteries of Rebellion* and *Fought Like Devils*. His first guest post on the Emerging Civil War Blog appeared on July 10, 2017, and his first post as a member on September 3, 2021.

Sean Michael Chick is a New Orleans native. He holds an undergraduate degree from the University of New Orleans and a Master of Arts from Southeastern Louisiana University. He is currently a New Orleans tour guide, giving one of the only guided tours of the French Quarter concentrating on the American Civil War and slavery. His first book was *The Battle of Petersburg, June 15-18, 1864*. He joined the Emerging Civil War blog in the summer of 2017 after making several guest contributions to the blog.

John Coski is the former historian and director of research and publications at the American Civil War Museum. Prior to that, he served in a variety of positions, including historian and director of the library and research, at the Museum of the Confederacy. He's the author of dozens of publications, including the groundbreaking *The Confederate Battle Flag: America's Most Embattled Emblem* (Harvard University Press, 2005).

Stephen Davis of Cumming, Georgia, is author of seven books related to the Atlanta Campaign, including the Emerging Civil War paperbacks *A Long and Bloody Task* (2016) and *All the Fighting They Want* (2017). His two recent volumes on John Bell Hood (Mercer University Press, 2019, 2020) have won the Fletcher Pratt Award of the New York CWRT, the Richard Barksdale Harwell Award of the Atlanta CWRT, and the Douglas Southall Freeman Award of the Military Order of the Stars and Bars.

Jon-Erik Gilot has worked in the field of public history for more than 15 years, and is active in numerous historical organizations. A regular contributor at Emerging Civil War since 2018, his work has also been published in books, journals, and magazines. Today, Jon-Erik serves as curator at the Captain Thomas Espy Grand Army of the Republic Post in Carnegie, Pennsylvania, and works as an archivist and records manager in Wheeling, West Virginia.

Meg Groeling received her Master's degree in Military History, with a Civil War concentration in 2016 from American Public University. She is the author of *Aftermath of Battle: The Burial of the Civil War Dead* and *First Fallen: The Life of Colonel Elmer Ellsworth*, both published by Savas Beatie. She and her husband live, with three cats, in a 1927 California bungalow covered with roses on the outside and books on the inside. Meg started writing for the blog in 2011.

In 1990, **Chris Heisey** began photographing American battlefields. He has published images in more than 250 worldwide publications and media venues, and his images have garnered numerous awards including four national merit awards. He has collaborated on three previous books: *In the Footsteps of Grant and Lee* with Gordon Rhea; *Gettysburg: This Hallowed Ground*; and *Gettysburg: The Living and The Dead* with Kent Gramm. He started writing and contributing photography with Emerging Civil War in June 2020.

Richard Heisler is the founder of Civil War Seattle, a public history project about the lives and legacy of Seattle's Civil War veterans. Raised with a love of history on battlefields and museums in the east, Richard has resided in Seattle for over 30 years. When not researching Civil War history, keeping up a 25-year career as an artist occupies any remaining time.

Steward Henderson is a park ranger/historian with the Fredericksburg and Spotsylvania National Military Park after having retired from a 35 year career in the financial services field. He has had a life-long interest in the Civil War and is a co-founder of the 23rd Regiment United States Colored Troops. Steward is also a member of the 54th Massachusetts Volunteers Co. B, the Civil War Trust, and the Central Virginia Battlefield Trust.

Dwight Hughes is a retired U. S. Navy officer, Vietnam War veteran, and public historian who speaks and writes on Civil War naval history. He is author of two books and a contributing author at the Emerging Civil War blog. Dwight has presented at numerous Civil War roundtables, historical conferences, and other venues. You can find out more about Dwight's works at https://civilwarnavyhistory.com. His first guest post on the ECW blog was in December 2014, and since that time has contributed more than 66 posts.

Frank Jastrzembski studied history at John Carroll University (B.A.) and Cleveland State University (M.A.). He's written dozens of articles and two books. He's also a regular contributor to Emerging Civil War's blog. He runs "Shrouded Veterans," a nonprofit mission to identify or repair the graves of Mexican War and Civil War veterans.

Brian Matthew Jordan is Associate Professor of Civil War History and Chair of the History Department at Sam Houston State University. He is the author or editor of several books, including *Marching Home: Union Veterans and Their Unending Civil War*, which was a finalist for the Pulitzer Prize in History.

Christopher L. Kolakowski has spent his career interpreting and preserving American military history, and is currently director of the Wisconsin Veterans Museum in Madison. He has written and spoken on various aspects of military history from 1775 to the present, including five books on the Civil War and World War II. He started blogging for Emerging Civil War in May 2013, and served as ECW's chief historian from 2017 to 2021.

Kevin M. Levin is a historian and educator based in Boston. He is the author of *Remembering the Battle of the Crater: War as Murder*, *Searching for Black Confederates: The Civil War's Most Persistent Myth* and editor of *Interpreting the Civil War at Museums and Historic Sites*. He is currently completing a biography of Robert Gould Shaw for the University of North Carolina Press. You can find his online at: https://kevinmlevin.substack.com/.

Chris Mackowski, PhD, is the editor-in-chief and co-founder of Emerging Civil War. He is the series editor of the award-winning Emerging Civil War Series, and author, co-author, or editor of more than twenty-five books. Chris is a professor of journalism and mass communication in the Jandoli School of Communication at St. Bonaventure University in Allegany, New York, and historian-in-residence at Stevenson Ridge, a historic property on the Spotsylvania battlefield in central Virginia.

Contributors' Notes   287

Derek Maxfield is an associate professor of history at Genesee Community College in Batavia, New York. Author of *Hellmira: The Union's Most Infamous Civil War Prison Camp—Elmira, NY,* and *Man of Fire: William Tecumseh Sherman in the Civil War,* Maxfield has written for Emerging Civil War since 2015. In 2019, he was honored with the SUNY Chancellor's Award for Excellence in Teaching, and in 2013, he was awarded the SUNY Chancellor's Award for Excellence in Scholarship and Creative Activities.

Tyler McGraw's passion for the Civil War began at a young age when his father handed him a copy of the *Centennial Civil War Handbook* and a VHS set of the series *Civil War Combat.* He interned at the Fredericksburg and Chancellorsville battlefields from 2015-16. In 2021, he started the Unfiltered Historian, an online blog and podcast with a focus on history as a conversation.

Tom McMillan is the author of three books, including *Armistead and Hancock: Behind the Gettysburg Legend of Two Friends at the Turning Point of the Civil War* and *Gettysburg Rebels,* which won the Bachelder-Coddington Literary Award (2017) as the best new work on the Gettysburg campaign. He has served on the Board of Trustees of Pittsburgh's Heinz History Center and the Board of Directors of the Friends of Flight 93 National Memorial.

Ohio native **Scott L. Mingus Sr.** is the author of nearly two dozen books and numerous articles. His biography *Confederate General William "Extra Billy" Smith* won multiple awards, including the 2013 Dr. James I. Robertson, Jr. Literary Award for Confederate history. Scott is also the author of many articles for a wide variety of publications, including *Gettysburg Magazine.*

Jon Tracey is a public historian focused on soldier experience, medical care, and veteran life in the Civil War era. He holds a BA in History from Gettysburg College and an MA from West Virginia University in Public History with a Certificate in Cultural Resource Management. He has also worked several seasons as a Park Ranger at various sites and is now a Historian with the National Park Service. He began writing for the Emerging Civil War blog in August 2020, and serves as the Editorial Board Chairman.

Patrick Vecchio, a classic rock enthusiast, is a retired newspaper editor and journalism professor. During his years as an editor, he was widely acknowledged as the handsomest man in American journalism.

Ashley Webb is the curator of collections and exhibitions with the Historical Society of Western Virginia in Roanoke, Virginia. She also acts as the registrar for the Moss Arts Center at Virginia Tech and is a museum collections specialist and dress historian with Bustle Textiles. She received her BA in History and Anthropology from Longwood University and holds an MA in Museum Studies from Bournemouth University, England. She is the author of *Botetourt County: 250+1 Years of Delight*, highlighting the history and material culture of Botetourt County, Virginia, through the decorative arts.

Dan Welch, a public school teacher and seasonal park ranger at Gettysburg National Military Park, is the editor of *Gettysburg Magazine* and managing editor of the Emerging Revolutionary War Series. He received his BA in Instrumental Music Education from Youngstown State University and an MA in Military History with a Civil War Era concentration at American Military University. He is the co-editor of *The Summer of '63: Gettysburg* and *The Summer of '63: Vicksburg & Tullahoma*, both part of the Emerging Civil War Tenth Anniversary Series. He has been a contributing member at Emerging Civil War for more than seven years.

Brian Steel Wills is the director of the Center for the Study of the Civil War Era and professor of history at Kennesaw State University in Kennesaw, Georgia. In addition to leading tours, offering lectures, and conducting programs, Dr. Wills is the award-winning author of many books relating to the Civil War, including a book about the Civil War in movies. He has also written the biography *Running the Race: The "Public Face" of Charlton Heston*. Dr. Wills is a graduate of the University of Richmond, Virginia, and the University of Georgia. He spends time on his farm in Virginia when not teaching and working in Kennesaw.

Cecily Nelson Zander, Emerging Civil War's chief historian, is a postdoctoral fellow at the Center for Presidential History at Southern Methodist University. She received her PhD in History from the Pennsylvania State University in 2021. She has published her work in *Civil War Times* magazine, *The Journal of Civil War History*, and has written essays for several edited collections. Her first piece for ECW appeared in June 2020.

Postscript

SB The Savas Beatie Concert Series
presents

TED SAVAS
SINGS THE CIVIL WAR

"This ain't your grand-pappy's 'Dixie.'"
— *Civil War News*

LIVE
ON TOUR

featuring
the 2nd Northern California String Band
and the Mark Wade Singers

Index

Adams, Richard, 206-08, *207*
African American Civil War Monument, 125
African American folktales, 185-92
Alcott, Louisa May, 182-37
American Civil War, The, strategic wargame (1974), 237
Andersonville, 109, 201c
Andersonville by MacKinlay Kantor (1955), 198-204
Andrews, James J., xxxiv-xxxvi, 94-95
Armistead, Brig. Gen. Lewis A., 131, 132, 133, 135
Art of War, The (The *Sun Tzu*), 223
Association of Lincoln Presenters (ALP), 267
Beauregard, Gen. P. G. T., 203-205
Beauregard-Keyes House, 203
Battle above the Clouds, wargame (2010), 238
Battle Cry of Freedom by James McPherson, 84
Battle Cry of Freedom, videogame, 243
Ben-Hur, 108, 109, 109c
"Ben McCulloch," song, 160-162
Berenger, Tom, 131, 139
Birth of a Nation, The, movie (1915), xxx, 18, 61, 63, 85-93
Birth of a Nation, The, movie (2016), 93, 119
Bowers, Tom, *257*-260, 265, 268
Brer Fox, 185-195, *188*
Brer Rabbit, 185-195, *188*
Bring the Jubilee by Ward Moore (1952), 214
Brother against Brother, miniature wargame, 226

Buford, Brig. Gen. John, 65, 131, 228, 242
Bunny, Bugs, 24, 191
Burns, Kenneth L., xviii footnote, 12, 35, 61, 65, 70 caption, 72-77, 131, 151, 272, 280, 281
Butler, Maj. Gen. Benjamin F., xxvi-xxvii, 237
Butler, Rhett, 103
C.S.A., movie, 83
Catton, Bruce, xvii, xxxiv, 36, 37, 61
Chamberlain, Maj. Gen. Joshua L., 65-67, 131-132, 133, 145, 164, 281
Churchill, Winston, 113
Civil War Campaign Series, operational wargame series, 236
Civil War Interpretive Center, Corinth, Mississippi, 275-279
Civil War, The, strategic wargame, 237, 238
Civil War, The, TV series, 12, 35, 65, 70c, 72-74, 131, 280, 281
Civil War: A Narrative, The by Shelby Foote, xvii, xxxi, 67, 68-72, 140
Civil War: A Nation Divided, The, videogame, 241-242
Clansman, The by Thomas Dixon (1905), 86, 90
Coal Black Horse by Robert Olmstead, 81-82, 209-210
Cold Mountain by Charles Frazier, 81, 114
Cold Mountain, movie, 114-115, 118-120
Crane, Stephen, xxxi, 193-197, *196*, 208
Daguerre, Louis, 3

Davis, Jefferson, xviii, xix, xxi, xxiv, 71, 152-173, 205, 212, 240
Davis, William C., xvii-xviii
de Havilland, Olivia, 99, 101, 104
Dickinson, Emily, 181-184, *182*
Dickinson, TV series, 176-178
Disney, Walt, xxxiv, 39, 42, 95, 183-186, 260
"Dixie," song, 24, 34, 36, 56, 153, 166-168, 169
"Dixieland," song, 160, 160-165
Dixon, Thomas, 86, 90
Django Unchained, movie (2012), 240
DuBois, William E. B., xvi-xvii
Dukes of Hazzard, The, TV program, 15, 16 caption, 28, 29, 31
Dunning, William, 91
Earle, Steve, 160-162, 163-165
Early, Lt. Gen. Jubal A., 64, 265
Edelman, Randy, 144-146
Emancipation, movie, 119-120
Enemy Women, by Paulette Jiles, 82
Faulkner, William, 71, 188, 202, 211-212, 215, 234
Fire & Fury, miniature wargame, 224, 225
Foote, Shelby D., Jr., xvii, xxxi, 61, 67, 68-72, 76, 140
For the People, strategic wargame (1998), 237, 238
Free State of Jones, movie (2016), xxx, 119
Freeman, Douglas Southall, 34, 35, 203
Gable, Clark, 100, 101, 103, 104, 106
Gallagher, Gary W., xxiv, 43, 60, 74n
General, The, movie, 94-96
"General Lee," racecar, 15, *16*, 28
Gettysburg by Peter Tsouras, 83
Gettysburg Miniature Soldiers, miniature wargame, 226
Gettysburg, movie (1993), 60, 65, 118, 130-31, 136-141, 142-146, 164, 263, 272, 280-78
Gettysburg, wargame (1958), 231-232
Gettysburg: A Novel of the Civil War (2003) by William R. Forstchen, 83, 215-216
Glory Road by Bruce Catton, 36

Glory, Hallelujah!, miniature wargame, 226
Glory, movie (1989), xxxvii, 35, 93, 112, 121-129, 140, 241, 272, 280, 281
Gods and Generals by Jeff Shaara, 63, 68
Gods and Generals, movie, 63, 68, 118, 140, 151
Gone with the Wind, movie (1939), xxvii, xxxi, xxxv, 18, 34, 37, 46, 61, 62, 80, 88, 92-3, 97-107, 118, 202, 240, 265, 273, 280-81
Gorman, Patrick, 134, 136-41, *137*
Grant, Ulysses S., 12, 37, 46, 64, 77-80, *78*, 83, 84, 87, 140, 213, 235, 237-38, 263, 266, 268c, 304c
Gray Ghost, The, TV program, 34, 37, 38c, 42-58
Great Locomotive Chase, The, movie, xxxiv, 42, 95
Griffith, David W., xxx, 18, 85, 86-93
Guns of Gettysburg, miniature wargame, 226, 238
Guns of the South, by Harry Turtledove, 82
Hammerin' Iron, miniature wargame, 224
Hancock, Maj. Gen. Winfield S., 131, 132, 133, 135
Harriet, movie (2019), 119
Harris, Joel Chandler, 185-93
Hateful 8, The, movie (2015), 240
Heston, Charlton, 108-113, *109*
Historical Miniatures Gaming Society, Inc. (HMGS), 226-27
Historicon, gaming convention, 226
Hodge, Robert Lee, 261
"Homespun Dress, The," song, 169, 175-76
Homestead Act, 250-51
Hood, Lt. Gen. John B., 126, 140-44
Horse Soldiers, The, movie (1959), 42-3
How Few Remain by Harry Turtledove, 83
"How Mr. Rabbit Was Too Sharp for Mr. Fox" by Joel Chandler Harris, 186-87
How to Play War Games in Miniature by Joseph Morschauser, 225
"I Heard the Bells On Christmas Day," poem/song, 177-180
"I Sang Dixie," song, 166-168

If the South Had Won the Civil War by MacKinlay Kantor, 83, 211-214, 216
If the South Won Gettysburg (1980) by Mark Nesbitt, 214-15
In the pursuit of the General: A History of the Civil War Railroad Raid by William Pittenger, xxxiv, 95
Intruder in the Dust by William Faulkner, 211-12, 215, 234
Jackson, Thomas J. "Stonewall," xxx, 13, 36, 68, 82, 83, 263, 272, 273,
Johnny Reb, miniature wargame, 224, 226
Kantor, MacKinlay, 37, 83, 202-05, 211-16
Keaton, Buster, 94-96, 164
Keyes, Frances Parkinson, 203, 204, 205
Killer Angels, The, novel by Michael Shaara, xvii, 60, 63-68, 80, 131, 135-36, 137, 140, 164-65, 265, 282
Kilrain, Sgt. Buster, 66-7, 133, 160, 163-65
King, Grace, 202-03
Kipling, Rudyard, 189-190
Kreutz, Dave, 263, 266-267
Ku Klux Klan, xxv, 22, 23, 30, 89-93, 102
Kunstler, Mort, 273
Lee, Gen. Robert E., xviii, xxiv-xxv, xxx, xxxiv, xxxvii, 12, 18, 20, 25, 55, 56, 64-65, 77, 82, 83, 87, 114, 115, 116, 117, 120, 122, 130, 131, 133, 137, 138, 142, 156, 157, 205, 206-08, 213, 214-15, 228, 235, 242, 249, 263, 264, 266, 273
Lee, Jennie, 89
Lee, Maj. Gen. Fitzhugh, 64
Leigh, Vivian, 99, 101, 103, *105*, 106
Lincoln, Abraham, xxiii, xxvii, xxxvi, *xlii*, 45-46, 47, 70c, 71, 76, 83, 87, 88, 91, 113, 115, 118-119, 127, 143, 145, 150, 212, 214, 237, 251, 263, 274, 266-67
Lincoln, Mary, 267
Lincoln, movie (2010), 118, 240, 280, 282
Lincoln's War, strategic wargame (2013), 237, 238
Little Wars (1913) by H. G. Wells, 223, 231
Little Women by Louisa May Alcott, 182

Longfellow, Charles A., 179-80
Longfellow, Fanny, 179
Longfellow, Henry Wadsworth, 177-180, *178*
Longstreet, Maj. Gen. James, 64-65, 83, 130-33, 139, 214-215, 242, 264c, 281
Longstreet, miniature wargame, 226
Lost Cause, xix, xx, xxiii footnote, xxx, 64, 74, 79, 85, 91, 93, 98, 103, 106, 118, 175, 182, 191, 203, 236, 227, 244, 265-66, 273, 281
Lynyrd Skynyrd, rock band, 27, 30
Madame Castel's Lodger, novel (1962), 203-205, *204*
Major Dundee, movie (1965), 108-09, 110, 111-13
Massachusetts Regiments
  54th Massachusetts Volunteer Infantry Regiment (living history), *122*-28, *126*
  54th Massachusetts Volunteer Infantry Regiment, xxxvii, 118, 121-28
McCulloch, Brig. Gen. Benjamin, 160-62
McCullough, David G., 59, 76
McDaniel, Hattie, 97-104, *99*
McPherson, James M., xviii footnote, 67, 84
McQueen, Butterfly, 103
Mitchell, Margaret M., xxvii, xxxvi-xxxvii, 18, 34, 37, 102-07
Morrill Land Grant Act, 250-51
Mosby, Maj. John S., *38*, 43-58, 212
"Night They Drove Old Dixie Down, The," song, 155-59
National Association of Stock Car Auto Racing (NASCAR), 15, 23, 29, 31
New Orleans, Louisiana, 202-03, 204-05
North Star, The, movie (2018), 119
O'Hara, Scarlett, xxvii, 34, 102, 104, 105
Official Records of the War of the Rebellion, xxiii-xxiv
Olmstead, Robert, 81-82, 209-10
On the Plantation by Joel Chandler Harris (1892), 188
On to Richmond, miniature wargame, 225

Index   293

"Paul Revere's Ride," poem, 178
Peckinpah, Sam, 112
Personal Memoirs of U. S. Grant, The, 64, 77-80, 239
Potter, Beatrix, 189-90
Price of Freedom The, strategic wargame (2008), 238
Pulitzer Prize, xvii, xxi, 59, 60, 72, 83, 84, 102, 198, 286
Reconstruction, xix, xxvii, xxx, 86, 88, 90, 91, 98, 107, 186, 188, 192, 250
Red Badge of Courage, The by Stephen Crane (1895), 80, 193-97
Red Badge of Courage, The, movie (1951), 42
Red Dead Redemption 2, videogame, 243-244
Reliving the Civil War: A Reenactor's Handbook by Robert Lee Hadden, 255-266
Republic of Suffering, This by Drew Gilpin Faust, 84
River Wars, miniature wargame, 224
Roots, TV miniseries (2016), 119
Roots: The Saga of an American Family by Alex Haley, xxxi
Schobert, Thomas, 263-266, *264*
Scourge of War: Gettysburg, videogame, 242-43
Scruby, Jack, 223
Selznick, David O., xxvii, 18, 34, 100-104
Shaara, Jeff, 63, 67-68
Shaara, Michael, xvii, 60, 63-67, 131, 133-135, 164, 165
Shaw, Col. Robert G., 13, 118, 121, 126, 127, 128
Shenandoah, movie (1965), 36
Sherman, Maj. Gen. William T., xx, xxvii, 150, 204, 213, 237, 238
Shiloh by Shelby Foote, 68, 80
Sid Meier's Antietam!, videogame, 242
Sid Meier's Gettysburg!, videogame, 242
Smoke on the Water, miniature wargame, 224
Society for Correct Civil War Information, xix-xxx

Song of the South, movie (1946), 191-192
Stewart, Helen, xix-xxx
Stewart, Lucy, xix-xxx
Stoneman, Maj. Gen. George Jr, 156
Stonewall Jackson at Gettysburg by Douglas Gibboney, 83
Stream of American History, 1770–1870, The, exhibit, 275-79, *276*, *277*, *278*, *279*
Sun Tzu, 223
Traveller, by Richard Adams, 206-08
Troiani, Don, 272c, 273
Turner, Nat, xxx, 93, 117, 119
Turner, Ted, 201
Twain, Mark, 188, 202, 210
Twelve Years a Slave, movie (2013), 240
U.S. Civil War, The, wargame (2015), 238, 240
Uncle Remus, 185-92
Uncle Remus, His Songs and Sayings by Joel Chandler Harris, 187-88
Unfiltered Historian, The, podcast, 245
United States Colored Troops (USCTs), 114-17, 121-29
  23rd USCT (living history), *122*, 125, 127
  23rd USCT, 122-23
  54th Massachusetts Volunteer Infantry Regiment (living history), *122*-128, *126*
  54th Massachusetts Volunteer Infantry Regiment, xxxvii, 118, 123-28
United States Colored Troops Living History Association (USCTLHA), 121, 125, 129
Wallace, Lew, 109, 109c
War Between the States, strategic wargame (1977), 237
War Games through the Ages by Donald F. Featherstone, 224, 225
War of Rights, videogame, 244-245
Wells, H. G., 223, 231
Wirz, Henry 109, 199-200
"Wonderful Tar-Baby Story, The" by Joel Chandler Harris, 186
Yoakam, Dwight, 166-168

Grant and Lee with *Grant vs. Lee*—Curt Fields and Thomas Jessee at Spotsylvania Court House with copies of their favorite book from the Emerging Civil War 10th Anniversary Series. Fields and Jessee are living historians nationally known for their portrayals of the two generals. *Chris Mackowski*

www.emergingcivilwar.com